# AMERICAN MYTHOS

ROBERT WUTHNOW

# AMERICAN MYTHOS

WHY OUR BEST EFFORTS TO BE A
BETTER NATION FALL SHORT

PRINCETON UNIVERSITY PRESS
PRINCETON AND OXFORD

Copyright © 2006 by Princeton University Press
Published by Princeton University Press, 41 William Street,
Princeton, New Jersey 08540
In the United Kingdom: Princeton University Press,
3 Market Place, Woodstock, Oxfordshire OX20 1SY

Library of Congress Cataloging-in-Publication Data

Wuthnow, Robert.
American mythos : why our best efforts to be a better
nation fall short / Robert Wuthnow.
p.   cm.
Includes bibliographical references and index.
ISBN-13: 978-0-691-12504-6 (hardcover : alk. paper)
ISBN-10: 0-691-12504-X (hardcover : alk. paper)
1. Social values—United States. 2. Social ethics—United States.
3. United States—Moral conditions. 4. Immigrants—United States. I. Title.
HN90.M6W867 2006
303.3′72′0973—dc22        2005018789

British Library Cataloging-in-Publication Data is available

This book has been composed in Aldus and Copperplate Gothic

Printed on acid-free paper. ∞

pup.princeton.edu

Printed in the United States of America

3   5   7   9   10   8   6   4   2

# CONTENTS

A C K N O W L E D G M E N T S

Much of this book was written during a sabbatical year provided by Princeton University and a fellowship from the John Simon Guggenheim Memorial Foundation. I am grateful to the university and the foundation for their support. My editor at Princeton University Press, Tim Sullivan, was a joy to work with and provided valuable editorial advice. The two anonymous readers he secured were enormously helpful, both with specific suggestions and in giving me the confidence that I had something important to say. Parts of the book were initially presented at the Montreat Conference Center in North Carolina and as my presidential address to the Eastern Sociological Society. Both audiences offered comments that have helped me to clarify my arguments. Natalie Searl and Karen Myers played a very important role in conducting interviews for the New Elites Project, transcribing the interviews, and organizing the information from the transcripts. I want especially to thank the men and women who made time in their busy schedules to be interviewed. Indirectly, this book reflects the fact that I work in a department that includes leading scholars of immigration, especially Alejandro Portes, Patricia Fernandez-Kelly, Marta Tienda, Doug Massey, and Tom Espenshade. Their presence contributed to my interest in learning more about the place of immigrant narratives in American culture. This interest was also reinforced by my working with a number of graduate students whose projects have focused on the intersection of immigration and religion. Conversations with Wendy Cadge, Elaine Ecklund, and Margarita Mooney were especially helpful. While writing this book, I convened a group of graduate students who helped me survey the literature on immigrant success. This group included Cristina Mora-Torres, Jim Gibbon, and Sara Nephew. After completing a first draft of the book, I benefited from teaching a graduate seminar on civil society and another seminar on sociology of religion. In both, we read and discussed many of the important works that have been influential in my thinking about the issues considered here. Many of these are identified in bibliographic notes, but these references cannot begin to indicate the deep personal and intellectual debts I owe. In this regard, I want to thank Richard Alba, Jeffrey Alexander, Peter Berger, Randall Collins, Paul DiMaggio, Jean Bethke Elshtain, Amitai Etzioni, Charles Glock, Wendy Griswold, Nathan Hatch, James Davison Hunter, George Kateb, Michele Lamont, Wilfred McClay, Mark Noll, Robert Putnam, Michael Schudson, Neil Smelser, Paul Starr, Jeffrey Stout, Ann Swidler, Alan Wolfe, and Viviana Zelizer. Finally, I especially want to thank Robert Bellah, whose teaching was formative many years ago when I was a graduate student, and whose ideas and writing have continued to be a wellspring of inspiration.

# AMERICAN MYTHOS

# INTRODUCTION

The deep narratives that shape our sense of national purpose and identity are so firmly inscribed in our culture that we usually accept them without thinking much about them. These are the stories we tell ourselves about the moral responsibilities of individuals and about success and failure, about immigration and diversity. Through them we find easy ways of believing that the enormous privileges we enjoy as Americans are privileges we deserve. The deep meanings of these stories provide us with common ways of thinking about who we are. At the same time, they bias our perceptions. For instance, they encourage us to think that we are more religious than we really are. They result in ideas about how to escape from materialism and consumerism that are usually more wishful than effective.

This is the first premise of the book. The second is that we would be a better nation if we paid closer attention to these stories, understanding their effect on us and how they constrain our efforts to be better as a nation—to adhere more closely to the ideals we profess.

How do we identify these stories? Thoughtful observers have had much to say about them and—from Alexis de Tocqueville to David Riesman to more recent observers such as Robert Bellah, Herbert Gans, and Robert Putnam—have produced a long tradition of scholarly inquiry. Beyond this literature, though, stand the stories of recent immigrants, which are particularly illuminating. Through their distinctive voices, immigrants make the familiar strange. The stories they tell come with different accents and valences, but they are thoroughly American. They reveal anew why we think America is good and why we are so often unable to move beyond the shortcomings of its past.

That we ignore these deeper stories isn't to say that we don't reflect at all. Far from it. Much of our public discourse is devoted to examining the state of American democracy. In many ways, the United States has gotten better. Take, for example, the fact that since 1965 approximately 22 million immigrants have entered the United States legally (perhaps 7 to 10 million more if all immigrants are counted). The American population is consequently much more diverse than it was. The number of Latinos has risen threefold, the number of Muslims and Hindus fourfold, and the number of Asian Americans fivefold. During the same period, we have undergone a major shift in values. We have become more accepting of diversity. Prejudice against Catholics and Jews has dropped dramatically. Racial discrimination has declined; interethnic and interracial marriage and friendships have increased. Gender equality has expanded. The number of women in the paid labor force has risen. We have also become a society in which individual rights are championed on an unprecedented scale.

In view of these changes, it would be appropriate to say that American culture has undergone the kind of democratic renewal that observers from Plato and Aristotle to Thomas Jefferson and Alexis de Tocqueville imagined as necessary to keep democracies strong. This period of reinvention has brought us closer to our ideals. We are a more inclusive nation, a nation that more nearly upholds the rights of minorities, and that more actively pursues equality and justice for all.

At the same time, a quick look at newspapers, magazines, and blogs reveals observers at both ends of the political spectrum arguing that American democracy is in danger. The threat is not just from foreign powers or terrorists. It is internal. It stems from complacency, from declining civic participation, and from self-interest.

Culprits are not hard to find. Some blame traditionalists dragging their feet. Or the untutored, the bigots, and fundamentalists, who have managed to avoid enlightenment. Others argue that reforms were too idealistic in the first place or carried unforeseen consequences that caused people to think twice. Other culprits share the spotlight: political gridlock, a sluggish economy, poor planning, partisan polarization, and diverted resources, such as those poured into national security. A case can be made for any and all of these. Yet to focus only on explanations such as these is to miss the most essential consideration.

That consideration is the deep character of our culture itself—what we might call the American mythos. The reason our best efforts to become more inclusive, more diverse, and more democratic have fallen

short, I argue, is that our collective thinking is grounded in widely accepted narratives that almost always go unexamined. These are the deep
meanings of which our culture is composed, the tacit knowledge we use
to make sense of our worlds. They are fundamentally about *morality*.
Not a list of dos and don'ts but rather one of expectations, of rights
and responsibilities. They are seldom spelled out explicitly in rational
arguments. They are instead stories—stories about individual success,
about why immigrants flocked to America, about ethnicity and religious
pluralism, and about how to divert our attention from materialism. They
are the stock of political rhetoric but also of our private understandings
of our nation. They vary among different ethnic groups and from one
region to another, and yet they provide us with common narratives
about our shared existence. They tell us what it means to be Americans,
how America is good, and why some people are more successful than
others. They reassure us that our privileges as individuals and as a nation
are well-deserved. They tell us how to worship and how to identify ourselves ethnically and racially. They help us understand our love-hate
relationship with material possessions—and keep us from doing much
to change this relationship. On the surface, there is a lot of talk about
these issues. Such talk, though, tends to remain on the surface.

There are also deeper assumptions implicit in these stories that merit
closer examination. For better or worse, these assumptions keep us from
changing quite as much as we wish. They keep us from realizing our
ideals as a nation and as a people. This is the focus of *American Mythos*.[1]

Cultural narratives and collective mythologies play such a powerful
role in the shaping of social life that we must be more reflective about
them. This idea differs from one standard way of thinking about democracy. In that view, the deep symbolism of which narrative and myth are
composed is a kind of sideshow—the focus of cheap political rhetoric,
television, and uninformed public opinion—while the real work of democracy is carried out in enlightened circles, presumably by canny bu-
reaucrats and legal experts. Proponents of this view seldom give serious
attention to the way ordinary people think about their lives. In the alternative view suggested by the term "reflective democracy," it becomes
important to bring the two forms of public discourse together. The
mythic dimensions of culture need to be taken seriously enough for us
to reflect on their meaning. In doing so, we gain the chance to decide

whether these are the assumptions we want to govern our lives. We can more effectively seize opportunities to renew our nation and ourselves.

My discussion of the deep narratives of American culture begins with an examination of what it means to engage in democratic renewal. Chapter 1 traces the history of calls for democratic renewal and shows how these calls necessarily raise questions about the basic cultural assumptions that come into play when people try to renew their society. Chapter 2 examines the changing arguments that have been made about the role of the individual in American culture. Social scientists and other social observers are conflicted about how much and what kinds of attention to focus on the individual. For instance, Robert N. Bellah and his associates argued in *Habits of the Heart* that there is an overweening emphasis on the individual in our society. In their view, we need to pay a great deal of attention to the role of the individual, if only to demonstrate in the end that we should de-emphasize this role and focus more on groups, communities, and institutions. Robert Putnam takes that perspective a step further, focusing almost entirely on communities and the attachments of individuals to their communities, rather than dealing very much with the individuals who make up those communities. Yet in the final analysis, he reveals that it is impossible to escape making the individual central: he argues that the renewal of communities will happen most basically through moral decisions made by individuals (such as deciding to watch less television).

Other social scientists take quite different approaches. It has become common in my discipline, sociology, to argue that social arrangements matter much more than anything done by individuals. If people buy widgets, it is not because they choose to do so, but because there is a market for widgets and this market is embedded in social arrangements. Through similar logic, inequities in job opportunities and income between African Americans and white European Americans are not the result of racism or anything that individual decisions might influence; rather they are macro processes evident only in patterns of residence and job location and thus remedied only through public policy. Still, there has been a rebirth of interest in questions about human agency and the self in recent years, and social scientists who propose policy solutions to the macro problems they study implicitly acknowledge that policies are made and supported or opposed by individuals.[2] My discussion of the individual aims not simply to show that individuals are important but also to suggest that our culture is imbued with certain understandings of the individual. These enduring understandings constitute one of the reasons that efforts to renew and improve the society often turn out to reproduce the status quo.

In chapters 3 through 6, I take as an extended case study the ways in which new immigration has renewed—and failed to renew—American culture. Immigration is oddly similar, in terms of its potential effects on a society, to the birth of new generations. Just as new cohorts of citizens need to be socialized into the society's ideals and yet bring fresh ideas of their own, so do immigrants become absorbed into the dominant culture and at the same time challenge it by bringing in new perspectives. As a society of immigrants, the United States has been especially influenced by thinking about how and to what extent American democracy was renewed by the inclusion of immigrants. "I have heard people say that the reason for America's greatness, in fact probably the reason for America's greatness other than the founding values, is the immigrants," says a Muslim immigrant from Pakistan. He subscribes to the long-held belief in American culture that new blood brings added vitality. He goes on, "The constant influx of people who take the risks and are resilient and bring in new challenges with them challenges the rest of the society."

The inevitable downward trajectory that Plato imagined is, in this view, a function of people's becoming too complacent or lethargic. Just as large business firms become lazy and need to be challenged by upstart competitors, so, too, does the general population. Its members become soft and begin to think too much alike, as Tocqueville predicted. The comforts of middle-class life and the opportunities provided by democratic government eventually become so commonplace that people no longer work as hard to attain them or preserve them. Immigrants have experienced hardship. They renew the culture by appreciating it more. "When you become comfortable," the man from Pakistan says, "you just start taking things for granted. You need the new blood to keep it going." Immigration is thus a challenge, as some argue, because it brings in new people who have not been exposed to the same values as native-born Americans. To an even greater degree, it represents possibilities for renewal because of greater diversity and fresh ideas. Recent immigration to the United States also offers chances to get it right, so to speak, by transcending the nativism of the past and by providing greater opportunities for inclusion and upward mobility.

The sheer act of coming to America, I argue in chapter 3, is rich in cultural connotations about renewal. Coming to America represents a decision to leave something behind in the hope of finding a better life. The transition itself is sometimes a passage fraught with danger and accomplished at considerable cost. American history is of course filled with narratives about immigrants who undertook such trips, and these narratives have become the basis for myths about the deep meaning of our nation. They tell us why people sought to become citizens and what hardships they were willing to undergo in order to live in the United States. As such, these stories are capable of functioning like the sorts of renewal rituals that interested Émile Durkheim, one of the fathers of modern studies of society. Through the telling and retelling of these stories, we remind ourselves that America is a place that attracts new-comers. Such stories offer a way to examine in some detail how narratives are constructed and to see how tacit understandings are embedded in these narratives. I rely on interviews with immigrants and children of immigrants, as well as on published accounts, to examine the content of such stories. These sources provide a rare vantage point from which to see the cultural assumptions about America that we so commonly take for granted. The question is whether these accounts, which are often rich in imagery of renewal and new life, replicate old patterns, leaving the meaning of America much the same, or whether they include significant new elements. One clue, for instance, is the fact that journeys to America in recent decades are (with some notable exceptions) seldom as dangerous as they were a century ago for immigrants who crossed oceans in steerage. Does that difference, though, result in significantly different narratives?

The stories immigrants tell about success once they are here provide another way of understanding how culture influences our efforts to be a good society. We may have grown familiar with such stories, reading about them through historians' accounts or the legends fictionalized by Horatio Alger a century ago. But now we can consider them afresh through the words of Muslims and Latinos and Korean Americans who have come to the United States in recent years to make their fortunes. Newcomers' ability to achieve their dreams is an ideal that has long been associated with the meaning of America. People who work their way from rags to riches demonstrate that America is an open society, a place that rewards hard work and moral virtue. At least those were the connotations of rags-to-riches stories a century ago. If even some of the millions of immigrants who have come to America in recent decades can be the subject of such stories, then we can collectively reassure ourselves that America is still a land of opportunity. Or better. Perhaps America is now more accepting of racial and ethnic diversity than in the past, less fraught with discrimination, and more willing to embrace cultural pluralism. Both the fact of upward mobility and the stories that can be told about it, therefore, are ways of renewing our society. But what happens if the path to success is different now from in the past—if, for instance, those who make it into the upper echelons of their respective fields were already successful in their countries of origin? Or had special advantages? Or prospered by virtue of education instead of moral luck? Are we in the process of inventing new myths about American prosperity?

Religion is the vehicle through which many Americans achieve personal transformation. This is especially true of those who say they are spiritually reborn. In other cases, religion serves as a source of hope or provides role models. The vitality of American religion is, in other ways, widely assumed to be a beneficial feature of American democracy. When religion flourishes, it suggests that separation of church and state, guarantees of religious freedom, and the resulting spiritual marketplace are all working effectively. When immigrants come to America and start new churches or temples or mosques, it reaffirms our faith that religious vitality will continue and that this vitality will probably benefit civil society. New congregations provide a more diverse space in which citizens of many faiths and ethnic backgrounds can meet. People overcome isolation in these places and learn how to be good citizens. In those ways, religion is reinvented to be more inclusive than in the past. But is this picture quite as rosy as it seems? Religion among native-born Americans is often a means of retreating from civic responsibilities. It is so highly personal and so deeply private that it fails to generate the frank give-and-take in the public arena that is probably necessary to enrich the culture. Examining the religious beliefs and practices of new immigrants is thus a way of seeing whether the prevailing culture of spiritual privatism is being transcended or whether it is simply being reproduced.

Ethnicity itself is another important dimension of what it means to be an American. Our understandings of ethnicity are, by many accounts, the part of our culture that has changed the most in recent decades. An earlier model of ethnicity assumed that American democracy would be preserved to the extent that immigrants abandoned their ethnic identities and became like everyone else. More recent understandings have championed pluralism instead of assimilation. According to the pluralist vision of America, we are living closer to our ideals of inclusiveness than ever before. The shift from the older perspective to the newer one amounts to a significant reinvention of America. In addition, evidence suggests, as I show in chapter 6, greater ethnic diversity. Immigration and new understandings of diversity have both contributed to this increase. Yet there is also resistance to diversity. It comes not only from nativists but also from assimilationists. The pressures to assimilate to the point of abandoning ethnic loyalties are quite powerful, especially among those who gain educational and occupational success. I consider the idea of symbolic ethnicity as an example of how we have moved toward a more pluralist understanding of America without abandoning the past quite as much as we may have thought.

The other question about renewal that I consider (in chapter 7) concerns our love-hate relationship with material possessions, a theme that goes back to the country's founding. There is a deep strand in American history that pits materialism against democracy. It does not deny that marketplace economics and economic prosperity are compatible with—perhaps even conducive to—democracy. But this critique suggests that materialism erodes civic virtue, or at least replaces it, and in the extreme leads to the kind of least-common-denominator culture that worried Tocqueville. Materialism, along with its critique, is more about culture than it is about economics. Over the years, we have invented many kinds of ideas about who or what would save us from materialism. New immigrants have been among those saviors. Coming to America from the outside and supposedly bringing with them more authentic values, immigrants symbolize the possibility of cultural rebirth. This hope has again been voiced in recent years. Yet there are other understandings of materialism that prevent these hopes for escaping it from making much difference at all. This part of our culture is, I suggest, a clear instance of cultural drag getting in the way of our desires to achieve higher values.

I conclude in chapter 8 by considering what I refer to as reflective democracy. The unreflective background assumptions that guide behavior are, by definition, ones that we do not pause to think about very often. I suggest that culture as deep meaning is sufficiently powerful that we can transcend it only by focusing more intentionally on it. Democracy has never worked well simply because people came out to vote or took part in civic organizations. Nor has it worked well only because of good laws and responsible policy makers. Democracy requires deliberation, as political theorists are prone to say. Even more, it requires deliberateness. We need to reflect on the cultural assumptions that hold us back when we aspire to be better. Our best efforts to do better do not fall short only because we lack material resources or qualified leaders. They falter because we are creatures of our culture—a culture that not only elevates ideals but also constrains our attempts to realize those ideals. There are, nevertheless, venues in which cultural criticism routinely takes place. We need to understand these venues and encourage greater participation in them.

The evidence I present in support of these arguments comes from a variety of sources. Some of it is new. It comes from in-depth interviews with recent first- and second-generation immigrants. They spoke candidly and at length about their experiences coming to America, their careers, their families, and their values.[3] I selected new immigrant elites because they provide a particularly interesting informational context in which to examine ideas about cultural renewal. Successful immigrants have stories to tell, if anyone does, about why it was good to come to America and how America helped them to succeed. They are thoughtful, articulate, and in most cases well-educated people with potential for revitalizing the culture through their own leadership and work. Their numbers include artists and leaders of ethnic organizations who aspire directly to cultural influence, as well as professionals in government and business who serve as role models in their respective fields. Raised in other countries and often deeply dedicated to religions other than those traditionally represented in the United States, these elites do contribute to an expanded vision of American ideals. Yet they also reveal the enduring power of the prevailing assumptions that have characterized American culture in the past. In addition to the evidence from these new interviews, I draw extensively on published literature in the social sciences, on polls and surveys, and on historical and journalistic sources.

This book is less about the mere presentation of evidence, though, than it is about cultural interpretation. Social scientists sometimes argue that we who work in these fields should refrain from making normative arguments because we are not very good at it. They see the purpose of social science as the accumulation of information—information that is personally interesting and that may prove useful to someone else, although a scholar should not be unduly concerned with those uses as long as the information is vetted by specialists in one's discipline. I reject that argument. Not because I think we social scientists are better at making normative arguments than my peers acknowledge, but because I think we have an obligation to try. After all, we devote our professional lives to collecting and analyzing evidence about social activities and conditions. We claim to know more than the average journalist or policy maker about the underlying factors that influence human behavior. If this knowledge amounts to anything other than fact gathering, it should have bearing on our thinking about what constitutes a good society.

To my fellow social scientists, then, my argument is this: Consider the ways in which social programs, policies, or movements fail to achieve their stated objectives. One possibility is that they fail because of resistance from their opponents. This possibility is widely acknowledged and even more commonly studied. It occupies a central place in the literature on social movements and countermovements, and in the literature on social conflict. A second possibility is that well-intentioned efforts fail for lack of planning. This is a possibility that social scientists like to entertain. It says, in effect, if you knew what we social scientists now know, you would have been more effective. I hope that there is truth in this argument. At least it is the reason much of social science is concerned nowadays with policy analysis. A third possibility focuses on unanticipated consequences. According to this argument, efforts that appear to have succeeded may in fact have failed once we recognize the full range of their consequences. There is a kind of supersleuth mentality to this approach. It is attractive because it again shows that social science can uncover things that people on the front lines may have missed. My argument is different from any of these standard approaches to explaining social failures. I do not deny the validity of any of the other arguments. I claim, however, that our best efforts typically fail to be quite as effective as we had hoped because there are unexamined assumptions in our culture that prevent us from exploring as many possibilities as we should. The implication of this argument for scholarship in the social sciences is that we must recognize the power of culture, as well as culture's durability. The stabilizing aspect of culture may prevent us from realizing some of our aims, but stability itself is something societies need.

For policy makers and other interested community leaders and fellow citizens who may not be social scientists, my argument is that we need to be more reflective about the stories we tell to make sense of our nation and ourselves. Too often, in my view, when we hear public officials and broadcasters tell stories about success or failure, about newcomers or old-timers, and about social problems or social triumphs, we simply accept these as sweet, familiar stories. We take them at face value, rather than questioning their implicit messages. Fortunately, we have cultural critics who do examine these underlying messages. I say, hooray for these critics. Let us give them more space in our newspapers. Let us also more often be critical ourselves. If an examined life is good for an individual, it is also good for a society.

## CHAPTER 1

# DEEP CULTURE AND
# DEMOCRATIC RENEWAL

How does a society renew itself? What exactly does renewal mean? The news media daily tell us of serious national problems that require our attention. The message of these headlines is that the public, our leaders, and we individually must rekindle our efforts to solve these problems. Today's newspaper, for instance, informs me that the number of Americans unable to find jobs has been growing even though consumer spending, factory orders, new equipment, and a rising stock market all point to a stronger economy. The question is whether our commitment to full employment is flagging and, if so, what we should do about it. Lawmakers are debating whether to support another round of efforts to pass gun control legislation, while a suspect in one western state is accused of having murdered forty-eight people. Disgruntled personnel at the Justice Department have released an internal memo suggesting that racial discrimination is still a problem in that agency. U.S. officials question how long the military may have to remain in one of the countries the United States has invaded; other officials are being accused of cronyism in handing out government contracts. Public opinion polls supply further indications of the problems we experience. When asked what the most important problem is, the public typically puts economic concerns, such as unemployment, taxes, the national deficit, and inflation, at the top of the list, followed by worries about corporate corruption, terrorism, crime, and the dearth of affordable health care. Yet the question of renewal transcends such specific problems as these. Concerns about unemployment, crime, and cronyism come to our attention through journalistic exposés and sometimes through routine statistical investigations. Social science sometimes plays a role in identifying the scope and sources of social problems. Under favorable circumstances, task forces are formed and legislation is passed to remedy these problems. However, the question of renewal is not so easily addressed. It implies a need to think about the whole of society, rather than the specific problems trumpeted in the daily press.

The United States has a well-established tradition of thinking about renewal in somewhat broader terms than those of the morning's headlines. Much of this thinking has taken shape through social reform movements. Many of the framers of the Constitution were still alive when the first national reform organizations began demanding that the nation turn from its erroneous ways. Bible societies emerged in the early decades of the nineteenth century to redress the worrisome state of morals on the expanding frontier. Antislavery agitators called for the abolition of what they described as an evil institution. In subsequent decades, other reform movements emerged—suffragists, free traders, missionaries, nativists, the single tax movement, the anti-imperialist league, prohibition, and of course the labor movement. As a society, we have often held the reformer in high regard. "Though the life of the Reformer may seem rugged and arduous, it were hard to say considerately that any other were worth living at all," wrote Horace Greeley in 1869. "The earnest, unselfish Reformer—born into a state of darkness, evil, and suffering, and honestly striving to replace these by light, and purity, and happiness—he may fall and die, as so many have done before him, but he cannot fail."[1] Reform movements, as Greeley asserts, are a struggle between good and evil. Their leaders call for renewed dedication against the forces of darkness, often drawing explicitly on the religious imagery that pits evil and darkness against goodness and light. Historians suggest that the reform tradition has been especially strong because the nation's self-identity has been so closely associated with this biblical imagery. The United States was to be a new Eden, a paradise in the wilderness, and a place where life would be better than it had been before, and where God's purposes could be more fully realized. Americans, the literary critic R.W.B. Lewis wrote, saw "the world as starting up again under fresh initiative, in a divinely granted second chance for the human race, after the first chance had been so disastrously fumbled in the darkening Old World."[2] America was, in this view, *itself* an important instance of social and cultural renewal. Yet the business of reform is usually concerned with correcting a specific wrong, such as slavery or prostitution, rather than renewing an entire society. Especially in the more secular context of contemporary politics, reform movements are like task forces and policy recommendations, only rooted more broadly in grassroots mobilization.

The question of renewal is less about politics and fundamentally more about *culture*. It is concerned with basic values and with taken-for-granted understandings of what it means to be good people and to live responsibly in a good society. Renewal in this sense is seldom concerned with anything as specific as public policy or social reform, although it may accompany both of these.[3] Renewal can sometimes be associated with a particular call by a community leader or an appeal by a public figure, such as a television preacher calling on the nation to repent. However, cultural renewal is usually harder to identify because it consists of many calls and many appeals, often focusing on specific problems but implicitly raising hope that we can be better in the future than we have been in the past.

The search for renewal arises from profound unease about the way things are going, as when a public opinion poll finds that a large segment of the population believes the nation is on the wrong track. "It's clear that the true problems of our nation are much deeper—deeper than gasoline lines or energy shortages, deeper even than inflation or recession," President Carter said in his famous "malaise speech" on July 15, 1979. "The threat is nearly invisible in ordinary ways. It is a crisis that strikes at the very heart and soul and spirit of our national will." When the problem is a matter of the heart, the call for renewal becomes an appeal to reexamine our deepest commitments—"the path of common purpose and the restoration of American values," Carter said.[4]

The search for renewal is often prompted by an accumulation of bad news suggesting that something more is wrong than any of the specific indicators suggest—indicators such as declining voter participation, weakening involvement in voluntary associations, rising crime rates, and high levels of child and spousal abuse. Carter's speech was inspired not only by energy shortages and inflation, but also by the lingering mistrust of government engendered by the Watergate episode and America's worsening situation in the Middle East. On such occasions, it is common for writers and public leaders to ask whether something is amiss with how we are spending our time and how we are raising our children. In their widely read *Habits of the Heart*, the sociologist Robert N. Bellah and his coauthors argued that America was in growing jeopardy from what they termed "expressive individualism," a public language of feelings and self-interest that made it difficult even to speak intelligently about the common good.[5] They were not arguing that tax reforms or better leadership could heal the nation's woes; the problem was deeper, buried in cultural assumptions and in language so familiar that we failed to realize its consequences. The book's popularity suggested that it resonated with many Americans' intensifying worries about the direction of our society. As the twentieth century ended, many observers also wrote about the need to renew our communities and our sense of civic purpose. Few of these writings were as empirically grounded as the political scientist Robert D. Putnam's *Bowling Alone*, which examined numerous indicators of declining civic participation and called for Americans to rebuild their communities one church picnic, one soup kitchen, and one bowling league at a time.[6]

In recent years, questions about the need for renewal have also increasingly arisen from reports about how our nation is perceived abroad. It is harder to be complacent about the American way of life when polls in other nations show widespread criticism, not only of American policy, but also of American lifestyles and values.[7] The public's response may be to hunker down or to argue defensively that others are just envious of our freedom and affluence. Such criticism nevertheless strikes a nerve. If we truly want to be a good people, we may respond by asking how we can come closer to achieving that ideal.

Apart from specific problems or criticisms, the question of renewal is evoked by the progression of life itself. Things tend to wind down or become outdated. We realize this at least in retrospect. We understand that social life is no longer centered in small towns and rural communities; somewhere along the way, we had to renew our patterns of life, just as we do now in coming to terms with new information technologies and globalization. We know, in addition, that institutions ossify. People fall into routines, and organizations—like the postal service or automobile manufacturers—develop structures that are difficult to change. We need ways of reinvigorating institutions, of rekindling our commitment to making them work as well in the future as they have in the past—if not better.

Usually the call for renewal comes when something is clearly awry, such as declining civic participation, an economic crisis, or mistrust of government officials. In those instances, it becomes possible to make the case for renewal by pointing to empirical evidence showing that things have gotten worse—that there is a downtrend in voter participation, for example, or an increase in crime. Social research serves usefully for making normative arguments. However, questions about the fundamental values of a society can be raised even more forcefully when our best efforts seem to fall short. America's military intervention in Afghanistan and Iraq after the September 11, 2001, attacks is an interesting case in point. The horrific events of that day inspired the Bush administration to resolve that its number one priority would be protecting the nation from terrorist offensives in the future. To that end, and with overwhelming public support, a new administrative agency was formed to coordinate homeland security. American foreign policy was also redefined. Instead of relying on economic sanctions or UN resolutions to deal with potential threats from abroad, and instead of waiting to wage war until there was imminent danger, the United States would now engage in preemptive strikes against governments that harbored terrorists or that stockpiled weapons of mass destruction. Troops were sent almost immediately to Afghanistan and subsequently to Iraq. Billions of dollars were authorized to be spent domestically and abroad on intelligence and national security, on the military, and on reconstruction in Afghanistan and Iraq. Yet it soon became clear that the money, leadership, and national will that had inspired these programs were not producing the desired results. Terrorist groups attracted more recruits than ever, and democratic government in the Middle East proved more elusive than anticipated. It became easy for critics of the Bush administration to argue that its policies were misguided in the first place or had been initiated without sufficient planning. It was just as easy for defenders of administration policies to argue that more resources over a longer time span were needed. However, it was also difficult to ignore the fact that the more Americans tried to effect change with respect to homeland security and the Middle East, the more things stayed the same. We had tried hard to make the world better, or at least safer, and yet our best efforts fell short.

In the most favorable interpretation of these events, we were a democratic society, inspired both by democratic ideals and by a resolve to protect ourselves from terrorist attacks; we were a rich society with unri-

valed military power, and we hired the brightest and best-trained officials we could find to lead our efforts. Yet we failed to achieve our objectives. With perfect hindsight, it is clear that our options were limited.
More money could have been spent and a different administration could
have been in power—the results would probably have been much the
same, for no single nation, no matter how powerful, can dictate how the
rest of the world should behave. That much is understood.

However, our national efforts to create a better world are also constrained by our assumptions and values. We are a free society in which
freedom of travel, freedom to engage in economic transactions, and freedom from government surveillance of our private lives are deeply valued. We are also a society with vested economic interests in the Middle
East, above all in protecting our access to its supply of oil. These are
what social scientists call *structures*—social arrangements, especially of
an economic and political sort, that limit the range of options available
even to the best-intentioned people and their leaders. Less easily identified are the *cultural assumptions* that are often just as powerful as the
economic and political structures. Cultural assumptions are seldom articulated very clearly or explicitly. They are more likely to appear between
the lines or in stories and myths. America's assumptions about the Middle East, for instance, have been most evident in what the American
studies scholar Melani McAlister calls "epic encounters."[8] These are narratives told in religious settings and in motion pictures, as much as in
public policy, about the Holy Land, Mesopotamia, and Egypt. They have
been told in different ways to different generations, but there are also
continuities. McAlister suggests that in recent decades these stories have
been greatly influenced by changing views of race, gender, and diversity,
and yet the narratives have been powerful enough to incorporate these
new ideas without challenging how we think about the Middle East. For
instance, our sense of superiority with respect to Arabic culture has, if
anything, been reinforced by perceptions that we outdo them in promoting gender and racial equality.

What I am suggesting is that the power of deeply held cultural assumptions may be especially evident when a society mobilizes itself to
achieve some laudable end, even to the point of committing considerable
resources, and still finds itself a long way from achieving its ideals. In
recent memory, the civil rights movement is probably the clearest example of what I have in mind. That movement mobilized a large number

of people, gained widespread media attention, and resulted in major legislation concerned with, among other things, ending school segregation and eliminating discrimination in housing and employment. Although there was resistance to these changes at the time, hardly anyone now thinks they should not have been made. We knew that racial discrimination was in clear violation of the ideals of equality and justice on which the nation was founded, and we have been able in retrospect at least to regard the civil rights movement as an important step toward more closely realizing those ideals. Yet we also know that those efforts have not fully succeeded. Racism is still a significant part of our culture. We may blame the problem on history or on human nature, and we may argue about specific policies, such as affirmative action, but we know there is more to the problem than just rolling up our sleeves and formulating better policies.

## RENEWAL AND DEMOCRACY

The question of renewal is especially pertinent in a democratic society. Although democracies have mechanisms for renewing themselves through an orderly process of elections and representation, they are also precarious. I do not mean that well-established democracies like the United States are in danger of actually collapsing. This happens rarely, if ever.[9] I mean rather that the quality of life in a democracy erodes into something less than what democracy was meant to preserve. That has long been a fear among observers of democracy. In the eighth book of the *Republic*, for instance, Plato described democracy as "the fairest of States . . . an embroidered robe which is spangled with every sort of flower," but he also warned of democracy's succumbing to the temptations of power and money that lead to oligarchy, and the "freedom and libertinism of useless and unnecessary pleasures" that result in anarchy. It is from such observations that we inherit the concern that democracy is fragile and that it must renew itself periodically, fortifying the character of its citizens against the desire to rule absolutely or to follow too readily. Complacency is especially to be guarded against, for it turns citizens into drones who "keep buzzing about the bema" without engaging seriously in the give-and-take that must be present for differing opinions and interests to be properly represented.[10]

The founders of America's government were keenly aware that theirs was a precarious experiment. "Remember, democracy never lasts long," John Adams wrote. "It soon wastes, exhausts and murders itself. There never was a democracy yet that did not commit suicide."[11] James Madison, who described democracies as "spectacles of turbulence and contention," was equally doubtful about their longevity. They "have in general been as short in their lives as they have been violent in their deaths," he wrote.[12] Madison's solution to the problems posed by pure democracy was of course a republic—specifically a republic of states governed by representatives with "enlightened views and virtuous sentiments" capable of overruling local prejudices and factions. That republic inspired confidence among leaders like Madison and Jefferson. If ordinary citizens could not be trusted with the reins of government, a republic led by men of wealth and good breeding would ensure against anarchy. In his first inaugural address, Thomas Jefferson described the new republic not only as a "successful experiment," but also as "the world's best hope." Yet Jefferson's optimistic language is designed to counter those among his contemporaries who, he acknowledges, believed that American government was not strong enough and lacked the energy to preserve itself. Jefferson's remarks also show clearly that the success of the American experiment depended on other conditions' being met. Besides abundant land and the oceans separating America from other continents, the nation's survival was contingent on the continuing honor and confidence of its citizens and, above all, such virtues as honesty, truth, temperance, gratitude, and generosity. It was in this context, too, that Jefferson emphasized the need for justice, toleration, diffusion of information through a free press, and freedom of religion.[13]

In the 1830s, Alexis de Tocqueville rendered a mixed verdict about the future of American democracy. On the one hand, it was a flourishing system of self-rule that offered freedom, encouraged a strong sense of equality among its citizens, and thrived on voluntary participation and self-help. It was thus a form of government potentially capable of supplanting the aristocratic and monarchic systems of Europe. On the other hand, Tocqueville worried that citizens would shirk their civic responsibilities and look to government increasingly to do what they should do for themselves. If that happened, Tocqueville argued, it would magnify the likelihood that government would grow stronger at the expense of popular sovereignty. Tocqueville also worried that democracy would encourage everyone to be like everyone else. A tyranny of public opinion would emerge, shaping beliefs and lifestyles, and demanding conformity. That, too, would rob democracy of its vitality. There were, in short, two threats: one from above, in the form of totalitarian rule, and one from below, in the form of a debased citizenry that followed popular opinion too easily. Either threat would diminish the quality of life.[14]

In recent years, Tocqueville's concerns have been rediscovered. Observers of American democracy warn of the problems that now endanger the vitality of civic life. In *Democracy on Trial*, the political theorist Jean Bethke Elshtain describes "warning signs of exhaustion, cynicism, opportunism, and despair." Her view of recent decades' events reflects the pattern I have mentioned: things have seemed to go well and yet have fallen short of our ideals. We have enjoyed exceptional prosperity and emerged victorious from the long Cold War, Elshtain notes, and yet find ourselves somehow incapable of turning these achievements into the creation of a better society. The trouble is not so much Tocqueville's threat from above but the second threat, the erosion of civic virtue from below. A strong democracy, Elshtain writes, "depends on what might be called democratic dispositions [including] a preparedness to work with others different from oneself toward shared ends; a combination of strong convictions with a readiness to compromise in the recognition that one can't always get everything one wants; and a sense of individuality and a commitment to civic goods."[15] Instead, we have become a society in which the narrow self-interest that Tocqueville warned about has become so rampant that we find it difficult to work together for the common good. Even if Elshtain's analysis is overly pessimistic, it is difficult to ignore the evidence she recites about faltering schools, failing marriages, abandoned children, the victimization of women, continuing racism, and factionalism within the political system and among self-interested special interest groups.

It might be supposed—and has often been argued—that the precariousness of democracy is mainly a problem of government. In this view, the way to safeguard democracy is to maintain a balance among the several branches of government, uphold the First Amendment, and enlist the best scholarly arguments in interpreting the Constitution. The problems that face American democracy certainly have a governmental aspect. If power resident in the citizenry is an essential feature of democracy, then an arrogation of power by the few signals the end of democratic rule. That is Tocqueville's threat from above. It is the principal reason for America's system of checks and balances and for our insistence that no citizen, no matter how powerful, is above the law. We protect ourselves against totalitarianism through legislation, a strong judicial system, and periodic elections. These are forms of democratic renewal. They are built into the system itself and are meant to provide recurrent opportunities to cleanse ourselves of misguided policies and wrongdoing. When one group or faction becomes too powerful, the judicial system and free elections offer a vehicle through which abuses may be corrected. The threat from below, however, is not so easily handled in this manner. We hope that freedom of the press and free exercise of speech and religious expression will prevent a single set of values and beliefs from dominating public opinion. These same freedoms, though, can be used to argue against any regulation of or interference with the mass media and, for that reason, can lead to the very tyranny of public opinion that worried Tocqueville. An informed citizenry that takes responsibility for itself is also a matter of character formation and community building. We are less apt to consider these as legislative or judicial matters than as means by which we protect ourselves against totalitarianism. A basic principle of a free society is that individuals should be able to pursue whatever values they wish and be part of whatever communities they may choose. We hesitate to impose rules and regulations on these matters, even though we may fear that character is dying and communities are collapsing.

The search for democratic renewal is, therefore, only partly fulfilled by government. We believe there must be ways other than through the courts or legislation to strengthen the values and the self-identities that a strong democracy requires. These activities fall squarely within the realm of *civil society*. They take place in families and in houses of worship, at community associations, and in neighborhood gatherings. They are not disconnected from government; indeed, government is implicated in two important ways: through laws, regulations, and funding that make it possible for groups of citizens to meet voluntarily and carry out their business; and through the political activities of citizens, such as voting and the forming of political parties, that bear directly on who is elected to govern and what these representatives have a mandate to do. Civil society is nevertheless composed of activities conducted freely and supported privately, rather than through the coercive mechanisms of government. It is the centrality of civil society to the vitality of democracy from the bottom up, so to speak, that necessitates the attention we so often pay to questions about civic renewal.

The most basic way in which civic renewal takes place is through the transmission of values from one generation to the next. Transmission of this kind happens through families and is the reason that strong families are so often mentioned as a critical component of civil society. Civic education through public and private schooling plays an equally vital role in maintaining democracy. Specific knowledge about the Constitution, the Bill of Rights, and the voting process is important. Equally important are the broader socializing functions that education plays, such as exposing children to a common set of values through the study of literature and history. "The chief work of the school has been to operate as a cement in the social structure," John Dewey wrote, "or, to use a less mechanical metaphor, it has been the shuttle which has carried the threads across and woven the otherwise separate threads into a coherent pattern."[16] We may not think of schooling as a renewal process because it happens so routinely. However, democracy is renewed through the incorporation of successive cohorts, just as it may be through legislative or judicial reforms. Apart from its economic benefits, this is why we spend as much money as we do on public education and why we worry if studies suggest that children are not being well educated. Illiteracy is not only an impediment to employment; it also impedes the formation of the kind of informed public we think is required for a stable democracy. Renewal through education is also more than simply transmitting adults' values to children. As successive generations enter the public sphere, they bring youthful energy and new ideas into the democratic process.

Besides instilling values in the coming generation, we sometimes try to renew civil society by encouraging more active participation among the public at large in civic associations. Renewal through civic participation addresses Tocqueville's concern about democracy's eroding because of a passive electorate. Strong community organizations serve as "mediating structures" between individuals and government.[17] But maintaining a democracy through active participation in community organizations is always problematic. The difficulty, to paraphrase Oscar Wilde's famous quip about socialism, is that civic participation takes up too many evenings—evenings that are more easily spent watching television, if Robert Putnam is correct, or resting from an arduous day at work. Nonetheless civic renewal through associationalist, communitarian, and volunteer efforts has received a great deal of attention in recent years. This form of renewal has been inspired by the evidence, mentioned earlier, of declining civic participation, and by discussions about the importance of nongovernmental social programs as ways of curbing rising taxes and federal deficits. Associationalism is a strategy for renewing democracy in at least two ways. By bringing people out of their homes and encouraging them to be more involved in their communities, to take an interest in politics, and to vote, associationalism incorporates new groups into the society in much the same way that civic education incorporates new cohorts. Once they are incorporated, these groups and individuals then contribute to the vitality of civil society by helping the needy, mobilizing grassroots organizations, expressing their interests, and engaging in public debate about collective values. When civic participation wanes, it is thus reasonable for discussions of democratic renewal to seek ways to reignite interest in community associations.

The other means through which civic renewal occurs is public advocacy. Associationalism emphasizes the possibility of democratic renewal simply through people's getting to know their neighbors and overcoming feelings of mistrust. But associationalism assumes as well that people who become more involved in their communities may also become mobilized as advocates of particular public policies. Public advocacy is a more intentional means of attaining renewal, and advocacy on behalf of social justice is perhaps the clearest example. Unlike efforts that focus on specific policy concerns, such as clean air or lower taxes, social justice advocacy emphasizes that a healthy democracy requires efforts to promote equality and equal opportunities among citizens. Too much inequality is tantamount to rule by oligarchy, whether the wealthy actually hold public offices or simply manipulate public officials behind the scenes. Public advocacy is thus a way to renew democracy by empowering the powerless. It seeks to incorporate segments of the public who have been economically or politically marginalized, just as associationalism tries to encourage greater participation by those who have been socially marginalized. Public advocacy is typically pursued through public interest groups, watchdog organizations, and community organizing. It is worth recognizing, though, that public advocacy is also furthered through academic research. Studies of racial and gender inequality and efforts to monitor the gap between upper and lower socioeconomic strata provide examples.

Education, voluntary associations that reinforce civic values, and public advocacy have one thing in common. They all involve culture. They seek to rejuvenate democracy by communicating what a good society should look like and how ordinary individuals should behave. Much of what is communicated is explicit. Students learn about the three branches of government and how the history of our country and world has been shaped. Voluntary associations write mission statements, and public advocacy groups formulate calls to action. Implicit messages are also communicated: for instance, about authority and cooperation through classroom discussions, or about trust through neighborhood gatherings and community organizing. Social observers who write about the need to reinvigorate common values and who argue that civic virtue needs to be revitalized implicitly recognize that culture is at stake. Yet these discussions do not, in my view, take culture seriously enough. They focus too much on surface-level messages and on the programs that might encourage people to become more involved in their communities, and not enough on the more subtle ways in which we are governed by the taken-for-granted aspects of our culture.

## BRINGING CULTURE BACK IN

To understand the deeper ways in which culture is implicated in the search for democratic renewal, we will find it instructive to remind ourselves of an insight that animated Émile Durkheim's scholarship nearly a century ago.[18] Durkheim was persuaded that societies are held together at a very basic level by the myths they invent to explain the most powerful forces they encounter. These forces may become symbolized in rituals or amulets, in legends about powerful ancestors, or in beliefs about the sacred. Such rituals, legends, and beliefs are not invented deliberately, in the way a new technological device may be, or through the creative acts of a few people, as a new musical or literary genre might be. They emerge less deliberately, more gradually, and often through the separate activities of people in scattered locations. If they become popular, it is because they help a people make sense of its common origins and experiences. The explanations they provide are thus less cognitive than, say, an account of why an earthquake happened or a regime failed (although cognitive understanding is part of these explanations). They are rather narratives and narrative enactments that are *meaningful* because they tie events and experiences together in an intuitively appealing way.

Social scientists have emphasized this Durkheimian view of culture in studies of tribal rituals, religious symbolism, and nationalistic myths.[19] I want to take it in a different direction. What we might call culture as *deep meaning* is concerned with the tacit knowledge that guides human behavior without our needing to think very much about it. It is composed less of beliefs and values and more of orientations and understandings. We simply "know" that certain things *are*. For instance, we "know" that motorists on highways in the United States will drive on the right-hand side of the highway. We know this to be the case. I say "the case," rather than "true," because this kind of knowledge is generally not theorized or philosophically based in the way that truth is. It is an implicit understanding of reality, of how the world works. In this sense, it is more descriptive than prescriptive. Deep culture is nevertheless concerned with the way things *should* be as well. It includes assumptions about the desirable. I not only recognize right-hand driving as a reality; I consider it desirable because it prevents accidents. The assumptions we make about human rights, personal dignity, freedom, trustworthiness, and civic responsibility are not so easily summarized, but they compose the cultural infrastructure that makes common life possible. They provide what the political philosopher Michael J. Sandel calls the "unreflective background" to public discourse and public policy, the "assumptions about citizenship and freedom that inform our public life."[20] In emphasizing its depth and the fact that it is taken for granted, I am suggesting that deep culture lies beneath the surface of what is actually said or written. We might say that it is the cultural subtext, the background knowledge that must be accepted for the surface text to make sense.[21]

The relevance to democratic renewal of this way of thinking about culture is that renewal is most effective when it rejuvenates or redefines culture at the level of deep meaning. Durkheim recognized this potential when he argued that the collective consciousness of a society is typically shaped by the stories that grow out of major crises and other turning points in the life of a people—such episodes as the founding of their society, a crisis of succession in leadership, a natural catastrophe, or a violent conflict. Durkheim believed, as Tocqueville did more specifically in reference to democracies, that societies tend to run down or lose steam over time. People gradually forget the collective values and the events that infused these values with meaning. We need to be reminded and to experience events that plug new life into these values and meanings. Periodic rituals, such as national holidays and anniversaries, serve this purpose. The larger point is not about rituals, though. It is that renewal operates at the level of deep meaning. Unanticipated events, such as an economic crisis, can precipitate rethinking of tacit cultural assumptions about personal meaning, freedom, success, and what is good about the society in which one lives. So can planned rituals—national celebrations, for example—or scattered responses to new conditions, such as techno-logical change or the shifts in population associated with conquest or immigration. The connection with considerations about democracy is that civil society does not function simply through social networks or participation in voluntary associations. Civil society is not as static or as instrumental as these images suggest, and we cannot renew it simply by encouraging people to join more organizations. Nor can we understand civil society by paying attention only to nonprofit organizations, advo-cacy groups, and public policy. Civil society is of course composed of organizations and social networks, but it is also composed of deeply held assumptions about society and its individual members. These assump-tions are sometimes subsumed in analyses of civil society under the word *trust*.[22] We make assumptions about whom we can trust and about whether or not trust is a good thing. But trust is in turn rooted in tacit knowledge about such matters as affinity (whom am I like?) and respon-sibility (who will be there when I need them?). The unreflective back-ground assumptions of which civil society is composed include schemes of classification (such as race and gender) that influence our perceptions of whom we can trust and with whom we prefer to associate, and they include understandings of what is in our interest, what is in the common interest, and how we should behave in pursuing these interests.

Culture as deep meaning is relevant to questions about renewal, therefore, because culture at this level is both an impediment to and a facilitator of social change. It is an impediment because the stock of practical knowledge that is generally taken for granted is difficult to recognize and thus even more difficult to challenge. Deep meanings pro-vide cultural *drag* in the same way a ship's anchor does. They stabilize a society, giving it continuity with the past and permitting its members to make new decisions without having to reinvent the past. Deep meanings endure because they work. They make it possible to go about the daily business of personal life without stopping at every moment to think about what we are doing and why we are doing it. They are the kinds of assumptions built into everyday language itself, the sociologist Michael Schudson writes, that make us nod knowingly when a child asserts, "You can't make me eat my vegetables. It's a free country."[23] We know intuitively that our country prides itself on being free and that this is an understanding reflected even in the most ordinary dinnertime conversations. Deep meanings impede a society from changing too rapidly or in ways that imply different understandings of who we are. As facilitator, deep meanings convey visions of the good and of what behavior encourages attainment of the good. Social actors can thus invoke these visions and initiate reforms that seek to clarify them and bring behavior more closely into conformity with them. Apart from specific ideals, the deep meanings of which cultures are composed also facilitate renewal by holding forth hopefulness itself. Hopefulness is the possibility that life can be better in the future than it has been in the past. It is an assumption about the possibility of personal transformation and societal betterment.

There was a time when these sorts of arguments about culture would have seemed more familiar to social scientists and their students than they do today. From the 1920s through the early 1960s, social scientists wrote books and articles in which the power of cultural assumptions was emphasized. Readers of these books and articles learned that American culture was individualistic and achievement oriented, for instance, or that such broad patterns of values as universalism were becoming more evident. Social scientists argued that there were such things as "national character" or differences among civilizations that could explain why some countries or regions progressed better economically than others. It was possible to read, for instance, that some cultures followed a "Dionysian" pattern, while others were more "Apollonian," and that there were deep archetypes and mythical structures beneath the surface of our everyday behavior.[24] Those arguments were often overstated or based on sparse evidence and, as such, were difficult to sustain when subsequent generations of social scientists began engaging in more systematic research. More than being disproved, though, they were displaced.[25] The social and political turmoil of the 1960s severely challenged the idea that cultural patterns were powerful and enduring. It seemed more reasonable to argue that politics was the driving force, and if not politics, economics. These could more easily be changed. Social scientists' attention shifted to "state structures," "mobilization theory," social movements, and revolutions. When studies of culture began making a comeback during the 1980s, they were informed by a very different understanding of culture from that which had animated earlier scholarship. Culture was now produced, contingent, and fungible. It was produced by specific organizations, groups, and power structures. For instance, it was the product of the recording industry, the academic elite, or a particular configuration of power among scientists. Culture was thus contingent on these social arrangements and, indeed, was subject to being intentionally manipulated by people in power and by people resisting them. In the well-known phrase advanced by the sociologist Ann Swidler, culture was a *tool kit*.[26] The overall composition of this kit might be relatively enduring (a possibility that few who were attracted to the idea emphasized), but, if it was, the more interesting concern was why someone pulled out a wrench at one moment and a pliers at another. Culture was obviously fungible if people could choose to employ it in such instrumental ways. Today's tools could well be tomorrow's relics. Rather than being described in terms of long-lasting patterns of unreflective background assumptions, culture thus became an object of study in which the latest fads in music or sports and the rhetoric of television personalities drew more attention than a society's more enduring beliefs and values.[27]

But if we are to understand why a society's efforts to be different or more fully to realize its ideals fail so often to hit their mark, then the more enduring assumptions of which culture is composed must be emphasized. If culture has the power to continue informing the future in the same way it has guided the past, despite major upheavals and despite deliberate change-oriented activities, then it is a force with which to reckon. Unlike cultural acts that are almost completely fungible, deep culture is more than the epiphenomenal product of political and economic arrangements. Civil society is composed of a democratic cultural "code," as the sociologist Jeffrey C. Alexander has argued—or, perhaps more accurately, not so much a code, since that implies the possibility of its being understood through a single prescient act of deciphering, as layers of meaning that go unnoticed most of the time.[28] If these meanings are "given off" and implied more than they are stated directly, then the reason we fail in our collective ambitions is that we do not pay more deliberate attention to them. We enjoy the story, the campaign speech, or the sound byte, and then move toward policy analysis and legal discussion without realizing the serious extent to which life is guided by stories, speeches, and sound bytes. The search for renewal focuses on better policies and better data, while ignoring the fact that there is more to culture than policies and data, and more than mere entertainment as well. The most effective times of renewal are ones in which policies and programs challenge fundamental assumptions about individual identities and responsibilities. An example from early in American history and a more recent one will show how renewal of this kind happens—how it involves deep meanings and how its strengths and limitations are conditioned by these meanings.

The social transformation that took place during the half century prior to the Civil War—what historians call the democratization of American culture—provides an interesting illustration of the processes through which cultural renewal occurs, and of the limitations of these processes. Having emerged by the start of the nineteenth century as an independent, self-governing nation, the United States found itself, as Jefferson's inaugural address suggested, in the position of needing to ensure that it could indeed govern itself and do so in a way that lived up to its founding ideals of representation and equality. The republican part of what it meant to be a republican democracy had been formalized as a system of divided powers and representation of the federation's member states. The democratic part of the equation was harder to achieve. If the more elite interpretations of federalism prevailed, the growing population and expanding territory encompassed by the United States could easily spin out of control—as illustrated by the religious conflicts of the seventeenth century and the anarchy following the French Revolution—unless some form of oligarchic rule was imposed. The option of handing over self-government to the masses of diverse, largely uneducated farmers and laborers of which the population was composed was untried and seemed fraught with extreme danger. By the eve of the Civil War, though, a form of popular enfranchisement, as much cultural as political, had been achieved. Its success could in significant measure be attributed to the Jacksonian reforms in governmental practice, but it was also the product of such scattered organizations as Bible societies and temperance unions, revival meetings, Methodist camp meetings, Mormons, Millerite Adventist groups, and Baptist churches. "As mass popular movements," the historian Nathan O. Hatch writes, "churches came to be places in which fundamental political assumptions were forged: ideas about the meaning of America, the priority of the individual conscience, the values of localism, direct democracy, and individualism."[29] Some of these organizations and movements, such as the revivals led by Charles Finney and the temperance and abolitionist movements, were concerned with specific reforms, and their capacity to mobilize around these reforms was the result of new techniques of assembly. They drew people into the first truly national, or at least translocal, movements and organizations.[30] Their effectiveness was nevertheless based on more than skill and innovative organization. They articulated more clearly than at any time during the preceding half century the idea that every person was governed by an inner sense of morality and that this sense of morality was sufficiently invariable that persons of modest means and no schooling could function responsibly as citizens, just as persons of higher rank could. This was cultural renewal clear and simple. It redefined the moral capabilities of individuals in a way that rendered democracy possible on an enlarged scale. What became known as commonsense morality was worked out in philosophical and theological discussions at colleges and in seminaries, especially by scholars following the writings of the moderate Scottish moral philosophers Francis Hutcheson and Thomas Reid. Locating morality within reach of the human senses essentially undermined the more restrictive view of moral reason attached to the regenerate through divine revelation that had been promulgated as recently as the 1740s by Jonathan Edwards.[31] The new commonsense view of morality was widely communicated through sermons and in the rituals associated with religious and community organizations. Revival meetings that called for confession and offered hope of personal transformation were especially prominent among these means of communication. "A cultural mechanism combining the evangelical schemas of public confession and the special sins of the nation launched sustained and interregional protests," writes the sociologist Michael P. Young. This cultural mechanism was both public and private, challenging whole communities to think about such issues as drinking and slavery, but doing so in a way that encouraged self-transformative experiences on the part of individuals. "The intensive and extensive power of these confessional protests called individual and nation to repent and reform, and mobilized actors and resources within a national infrastructure of religious institutions."[32] The effects were in many ways enduring, as is revealed by the sociologist John L. Hammond's careful research on the long-term social and political differences between counties experiencing and not experiencing revival meetings.[33] At the same time, the cultural means through which these new ideas of moral responsibility had been communicated were also their limitation. The union of public responsibility and private morality masked gendered distinctions in popular understandings of virtue that would make this union difficult to sustain. "During the 1760s and 1770s, virtue usually implied something close to what it had meant in the civic humanist tradition—a public-spirited attitude that subordinated personal interest to the public welfare," the historian Mark A. Noll writes. But the democratization of virtue through religious conversion gradually associated it more with domestic life. "By 1830 virtue had become a much more private quality, a standard of personal morality, 'something that women guarded within the household, something that they protected against lustful males.' "[34] Abolitionist arguments that included African Americans among those who were endowed with moral responsibility did not prevail everywhere. A war between the states was waged over conflicting definitions of personhood and rights. Following the war, the Protestant consensus that had defined itself as a universal understanding of morality gradually lost force because of immigration, greater religious diversity, and industrialization. "The religious habits of mind that had built a Protestant Christian America divided and eventually petered out after the war," writes Noll. The result of "deeply entrenched patterns of thought" was, he argues, "a tragedy of worthy thinkers striving faithfully for noble goals who were brought down by the very synthesis of Christian theology and American ideology that had transformed their society."[35] The cultural synthesis that emerged around the idea of commonsense morality was thus an instance of democratic renewal, and yet one that imposed its own limits, especially through its implicit assumptions about religion, race, gender, and cultural homogeneity.

My second example of cultural renewal is the redefinition of nationhood and citizenship that occurred in conjunction with the Second World War. This example is quite different from the first. Because it took place during war, it was significantly influenced by an acute sense of crisis and by deliberate mobilization in response to this crisis. The changes that came about were more centrally coordinated. They suggest that substantial cultural renewal can be promoted by government. Yet they also exemplify changes that were lasting and significant, affecting hearts and minds, rather than only involving propaganda and other measures needed to fight the war. From the end of the Civil War to the beginning of World War II, the United States experienced an almost steady move toward greater national integration and a more distinct sense of its national identity. These changes were partly the result of railroad networks linking local markets, telegraph and telephone technology, a more dependable postal service, and a more extensive system of roads and highways.[36] Religious organizations became more centrally administered, fraternal associations were part of a vast federation of local and regional clubs, new civic organizations (such as Rotary and Kiwanis) emerged, and eventually radio provided a more unified national culture, as did catalog companies, mail-order houses, and mass-circulation magazines such as *McClure's*, *Ladies' Home Journal*, and the *Saturday Evening Post*.[37] At the start of World War II, the nation nevertheless had relatively little of the cultural integration that actually linked individual citizens with the federal government and with other national organizations of the kind that would be present by the early 1950s. Day-to-day life could still be lived in local settings, and moral obligations could be defined largely within those settings. This was true especially for the 40 percent of the population who lived in rural areas where rural electrification more often meant wind chargers and batteries in the attic than integration into regional power grids, and where long-distance telephone calls were impossible or prohibitively expensive.[38] It was true for different reasons in urban neighborhoods where poverty, segregation, ethnic loyalties, and language barriers reinforced local ties. The large-scale immigration that had taken place as recently as the 1920s and the economic hardships of the 1930s reduced the likelihood that local ties would be transcended. "Cornerville's problem is not lack of organization but failure of its own social organization to mesh with the structure of the society around it," the sociologist William Foote Whyte concluded from his study of an Italian neighborhood in the late 1930s.[39] There was intense loyalty and a great deal of generational continuity among its members, including an internal power structure that reinforced local norms;

Cornerville was, however, disconnected from the world around it. Other sociologists found a similar emphasis on local attachments. The small local unit "makes possible a spirit of neighborhood and unity which is difficult to attain over larger areas," Louis Wirth wrote in 1937.[40] Centralized government and mass communication threatened the autonomy of local communities, but these threats were more possibilities than realities. If veterans organizations drew people into wider networks, the number of Americans who had served in World War I was relatively small (less than a third) compared to those who would serve in World War II, and the ranks of Civil War veterans were rapidly diminishing. World War II mobilized the population on a larger scale and with greater unity of purpose than did anything else in the history of the United States. For 16 million Americans, or approximately half of the male population between the ages of fifteen and forty-five, volunteering for military service or being drafted forged a defining connection between themselves and Uncle Sam.[41] Nearly everyone else had a role to play in the war as well. Farmers and factory workers who received deferments did so because the goods they produced were considered vital to the war effort. Women were employed in wartime industry in record numbers, and other women helped by planting victory gardens and joining ladies' auxiliaries. Rationing of gasoline, tires, sugar, nylon, and other goods directly affected the daily lives of all Americans. Some estimates put the number who actually served on War Price and Rationing Boards and on Consumer Interest Committees as high as 3 million.[42] By the end of the war, Americans were also linked to the federal government as never before by taxes. In 1939, only 4 million people were required to pay federal income taxes; by 1945, that number had risen to 42.7 million.[43] The long-term consequences of this redefinition of the relationship between individuals and the nation may not have been fully recognized at the time. Yet by the 1950s, many of these consequences could be imagined. Veterans' benefits and pensions linked growing numbers of individuals to the nation financially. Announcements about veterans' benefits appeared regularly in local newspapers; approximately half of all veterans took advantage of the GI Bill for education, and more than a quarter purchased houses with VA loans.[44] A new system of interstate highways, touted as fulfilling part of the nation's need to be prepared for another war, connected local communities through more rapid and more comfortable transportation.[45] The Cold War necessitated continuing emphasis on the nation's distinctive identity and values, including its freedom and the religious zeal that was evident in a postwar boomlet in religious service attendance. Seldom had private faith been as closely associated with the national agenda. "If you would be a true patriot, then become a Christian," evangelist Billy Graham encouraged. "If you would be a loyal American, then become a loyal Christian."[46] A new national culture of conformity to bureaucratic and organizational hierarchies, identified by such observers as social critics William H. Whyte Jr. and C. Wright Mills, was related to business's borrowing leadership styles from the military and corporations' simply being organized on a larger scale. "The twentieth-century white-collar man has never been independent as the farmer used to be, nor as hopeful of the main chance as the businessman," Mills wrote. "He is always somebody's man, the corporation's, the government's, the army's."[47] A service ethic, too, seemed to have carried over from wartime to peacetime as America became known as a nation of joiners. A half century later, Robert D. Putnam observed, there was still evidence of a "long civic generation" that came of age during World War II and continued to serve civic associations throughout their lives. "The core of this civic generation," Putnam writes, "is the cohort born in 1925–1930, who attended grade school during the Great Depression, spent World War II in high school (or on the battlefield), first voted in 1948 or 1952, set up housekeeping in the 1950s, and saw their first television when they were in their late twenties. Since national polling began, this cohort has been exceptionally civic—voting more, joining more, reading more, trusting more, giving more."[48] If World War II was responsible for a significant civic renewal with these characteristics, it nevertheless was a renewal that bore the stamp of cultural drag as much as of cultural facilitation. The same energies that mobilized the national effort in World War II encouraged the mass marketing through television that Putnam believes became responsible for a subsequent decline in civic participation. The individualism and nonconformity that Mills associated with farming and small business soon reacted against the conformity required of GI Joe and the Organization Man—a reaction that would appear with a vengeance during the 1960s. In the early 1950s, Clark Kerr, chancellor of the University of California at Berkeley, urged "each individual to avoid total involvement in any organization; to seek to whatever extent lies within his power to limit each group to the minimum control necessary for performance of essential functions; to struggle against the effort to absorb."[49] Little could Kerr imagine how those words would appear a few years later as he struggled against the Free Speech Movement unleashed on the Berkeley campus by a generation of students governed less by conformity and more by a lingering commitment to freedom. In other ways, too, the civic renewal occasioned by World War II fell short of bringing about as much change as might have been hoped. Military service brought African Americans and white Americans into closer contact and achieved some racial equality, but it would take a civil rights movement to press for greater realization of these ideals. If white ethnics had been forced to abandon some of the local ties that had meant so much before the war, these local loyalties were also reborn, even in the Levittowns and other suburban developments that emerged after the war.[50]

The antebellum and World War II renewals illustrate the extent to which redefinitions of ourselves as Americans involve redefinitions at the level of deep culture. In both cases, it was impossible for individual Americans to think of themselves and to imagine their moral obligations in the same way as an earlier generation had done. More deliberate planning by far went into the second period of redefinition than into the first. Yet neither could be regarded as a time in which Americans consciously set out to reinvent themselves or their nation. The reinvention happened as an unanticipated but necessary consequence of efforts devoted to realizing the higher aims of the society, whether in bringing into being a more stable and truly representative democracy or in mobilizing that democracy in the struggle against totalitarianism. Because the process involved a significant refabrication of personal identity and moral responsibility, it came close to bringing about the desired realization of a better world. That neither era resulted in quite the success it might have cannot be understood solely in terms of resistance mobilized by opposing forces or, as historians have sometimes postulated, mere exhaustion from waging the good fight. The stabilizing power of cultural assumptions is considerable.

## REINVENTING AMERICA

The most recent period of American history—the decades spanning roughly the years from 1965 to the present—is a time in which the

United States has, by many accounts, reinvented itself. The period includes the civil rights movement and subsequent efforts, ranging from equal opportunity legislation to affirmative action policies, to promote greater equality across racial lines. It includes similarly profound efforts to promote gender equality, at least one result of which has been a huge rise in women's participation in the paid labor force and nearly equal gender representation in many fields of higher education. These and other changes in cultural self-understanding have led many observers to write about a "rights revolution" in which individual rights and the freedom to pursue or express these rights have become more pronounced.[51] The past four decades have also witnessed more immigration than has any period since the 1920s. Since immigration policies were reformed in 1965, some 22 million immigrants have come to the United States legally, and as many as 7 to 10 million have come as undocumented workers. The number of Americans who claim Hispanic or Asian ancestry has risen dramatically. On a smaller scale, the number of Americans who identify with religions other than Christianity or Judaism has also increased. Muslims, Hindus, and Buddhists have become citizens in larger numbers than ever before. Immigration has been a significant part of America's self-understanding about youthfulness, creativity, and rejuvenation from the beginning, and the recent wave of immigration is no exception. "The U.S. will be, through our lifetimes, young, ambitious and energetic," writes the columnist David Brooks. This "Great Rejuvenation," as Brooks calls it, is in no small measure attributable to our having absorbed so many immigrants in recent years.[52] Besides immigration, which has added cultural diversity in its own way, diversity itself has become a much more prominent value than it was for previous generations. Through schooling and the mass media, Americans learn that diversity is a good thing, and are encouraged to embrace it. In all these ways, American culture has been reinvented—or at least we have sought to reinvent it and have often been told by social observers that things are quite different from the way they were. The recent period is thus an interesting and important case study through which to examine the unreflective background assumptions that have facilitated but also impeded cultural renewal. This is especially so when we consider the narratives of new immigrants themselves. Despite differences in national origins, these immigrants have often adopted assumptions about the United States that sound strikingly familiar. Examining these assumptions can provide new perspective on what we so often take for granted. Indeed, the American mythos consists so much of stories about—and by—immigrants that understanding these stories is an excellent way of grasping how the deep meanings of our culture are constructed.

## CHAPTER 2

# QUANDARIES OF INDIVIDUALISM

I have suggested that the threat to democracy from below fundamentally concerns the individual. While the threat from above—the danger of takeover by the wealthy and powerful—requires legislative and judicial vigilance, the threat from below emerges from social conditions that discourage ordinary citizens from playing an active part in upholding democracy and in contributing to the common good. Tocqueville's ideal of self-interest *rightly understood* requires social conditions that maintain individual freedom *and* individuals who play a responsible role in their communities. When individuals become part of a nameless and faceless mass, democracy suffers. The mass conformity that worried William H. Whyte Jr. and other observers in the 1950s is one example. The Organization Man was a cog in a wheel, rather than an independent thinker capable of forming opinions and making moral judgments on his own. With World War II such a recent reminder, it took little imagination to glimpse in the look-alikes streaming from large office buildings an image of the masses assembled at Nazi rallies. In recent years, it has been more common to worry about individuals' losing their ability to function as thoughtful citizens because of consumerism and television. It is troubling to think that a few conglomerates control the publishing industry, and that television stations and newspapers are being bought up by the same companies. These are worrisome developments. They increase the chances of individual opinions' being molded by powerful corporate interests. It has been refreshing to imagine that diversity is at least being reinforced in other ways.

Evidence of increasing racial and ethnic diversity and of increasing respect for such diversity provides hope that we are not all becoming look-alikes. In that sense, the America of today is quite different from the one that social observers examined a half century ago. We have become a rainbow society. Against the homogeneity that consumerism and advertising promote, we are a nation of myriad tastes. Gender, race, religion, national origin, lifestyle, and region all encourage differences of opinion. This diversity generates individual identities that do not take their cues from any one source. Yet diversity produces concerns of a different kind. A diverse society is one in which centrifugal forces dominate. Not only are there special interest groups that create political conflict in the name of identity politics. Individual identities also proliferate as people identify with unique combinations of ethnicity or race or religion based on an increasing diversity of ancestry and national origin. Tiger Woods becomes the symbol of this new diversity. Instead of individual identities' being lost in a faceless crowd, individual identities now become so important that common purposes are difficult to pursue. We worry that democracy will falter under the burden of too much individuality. Being the only Tiger Woods can mean becoming a modern-day Robinson Crusoe. An "army of one" can be appealing if a person has moral courage and a strong desire to succeed. However, it can also connote a lonely life off fighting by oneself and, for that matter, an ineffective approach to warfare. The shift in opinions about the balance between individuals and communities is thus one in which we seem to have changed dramatically over the past half century and still come up short. We are much better off than we were in the 1950s in terms of respecting individual freedom and diversity. Yet we seem to have traded one set of problems for another. Having struggled to emancipate the individual from totalitarian control, we now find ourselves worrying that individual freedom has advanced to the point that community loyalties have been lost. The question, then, is what kind of individual persons do we want and need in order to be a good society?

There are no easy answers to this question, and my aim here is not to suggest that there are. Instead, it seems to me that we fall short of our aspirations as a society by expecting either too much or too little of individuals. Moreover, we expect too much or too little because we do not pay sufficient attention to the myths that swirl around in our society about individual freedom and moral responsibility. Thus we vacillate between worrying about a lack of individual freedom and condemning ourselves for not being loyal enough to our communities. What is good about these discussions is that we are least having them—up to a point. Individualism is an example of a topic that has received more attention than some of the narratives we shall consider in later chapters. And we learn from these discussions that any hope of probing deeper into the American psyche for answers to our problems must begin with the individual. That was clear in the examples I presented in the previous chapter. In the antebellum period and again during and after World War II, social renewal was accomplished—and limited—by a shift in narratives about the moral qualities of individuals and about their ability to make morally responsible decisions. In these early years of the twenty-first century, I believe we must again look closely at how we think about individualism. Doing so necessitates revisiting how the debate about individualism has shifted in recent decades, developing a clearer understanding of the importance of "embedded selves," and examining the role that narratives play in our ability to reflect on ourselves.

This chapter, then, is concerned with the various meanings of the *self*, as it is called, or perhaps better, the human person—the meanings that currently occupy much of our public discourse about individual rights, freedom, and moral responsibility. The examples from antebellum America and from the World War II era suggest that cultural change runs deepest when it influences our ideas about the rights and responsibilities of individuals. How much or how little to focus on the individual, though, is a contested question. Some theorists argue that we have become obsessed with the person and need to pay less attention to individuals, while others argue just the opposite. These arguments are part of a long debate, but the terms of debate have altered greatly since the mid–twentieth century.

Whereas scholarly opinion in the 1950s focused on too little individualism and too much conformity, the dominant view in more recent years has focused on too much individualism. This reversal of opinion is one of the more interesting aspects of the cultural change our nation has undergone during the past half century. We seem to have overcome the fear about losing our individual identities, only to have given birth to new fears that individualism is out of control.[1] I believe there is a middle ground, an understanding of the human person that emphasizes the *embedded self*. This view of the human person, I will try to show, provides a way of retrieving the moral dimension of traditional understandings of American individualism *and* of recognizing the continuing importance of individual responsibility in community-oriented appeals. At the same time, it stresses the social arrangements, networks, and organizations that facilitate (or impede) moral conduct. If the individual is of continuing significance in discussions of American democracy, we also need to move beyond philosophical arguments about rights and responsibilities. To do that, I suggest we pay closer attention to personal narratives and their role in framing cultural assumptions about the individual. My further aim here is to provide a context in which to introduce the more specific themes about individual journeys and success that I will take up in chapters 3 and 4, and to set the stage for considering what it means to be more reflective about our roles as citizens.

The Tocquevillean tradition offers a first step toward answering the question about what kinds of individuals are needed to ensure a strong democracy. The answers are most clearly stated in the negative. A good society is one in which individuals do not blindly follow their leaders or conform blindly to popular opinion. In a strong democracy, individuals do not depend on government to do everything for them, nor do they depend too heavily on others. The individuals who constitute a good society are not driven by narrow self-interest. And they are not isolated from one another. Positively, the criteria for a good society include individuals who not only are engaged in the pursuit of happiness but to some extent realize that goal. They are people whose lives are respected by others and who themselves respect the lives of others. They are also individuals who do their part and are thus good citizens. They are self-sufficient, but they also depend on others to accomplish tasks that require cooperation. The political philosopher George Kateb calls this understanding of the human person "democratic individuality."[2] It involves recognizing that social conventions *are* conventions and thus open to change. Democratic individuals seek to liberate human energies and thus to live more intensely. A good society therefore protects the autonomy of individuals by respecting their freedom and their right to free expression. A good society also encourages individuals to form alliances and to engage in political activity. As an initial guiding principle, there is thus a kind of *both-and* quality to the individual—a delicate balance between the autonomous individual who pursues individual happiness and the responsible individual who contributes to the common good.

These desiderata overlap considerably with ideas about human flourishing in psychology. Individuals who flourish have an internal moral compass that guides their thinking about right and wrong. They have become differentiated from their families and communities. They take responsibility for their own happiness. At the same time, they seek support when they need it and they usually receive gratification from their social attachments and their efforts to help others. There is thus a balance between egoism and altruism, between self-fulfillment and caring for others.[3] Whereas psychologists typically ask only what helps individuals to be happy and achieve their goals in life, though, the question here is what is good for society. The basic argument is that particular kinds of individuals are required—individuals who, in the Tocquevillean vision, contribute to their communities but are also strong selves who embody what scholars of Tocqueville's era would have called virtue. Put negatively, it is not enough for a society to achieve a stable or growing economic base or to follow democratic procedures of government. Those are important, as are creative ideas about how to solve specific problems. But a good society requires good people.

But merely stating the desiderata identified in the Tocquevillean vision of democracy or in social psychological ideas about human flourishing begs the question of why these ideals are difficult to attain. We may agree that a good society requires good people and yet perceive the challenges quite differently, depending on how we view the dominant culture. If there has been a turnaround in these perceptions, as I have suggested, between those of the 1950s and more current ones, we need to see what that turnaround has involved and what it tells us about the social conditions that influence our understandings of the individual.

## INDIVIDUALITY, MORE OR LESS?

When social observers wrote about American society in the 1950s, they usually expressed concern that the individual was being replaced by the group. The triumph of groups over individuals took place at several levels and thus received differing treatment by different scholars. At one level, the growing emphasis on the group was evident in scholarly perspectives themselves; that is, in the theories and concepts that animated intellectual discussions, whether or not these reflected the realities of social life itself. Psychology had been deeply influenced by World War II. There was interest in mass psychology, the psychology of crowd behavior, the kinds of personalities or temperaments that might be conducive to totalitarianism, and the needs for mental health resources that would make people better adjusted to the demands of modern society. Sociology was more oriented toward collectivities than toward individuals, but observers also perceived a shift in emphasis within the discipline. "More than any other, it is the concept of the social group that has become central," Robert A. Nisbet wrote. "It contrasts sharply with the primacy of the individual in earlier American sociology."[4] This reorientation was, in Nisbet's view, symptomatic of growing influence from conservative social philosophy as opposed to the classical laissez-faire ideas that attached greater importance to the individual. At the same time, it was also a reflection of the times in which people lived. "A preoccupation with community and a fear of insecurity pervade almost every area of civilized life."[5]

It was not simply that intellectuals had become more interested in social life than in the needs of individuals or that people were somehow afraid to express their individuality. The larger concern was with an apparent trend toward conformity. The collectivity was more powerful than the individual because individuals conformed to the will of the majority. People knowingly or unknowingly imitated one another. Too much conformity means being like everyone else and thus not realizing one's particular talents. The society loses because people do not develop their special gifts. It also means that people do not think for themselves. Not only did people *become* like everyone else, they also *desired* alikeness (and thus gave up their freedom). Conformity helped the society to run smoothly but was not good for the individual. What had once been individual character, a bundle of attributes associated with the individual, now became "social character." People were so much alike that they could be lumped together into single national or cultural types. "By adapting himself to social conditions man develops those traits which make him *desire* to act as he *has* to act," the psychologist Erich Fromm wrote. "The energies of people are molded in ways that make them into productive forces that are indispensable for the functioning of that society."[6] Conformity meant that work was done and social order was maintained. The trains ran on time and factories filled their orders. But individual freedom was bargained away. The unique reflections and experiences of the individual were lost, and lost with them were the independent decisions that keep a democracy on track.

The sociologist David Riesman captured the spirit of the times better than anyone else did. Riesman depicted the rise of social conformity as a shift from an "inner-directed" to an "other-directed" character type. An inner-directed person was guided by his or her own values. There was an interior reservoir of strength, autonomy of thought that came from critically reflecting on differences of opinions and trusting firmly in one's own decisions. Inner-directed Americans were people of virtue. They had strong convictions and were not afraid to voice these convictions to their friends and families or at town meetings. They were the pioneer men and women, the trappers and traders, and the entrepreneurs who had made the nation great. Other-directed Americans, in contrast, waited to sense where the majority opinion lay and then went along with it. Instead of making decisions based on what they knew to be right or wrong, they tried to get along. Other-directed people had friends, and they were willing to sacrifice anything to keep them. They desperately wanted to fit in and to be liked. But they did so at the cost of thinking for themselves.[7]

The most troubling part of all this was not just that individuals caved in to social pressures. It was that Americans no longer realized they were caving in. As Fromm observed, they *desired* to be like everyone else. In an ironic twist, it thus became possible to assert one's individuality by *choosing* to be like everyone else. William H. Whyte Jr. understood that conformity was not so much an abnegation of individual virtue as a new way of defining virtue. It was a "social ethic," he wrote, meaning that Americans believed it to be their moral responsibility to go along with the crowd. The social ethic was "that contemporary body of thought which makes morally legitimate the pressures of society against the individual." It was composed of three major propositions: "a belief in the group as the source of creativity; a belief in 'belongingness' as the ultimate need of the individual; and a belief in the application of science to achieve the belongingness."[8] The social ethic was thus a definition of commitment. It demonstrated how easily transformed understandings of the individual were. A person could be an unthinking automaton and still feel like a person with strong convictions. The social ethic, Whyte wrote, "rationalizes the organization's demands for fealty and gives those who offer it wholeheartedly a sense of dedication in doing so—*in extremis*, you might say, it converts what would seem in other times a bill of no rights into a restatement of individualism."[9]

Despite the seeming ease with which people adapted to the social ethic, there was nevertheless a quality about it that proved unnerving. This was the fact, quite simply, that conformity was becoming increasingly difficult. Were it just a matter of following the lead of one's peers, conformity would be easy. But the society to which one was expected to conform was increasingly composed of large, impersonal organizations. Confronted with them, the individual felt powerless. There were too many responsibilities. People were faced with new rules and regulations that quashed their personal freedom. They tried hard to live up to their responsibilities but found it difficult to do so because the rule-makers were impersonal and thus impossible to negotiate with. "From the executive's suite to the factory yard, the paper webwork is spun," C. Wright Mills wrote; "a thousand rules you never made and don't know about are applied to you by a thousand people you have never met and never will."[10] Faced with such odds, the individual becomes alienated and feels incapable of changing them. A fatalistic view of life results. Things happen to a person because of outside forces, rather than being made or controlled by a person's decisions. Besides the fact that society was more complex and impersonal than ever before, the individual was also weaker. The lonely person in a crowd is an image of weakness. There is no support, no protection against large-scale institutions, such as the corporation, the media, and government. Democracy is endangered because the decisions made by individual members of the electorate are more easily manipulated by people in power. If conformity could become a conviction, consent could also be manufactured. "We cannot today merely assume that in the last resort men must always be governed by their own consent," Mills wrote. "For among the means of power which now prevail is the power to manage and to manipulate the consent of men."[11]

Although the submersion of individuals keeps the society functioning, there is in these analyses a troublesome sense of injustice and inauthenticity about this loss of individuality. If people get ahead because of whom they know instead of what they know, the implication is that they are not succeeding justly. The old view of America—a good society that provides opportunities for good people to succeed—is threatened. Getting ahead because of social networks is inauthentic. It connotes not working hard or not actually adding value through one's labor. The person who socializes is a salesperson, a gossip, a freeloader. Similarly, a person unduly influenced by others is likely to be driven by image and by a desire to keep up appearances. Decisions are thus faulty because one sees only the surface appearances presented by others, rather than truly knowing one's friends and having inside information about them. Friendships and family relationships suffer because they are based on surface appearances rather than more intimate knowledge of the inner self. This concern about inauthenticity assumed, of course, that something about individuals could not be understood in terms of culture. There were underlying personality types or character traits. These were diverse and needed to be expressed, rather than being reshaped by a common mold. "Until the psychologist knows what the norms of behavior imposed by a particular society are, and can discount them as indicators of personality, he will be unable to penetrate behind the facade of social conformity and cultural conformity to reach the authentic individual," wrote the anthropologist Ralph Linton.[12] Culture was a barrier to perceiving or realizing what this individual authenticity was. The assumption implicit in this critique of cultural conformity was that individuals have distinctive gifts and potential buried within them, but as long as they do what everyone else is doing, this potential remains unrealized.

Besides inauthenticity, the social ethic posed a danger of emasculation. In the "old days" against which contemporary society was always measured, people were willing to suffer, endure hardship, and experience pain in the service of a cause or simply to achieve their life's ambitions. Having lost that vigor, people now wanted instant gratification, were unwilling to sacrifice for it, and pursued short-term gains by cutting corners and cultivating their friends. Whereas in earlier times competition promoted individuality, strength, and achievement, it now took place in rigid organizational hierarchies that stifled creativity. No longer was competition "a testing field for heroes," Mills wrote.[13] Even good citizenship was suspect because it was more likely to be motivated by social climbing than by a genuine desire to serve. Joining social clubs was something the Organization Man did to make good in the company. The fear of emasculation carried the term's gendered connotation as well. The man in the gray flannel suit had become soft, effeminate, because he was no longer on the prairie or in the factory doing physical work. He was no longer dressed in buckskin. Women were conformists in their own way, going to coffee klatches and buying the same consumer products as everyone else. Yet they were, in another sense, the solution to the problem of mass conformity. Being outside the labor market, they were at home, fixing up the home in intimate and personalized ways, making it a haven to which the Organization Man could escape, and providing decent values for the children. All that, of course, would change as women began entering the labor market in increasing numbers and the concern about individuality shifted from too little to too much.

During the 1960s and 1970s, the concern about mass conformity was still sufficiently in mind that clearer expressions of individuality were generally welcomed. The civil rights movement especially came to be regarded as an articulation of individual freedom—as a triumph over the racial strictures of a society dominated by whites. The quest for gender equality carried similar connotations. It was a struggle for freedom to enter the labor force, to pursue a career of one's choice, and to control one's choices about reproduction. With some misgiving, the youth culture of the period was also welcomed by social observers as an expression of individuality—despite the fact that countercultural styles of dress and music demonstrated as much conformity as they did individuality. But by the 1980s, there was a widespread sense that individuality had gone too far. The trouble was no longer that of society's having triumphed over the individual, but of individuals' having triumphed over society. Whereas there had been too much homogeneity in the 1950s, now there was too much diversity. If people had been subservient to social expectations before, now they defied those expectations to pursue their own interests.

Too much emphasis on the individual means that people are selfish and focused narrowly on pursuing their personal interests. They are free riders who reap the benefits of society but are unwilling to do their part to sustain the common good. This orientation, writes the sociologist and communitarian advocate Amitai Etzioni, consists of "a strong sense of entitlement, demanding the community to give more services, strongly upholding rights [and entailing] a relatively weak sense of obligation, of serving the commons, and the lack of a sense of responsibility for the country."[14] The selfish individual retreats from civic involvement, stays at home, or works longer hours to achieve a higher income, but gives nothing back to the community. Such people are narcissistic, thinking too much about themselves, worrying about how to find personal fulfillment, and interested in doing so by expressing their feelings. They have trouble finding friends because when they socialize, they talk only about themselves. Whereas the conformist of the 1950s was driven by surface appearances rather than an inner self, the individualist of the present is guided almost entirely by the inner self. What the sociologist James Davison Hunter calls "the death of character" is a condition in which individuals are moved more by the quest for good feelings than by principles.[15] Character implied stability because the principles to which one was committed were enduring. They were rooted in cultural traditions that people believed to be true and in the accumulated wisdom of generations. Feelings, in contrast, focus attention on the moment. They are ephemeral and thus unreliable guides for individual behavior, let alone for collective responsibilities. When behavior is influenced by feelings, it may also be too little supported by the activities of others. Thus a person who attributes decisions to the fact that "it felt right" can avoid having to listen to the counsel of others. That same person can also experience too much guilt when things go wrong. Or no guilt at all, if one's conscience is guided only by an inner voice. Sheila Larson, the woman described by Bellah and his coauthors in *Habits of the Heart* who looks inside herself for guidance and creates her own religion ("Sheilaism"), exemplifies this kind of person.[16] She has no anchor, no way of knowing for sure whether she is doing right or wrong. In the limiting case, she becomes the ruler of herself, responsible to no one. "Kill when you must, and be killed the same: the *must* coming from the gods inside you," wrote D. H. Lawrence.[17] As moral guides, feelings are worrisome because they replace convictions rooted in cultural traditions. A focus on feelings leads also to self-delusion. Sheila can believe herself to be doing right even when she is not. She can imagine herself being in charge although she is a product of her times. Feelings imply that choices are entirely controlled by individuals, whereas in reality they are constrained by circumstances.

There is a continuing critique of power in these criticisms, too, but one of a different sort. The media, political parties, and the entertainment industry encourage narcissistic understandings of the individual. A therapeutic state shapes the public schools, drug courts, and legislation. It emphasizes self-esteem too much and enduring values too little.[18] There are also popular notions of individual rights that have become skewed. These notions are institutionalized in laws that focus only on rights and in mass media that champion freedom with venal intent. Extreme individualists assert their right to make choices but have little basis on which to make good ones. The quest to know one's inner self, one's authentic self, is misguided. Instead of gaining self-knowledge, and instead of putting oneself in contexts where a stable self can be developed, the person develops a mutable self, a shifting array of facades.

The mutable self is little more than a multiplicity of roles, a person engaged in the presentation of self, or, more accurately, in the presentation of a different self in each situation—a workplace self, a sports self, a lover self, a parent self, and so on.[19] The mutable self makes decisions based on what feels right at the moment, rather than making long-term plans and enduring commitments. "All I can see is wanting this job today. I do think this is what I want right now," says a young woman interviewed in a study of law students. She gets confused when she tries to think too far ahead. "Only when I stop and think do I think that maybe this lifestyle isn't what I want."[20] It is easier to not stop and think very often. Another student does think ahead, but being uncertain about the future, he thinks only in utilitarian terms. "I'm not going to invest a whole lot of energy in the company because I don't know what they're going to give me," he says. For the mutable self, relationships may be based more on the manipulation of one's image than on long-lasting convictions. As earlier critiques also saw it, the average person is duped, happily playing the game of pursuing individual happiness, but often with unhappy results. The individual may be relatively powerless in the face of such forces. Yet the assumption is that individuals can make moral choices if they see more clearly the consequences of their actions.

Why more recent criticisms differ so sharply from those of the 1950s is a matter of conjecture. The earlier criticisms were expressed by younger scholars who saw themselves as independent intellectuals and found the conformity they witnessed among their peers disconcerting. The recent criticisms have mostly been voiced by an older generation, many of whom were themselves products of the 1950s, and are directed at excesses they perceive mostly among younger Americans. Whereas the earlier criticisms focused on declining masculinity, the recent ones have included more nuanced gender connotations but have, if anything, been more critical of characteristics stereotypically associated with women—such as an emphasis on feelings and the inner self—than with those attributed to men. The possibility that Americans have actually become more individualistic or selfish is suggested by evidence of declining civic participation and rising interest, according to opinion polls, in individual fulfillment and personal freedom. The communities and organizations that generated loyalties in the past have become more uncertain. The children of the Organization Man, write social scientists Paul Leinberger and Bruce Tucker, are "more inclined to join many ever-shifting networks than to seek a niche in one immortal hierarchy."[21] If they have an identity at all, it has to come from within, not from a community or organization. The growing diversity and tolerance of diversity within the culture are undoubtedly factors as well. With more variety available, conformity seems less of a problem, while the time and energy that individuals devote to making choices has necessarily increased.

A surface reading of the literature criticizing American individualism in recent years would probably suggest that we simply need to pay less attention to individuals and devote more attention to groups, communities, and the society. Instead of spending time thinking about themselves, individuals would become better citizens—if not better people—by blending into the community. They would, as some proponents of strong communities argue, discover that it is more in keeping with human nature to belong than to be separate, and more natural to accept the community's rules than to constantly make choices of one's own. "Most people want a chart to follow and are not happy when they don't have one," the writer Alan Ehrenhalt asserts. "The uncharted life, the life of unrestricted choice and eroded authority, is one most ordinary people do not enjoy leading."[22] Insofar as growth toward personal fulfillment takes place, it occurs more naturally, according to this view, as people fit into the group, serve others, and receive support in return. Emphasizing the rights of human persons is off track because personhood is achieved only as people lose themselves in service to others. Life apart from the group is lonely, whereas the gathered community is where life is experienced most fully. Religious leaders, as the shepherds of gathered communities, are especially keen on making these arguments. Religion is, if anything, communal. It encourages people to spend time in congregations and to identify themselves fundamentally through narratives about a community of faith. "By working and playing together," one pastor writes, "by not being afraid to ask both the whimsical and the hard questions, by coming together, we can make our lives something like that famous mustard bush, with its great branch giving shade for the birds of heaven."[23] The same arguments can be appealing, too, if ethnicity or race is regarded as a basic community of identity or if democracy is thought to be strengthened mainly by vigorous, politically engaged associations. I call this a surface reading, though, because it misses what critics are actually saying about the continuing significance of the individual.

The deeper message in recent criticisms of American individualism is that an effective democracy, like an effective individual, requires what, for want of a better term, we might call *strong selves*. Strong selves are people who have what is variously termed inner strength, character, or moral resolve. They are people who know their mind, who have opinions, and who are willing to express these opinions. They are thus capable of making decisions, and they do so in terms of considered judgments about what is right and wrong. Yet they are not nonconformists who go against the grain simply for the sake of nonconformity. They strike a balance between inner conviction and cultural tradition, not simply as a via media approach to life, but more as a considered judgment that takes account of the changing complexities of situations and responsibilities. A strong self is someone who exercises discretion, rather than blindly rejecting or accepting social customs. Discretion suggests that strong selves make choices, but choices that are tempered by conviction. A conviction is not something we merely decide to adopt; it grips us and thus seems to be anchored more deeply within us.[24] It is that sense of being anchored that gives stability to the self. "My trouble is, I lack conviction," says one of the characters in John Barth's *Lost in the Funhouse*. "Many accounts of our situation seem plausible to me—where and what we are, why we swim and whither. But implausible ones as well, perhaps especially those, I must admit as possibly correct."[25] The problem here is that accounts are free-floating, delimited neither by cultural agreement nor by a clear personal identity. Being strong implies more even than learning principles of good conduct. "It is more a matter of trying to understand how general claims apply to us in particular, given our characters and circumstances, and how to balance the competing demands they make on the way we try to live our lives," writes the philosopher John Kekes.[26] A strong self is thus self-directed. Self-direction involves negotiating a balance between the deep inner promptings of conscience and the norms of one's community.

The value of strong selves can be seen in the case of Sheila Larson. She is already a person who appreciates the importance of inner strength and apparently has some, given that she is a nurse who cares for dying children. The criticism expressed by Bellah and his coauthors is not a suggestion that she give up her identity for the sake of becoming, say, a

Methodist. It is rather a concern that she will find herself running on empty at some point as she exhausts her inner reserves. If she listens for God and hears only herself, where can she turn when self-doubt arises? She needs group support, and she would benefit from knowing more about a religious tradition because the camaraderie and wisdom would give her additional strength. She would have others from whom to seek advice and a narrative tradition in which to find role models. She would not lose her identity by becoming like her friends or by blindly following these role models. She would compare herself with them and thus gain greater clarity about who she is and what she values.

Similarly, the idea of a strong self is implied in the story of Narcissus from which the concern about narcissistic personalities takes its name. Narcissus drowns because he sees his image reflected in a pool, confuses it with himself, and falls in. The problem is not that a person has too clear an identity; it is not having one that is clear enough. With no sharp line of demarcation between self and society, it becomes impossible to adjudicate between conscience and culture. One either follows conscience, failing to realize that it deviates radically from social norms, or follows social norms, imagining them to be the voice of conscience. People with strong selves are better able to distinguish themselves from others and thus are more capable of interacting confidently with others. People retreat from public life, in this view, not when they become too interested in themselves, but when they are unsure of who they are.[27]

The criticisms expressed by scholars in the 1950s help to keep those of more recent years in proper perspective. If the solution to narcissism, expressive individualism, and the death of character were simply to minimize the importance of the individual relative to the group, then the 1950s would be the ideal situation. The inner-directed Americans of today should once again become other-directed. An individualistic ethic should be replaced by a social ethic. But the critics of the 1950s recognized the shortcomings of those kinds of association. Peer groups can pose problems just as severe as the absence of peer groups. The solution to individualism therefore is not to become more fully identified with a group of one's peers. When that happens, individual identity is lost. The person becomes weak, not strong. What is needed is interaction with the group, not identification with it. Interaction implies give-and-take. In the process, individuals learn the group's values, but they also learn to disagree with the group. For its part, the group does not just expect conformity. It respects and empowers the individual.

Despite the 180-degree differences that seem to separate the more recent from the earlier discussions of individualism, there are also some underlying continuities that help us understand the moral meanings we associate with human personhood. An important one is the concern evident in both about power's subverting democratic institutions and, for that matter, weakening the individual. In the earlier discussions, this concern is evident in arguments that mass society leads to totalitarianism like that in Nazi Germany and Bolshevik Russia. The more recent discussions more commonly voice concern about fragmentation and chaos than about totalitarian rule. However, we still see evidence of the Tocquevillean conviction that too much individualism results in a power shift toward big government. The argument is not just that civic withdrawal on the part of individuals forces government to supply more services, although that argument is popular in some quarters. The argument connecting individualism with big government is rather one that views an emphasis on rights as the culprit. Rights need to be upheld universally instead of being defined differently in different communities. They cannot be one thing in Mississippi and another in California. "As rights and entitlements expand," writes Michael J. Sandel, "politics is therefore displaced from smaller forms of association and relocated at the most universal form—in our case, the nation."[28] In his view, this shift from localities to the nation is also evident in increased executive and judicial power at the expense of the legislative branch. But the important implication of this concern about individualism's eroding democracy is that the nation-state cannot define what is good any more than it can define what is right. For to do so would also require large-scale, centralized structures capable of harnessing and directing national energies. The criticism of individual rights is thus an appeal for greater power to be vested in local communities, local government, and other local organizations, such as churches, social clubs, and school boards. And that has two further implications: if there is to be a more appropriate balance between the individual and society, it needs to be found within local settings; and insofar as the national population is more ethnically and racially or religiously diverse, this diversity will inevitably be embodied in these local settings. In short, the concern about too much individuality necessitates rediscovering the mutual influences between individuals and local communities, which in turn necessitates taking greater account of cultural diversity.

## THE EMBEDDED SELF

The criticisms from the 1950s and in more recent years point to the need for an understanding of the self that acknowledges both its relationships to the community and its need for autonomy. I use the term *embedded self* to suggest precisely this balance. Selves are situated within communities and other social arrangements, such as the workplace, families, ethnic groups, and nations. Embedding implies that individuals are constrained by their social locations—by the resources inherent in these locations, such as wealth or power, and by the position a particular individual occupies within that location, such as being an executive in the workplace or a leader of a voluntary association. To be in one social location implies a commitment to that location. This is the moral dimension of embeddedness. I am constrained by the expectations built into the roles I play and by the internalized commitments I have made to abide by those expectations. Embedding, however, does not imply that I am simply the product of my circumstances. I have sufficient autonomy and am sufficiently self-directed to negotiate among the competing factors that have influenced me, and to set my own goals.

The recently popular idea of social capital captures some of what I mean to suggest by the concept of embedded selves. Social capital consists of the networks in which an individual is embedded and the norms governing those networks. Capital implies that these networks and norms serve as resources for accomplishing some of the ends an individual may wish to pursue.[29] Having such resources is part of what it means to be a strong self. Although the literature on social capital has not tended to emphasize this connection, an individual with social capital must also be a decision-maker. He or she makes decisions about the deployment of social capital, just as an entrepreneur does about economic capital. This decision-making capacity implies responsibilities. A person must decide when to make use of a network contact and must calculate what the cost may be. That much can be considered in utilitarian terms and thus is subject to the derogations of utilitarian calculations that have been common to nearly all criticisms of individualism. From a broader perspective, though, social capital does not consist only of utilitarian calculations that will benefit the individual. Social capital implies a network in which there will be long-term relationships. It implies behavior that will maintain trust. The good of others in the network must therefore be taken into consideration.

A person with social capital enjoys a certain kind of strength. Unlike the isolated individual, that person can rely on friends for support or information. Research suggests that people with social capital get better jobs, have fewer illnesses, and live longer. These are examples of personal strength. However, they do not exhaust the idea of strong selves. Strong selves make choices about which networks to cultivate, when to rely on their networks, and when to go their own way. An observation from the sociologist William Julius Wilson, who has studied social capital in low-income, inner-city neighborhoods, provides an interesting example. Economically successful parents in these neighborhoods generally had fewer friends in the neighborhood and were more likely to discourage their children from making friends there than were less successful parents. By deciding not to have friends, they shielded themselves and their children from what they perceived as bad influences, such as drug use or needy neighbors who would become drains on their time or money.[30] Persons with strong selves have their own goals well enough in mind that they can make such choices. They are also more deliberate about seeking out friends and sources of advice. A person with naturally occurring social capital, for instance, may have friends to rely on when the chips are down; a person who is more intentional about his or her social capital will be more likely to seek professional help. The idea of strong selves also implies the capacity to select contacts who contradict the norms of one's naturally occurring network. For instance, a mutual-funds trader may be driven by the norms of his or her peers to earn higher profits by cheating, whereas a trader with a more firmly developed sense of right and wrong would cultivate other networks (such as with family or through a religious congregation) for countervailing advice or to locate a different job. Overall, therefore, social capital is probably conducive to strong selves in most instances; yet knowing only that a person has social capital is no assurance of that person's having a strong self; the person's self-understanding and moral commitments must be taken into account as well.

These examples suggest a consideration that is not fully satisfied by the idea of social capital or by arguments about individuals' needs for community. Writers who emphasize community place great stock in the fact that throughout most of human history people have belonged to particular clans, tribes, and other local groups. Through these groups, people received an identity and learned to pursue the community's values by playing such roles as chief, hunter, shaman, father, mother, son, or daughter. Advocates of strong communities have trouble with the idea that individuals now can somehow be expected to have identities and conceptions of the good without such roles. They sometimes argue that it would be better if individuals subjected themselves once again to the authority of the group. What this view misses is the fact that everyone still plays roles and does so all the time. The problem is not a lack of roles or role commitments. The problem is that these roles are no longer the stable properties of clans and tribes. One can no longer say, "I belong to this clan or that tribe." Communities of identity are multiple, overlapping, and conflicting, and the roles we play in them are unstable. I may identify myself as a descendant of Scotch-Irish Presbyterians for certain purposes, as a descendant of German Baptists for other purposes, and most of the time in other ways entirely—as, for instance, an employee of a university, a resident of a particular state, or a consumer with certain tastes in literature and music. None of these roles fully defines what I believe to be right and good. I have had to make choices about them.

An embedded individual is thus one who lives within not a single community but several. "Layered loyalties," Etzioni writes, in which "members see themselves as, and act as, members of more than one community" become necessary.[31] The image of layers suggests a geographic hierarchy of communities, such as town, state, nation, and world. If my tribal loyalties conflict with yours, the way to resolve our differences is by switching reference to a larger community of which we are both a part. That solution, however, works less well in practice than in theory because communities usually do not exist in such neat layers. My loyalties to where I work and where I live are to entities that are not really communities at all, but social relationships of a very specific kind that influence me at some moments more than at others. I have to negotiate among these competing commitments. The fluidity of actual community attachments and roles does not result in complete individualism, however. I create unity and impose order on these attachments and roles through the *narratives* I use to make sense of them. Being associated with and influenced by multiple communities implies that discretion is an important part of the relationships between individuals and their communities. Individuals do not simply accept the definitions of goodness that are built into the traditions and functioning of communities. Individuals find it necessary to arbitrate among competing definitions of the good. We can also think of instances in which individuals find it necessary to call into question the values evident in the functioning of communities. We at least hope this will be the case because communities fall short of their ideals and in the extreme become ruthless and subservient to the interests of power. This is a point that proponents of stronger communities neglect. Communities come in the form of skinhead organizations and manipulative multinational corporations, not just neighborhood gatherings and civic associations. The role of the individual as moral decision-maker, therefore, is one that must be protected and encouraged.

The multiplicity and fluidity of communities is an issue that pertains especially to arguments about religion. A faith community may have a primordial claim on a person's identity by virtue of having played a formative role in his or her childhood socialization or by defining its beliefs as ultimate truth. In a pluralistic world, though, most individuals will be exposed to competing definitions of religious truth. We also live in a society that officially does not recognize one, or any, faith as being preferable to others. Thus it becomes incumbent on individuals to work out a satisfactory relationship to one faith community, or more than one. The balance here involves committing oneself to the moral obligations of the community, such as living according to its rules, participating in its worship services, and helping its social programs, on the one hand; and on the other hand, deciding that the community's teachings are also one's own beliefs, up to a point, and determining where that agreement ends. This iterative process requires renegotiation as a person's life situation changes and as his or her understanding and practice of faith change.

It is the reality of pluralism and of individuals' need to choose among competing communities and commitments that points to the requirement for autonomy. An embedded self is a person whose autonomy is sufficiently protected to guarantee the free exercise of conscience. This is why *rights* as well as responsibilities are important. A proper understanding of rights does not mean that the individual makes only those claims on the group that maximize his or her self-interest—claims such as freedom from being bothered by having to pay one's dues. The purpose of rights is to ensure that moral disagreements between individuals and the group are not always resolved in favor of the group. A minority of one is entitled to speak her mind, worship as she chooses, and receive fair treatment in the courts and by the police. A minority of one is subject to the law, like everyone else. But rights may also extend to questions about resources, such as fair employment and fair housing, on which the capacity to live and to choose depends.

An embedded self is not only situationally located but also *reflective*. "Self-identity," writes the sociologist Anthony Giddens, "is the self as reflexively understood by the person in terms of her or his biography."[32] Indeed, it is more even than this. We interpret our situations, responding to them and acting upon them in terms of the meanings we create. We construct a sense of our self-identity by pondering how we have responded to events in the past and what different courses of action we may take in the future. We tell stories that make sense of our lives and provide the occasions for self-assessment. These stories are not unrelated to the social contexts and networks in which we are embedded. The stories, though, are themselves a form of embedding. They create connections between self and society, and provide continuity between past and present and between present and future. *How* people understand themselves is thus a key to grasping the role of the individual in our society and to identifying the deep meanings that give stability to the society. It is through reflection that individuals gain the capacity to transcend the specific roles, rules, and regulations of their situation and thus the ability to make moral judgments about them. A view that encourages radical immersion of the individual into the group can offer possibilities for moral judgments only through the values and beliefs that are espoused by the group itself. For instance, a person who identifies solely with a religious community may believe with that community that taking lives is wrong. Yet the ability to make moral judgments in a pluralistic society requires *imagining* oneself outside of that community as well. It involves comparing the values of more than one community and, indeed, recognizing heterogeneity of beliefs within a particular community. This capacity permits individuals and communities to grow and to change. Within the confines of a single homogeneous community, individuals' second or subsequent experience of events still differs from their first. It is through the *narratives* they construct and the reflection in which they engage that they are able to respond appropriately, rather than being driven only by the moment-to-moment authority of the group. "As a self-interpreting being," Michael J. Sandel writes, "I am able to reflect on my history and in this sense to distance myself from it."[33] Self-interpretation of this kind requires living in imagined worlds, in the world as one chooses to remember it, and in future worlds that one can anticipate. Sandel is correct in observing that the distance between these imagined worlds and one's immediate situation is always provisional. Yet it is, not because the power of the group is so morally overwhelming, but because one's own moral reflections take account of the situation.

Narratives are the cultural frameworks in which individuals interpret their social situations, imagine themselves in other situations, and make choices about who they want to be and how to behave. Narratives contain moral principles (cautionary tales are a prime example), but telling stories is quite different from memorizing principles. Storytelling is deliberately multivalent. It evokes interpretations, rather than closing them down. Narratives spark the imagination, showing that conditions were different from what they seemed to be and that the self can be different. Storytelling and self-direction are intimately connected. "Self direction is open-ended," writes Kekes. "Self direction presupposes that while part of human nature, set by the facts of the body, self, and social life, is constant and universal, other parts can be and are being transformed."[34] Ultimately, then, it is not so much the social situations in which people live that provide clues about their understandings of themselves, but their narratives. This means that moral judgments are situated within the stories we tell about ourselves, the stories we hear others tell about themselves, and what we might call public narratives—the stories about celebrities, public officials, and characters in literature that make up the cultural stock of any society. Narratives typically include implicit references to the principle or principles at issue, the context in which questions about the application of those principles arise, an example of how decisions are made, and possibly an implied lesson about the consequences of these decisions. Narratives of this kind link the moral judgments of individuals with the norms and values of a community. They often bring in a tradition or a form of reasoning that provides warrants or legitimation. Folktales and narratives in religious texts are stories of this kind, but the tales that philosophers and students of jurisprudence tell about rationality and fairness, or that scientists tell about experiments and discoveries, are examples as well. They spin webs of meaning around the individual, explaining why certain actions are taken or not taken and what the consequences are.

## MAKING SENSE OF PERSONAL NARRATIVES

Narratives guide behavior, provide interpretations of it, and reveal what the culture knows and values. Narratives, as I have argued, hold the key to striking an appropriate balance between the individual and the community. If we are to understand the deep cultural meanings that propel us forward, on the one hand, and hold us back, on the other, we need to consider carefully what narratives are, how they function, and what they can tell us about our understandings of personal strength. Among social scientists who study culture, narratives often receive surprisingly little attention. It has been more common to dissect culture into small bits, such as frames, tools, scripts, symbols, boundaries, and genres, and to deny that culture has much coherence beyond what is revealed in particular situations. Yet we know that personal narratives play a large role in human behavior and are an important part of what it means to be human. We create and tell stories to make sense of our lives. Many of our best-selling books are biographies. Talk therapy consists largely of telling stories about ourselves. Television programming ranges from the long narratives that make up epic dramas to the shorter ones of which sitcom episodes and talk show interviews are composed. Historians and anthropologists insist that through most of human history storytelling was the principal means by which culture was transmitted from one generation to the next. Increasingly, social scientists themselves make use of in-depth interviews—often without much attention to the structure of the narratives that are obtained, but as a source of narrative information nevertheless. Personal narratives tell us how we think about ourselves in relation to the situations in which we are embedded. Creating these narratives, writes the psychologist Dan P. McAdams, "is an act of imagination that is a patterned integration of our remembered past, perceived present, and anticipated future."[35] Personal narratives constitute our outlook on the world. They are inside us.

The goal of narrative analysis is greater awareness of how we are shaped by our culture and heightened opportunities for self-reflection. We are generally aware enough of our personal narratives that we can tell stories about ourselves. This does not mean that we have thought much about our narratives or that these narratives necessarily provide accurate information. Individuals do not always know what guides their behavior and may delude themselves into thinking that they are better than they are. This point was taken more seriously when Freudian and Marxian assumptions dominated the social sciences than it is now. In that era, a hermeneutics of suspicion led social scientists to imagine that people were nearly always guided by unconscious drives or by false consciousness. Hardly anything could be taken at face value. Yet Freudians and Marxians also believed it was possible to unmask false ideas by examining the texts of what people said or wrote and by looking at them critically in relation to broader understandings of personality and society. We are less likely in the present era to believe that individuals are so often duped or that social science can so readily discover deeper truths. If assumptions about the individual are part of the deep meaning of culture, though, it makes sense to examine these assumptions. Personal narratives inform us about both the way individuals understand themselves and the way our culture understands individuals.

To see how personal narratives work, we will find it helpful to consider a specific example. This example comes from a woman talking to an interviewer who had asked her to tell about some of her experiences as a foreign-born person living in the United States. The woman, whom I will call Fatima Akhtar, is an immigrant from Pakistan.[36] She came to the United States with her husband in 1975. They live in a middle-class neighborhood in southern California where her husband works as an engineer and she divides her time between mothering their three children, who are now in high school, and participating in community organizations. The particular story she tells is an account of how and why she has played a leadership role in Women's Network, a group that combats domestic violence and tries in other ways to support Muslim women. As the narrative unfolds, it provides evidence about Mrs. Akhtar's sense of herself as well as about the organization. She says:

> A bunch of us used to gather at the mosque for classes or for some
> family night educational programs and we shared stories about how

women are suffering. They cannot talk to anybody and their husbands are abusing them and beating them. Some are beating them because they think it says to in the Qur'an. All kinds of horror stories. So it was like the anger in a lot of women against men. Those men sometimes are in high positions in the community, so the woman is totally trapped, cannot say a word because it will damage his reputation. We thought, "what can we do about it?" There were African American Muslim women, white converted Muslim women, Arab, Egyptian, Irani. So our cliquish Muslim women's group kind of evolved from there and we were all concerned for other women in our own communities. I am in a Pakistani community. There are Irani women who know what's going on in Irani culture. The Egyptians know how their women are suffering. So we thought that we should make a group and advertise and educate through Islam what their rights are, empower women by teaching them what their rights are, and also give them kind of practical ideas of how to deal with situations at home because we cannot ignore the male nature, their ego problems and all that. You cannot challenge them. We totally believe that we don't want to break up any marriages because Muslims strongly believe in the family. Children suffer if the marriages are broken. So that was our idea of making this network to help women. If a woman says, "I want to go see another woman," there is no objection. "This is a friend; we are getting together at a friend's house." So the husbands who are controlling are less threatened if the wife is going to see another woman. We thought this way we can have meetings and do things and there will be no threat to the husbands.

The interviewer then asks Mrs. Akhtar to say what motivated her to become involved in starting the group. This question gives her the opportunity to speak more personally:

I have seen women in Pakistan suffering from this type of thing. Not particularly the beating abuse. That, plus the other thing which makes me more mad, is the divorce trap. My young niece was married for a year and the guy was abusive. She was a beautiful young woman and her husband, a medical doctor, was an abusive man. She refused to go back to him and then he refused to give her a divorce. Things like that, closer to home, made me mad, and raised the question, "Is there justice?" Some other very close friends, similar things happened. It's like, here I am reading this Qur'an. It tells me about kindness and justice. But there is no match in real life. So who can do something? To tell you the truth, there were times when my own husband was not fair to me, before I got empowered with my own knowledge. He was a typical man and he wanted service from me all the time. I had little kids, I was working full-time, and he would come home and he would not help me in the household. If I was mad and demanded him to, he says, "I don't do this thing, I don't do this thing." That kind of made me mad. It's like what is this thing? He used to just say he is a man, he can't do it. Though he was never abusive.

I had a lot of questions. Why is being a woman the wrong gender? It's not my fault. It's not anybody's fault. I didn't do anything in terms of being a woman. There are so many other women, and what can we do about it? So that element, plus other women, just because they're women, men can give them a divorce if they want. There was another young woman in Pakistan, she was married for a year and she had a child. She came home and her husband sent her a divorce in the mail. Another woman we knew was married for six months and she was a working woman, she had a lot of money, and her husband wanted her to give him all the money. She refused so he gave her a divorce. There were things happening within our close circle of friends, relatives. I said, "Whatever I study is so rosy and so nice, but why are all these things happening?" I guess that gave me the energy.

Mrs. Akhtar pauses for a moment to catch her breath. Then she remembers that there was another experience that motivated her:

My kids went to a Catholic school. I joined a Bible study group there because I wanted to learn what my kids were learning! I became friends with these Christian Catholic women. They were so nice. They were doing things for other women, a sisterhood. And *that* motivated me also. Then I went and joined the mosque downtown. I started teaching there in the Sunday School. I got *so* discriminated against there because I was a woman, and a blunt, outspoken woman, very untraditional. I could do a lot of things that men were not doing there. The way they played tricks with me, the way they made me miserable in my own Islamic environment was very, very sad. But that motivated me to learn. I felt the barriers everywhere. It made me angry. I think that was probably God's plan, to make me angry, and that anger came out as a force for me to learn. Every time somebody was nasty to me I hit the Qur'an again and I learned. I have more than three hundred books on Islam now; I have my own library. All my women's books are all here, I have another room full of books. I sometimes laugh now. I say, "I should send thank-you letters to the mosque people who made me so angry that I learned more and more."

A narrative like this reveals a lot about Mrs. Akhtar's understanding of herself, the community with which she identifies, and her sense of responsibility toward it. Her story shows that not only is she of Pakistani origin, but she continues to regard herself as part of the Pakistani community. Her identity as a Muslim extends further, including her friends of different national backgrounds. She indicates that storytelling is one of the important activities in which she and her Muslim friends engage. She clearly identifies herself as a woman and is devoted to a cause that transcends particular ethnic or religious backgrounds, although in her case this is a cause that she strongly associates with interpretations of the Qur'an. The story reveals some of her values: she believes that it is wrong for women to suffer, she thinks it is possible to do something to alleviate this suffering, and she implies that gaining knowledge from books is one way of achieving this goal. She explicitly describes herself as a person who has been "empowered." Her narrative mentions energy but also conveys it, especially through the language she uses to describe her emotions. It might be possible to dissect a narrative like this, showing, for example, that it employed a "frame" of gender equality, that it drew a "symbolic boundary" between men and women, or that it deployed a "tool kit" of emotionally expressive words. But dissecting it like that makes sense only in the context of understanding that the whole narrative has coherence.

As this example shows, personal narratives typically provide important clues about the social networks in which people are involved. It is always nice to have independent evidence about these networks, such as that provided by ethnographic studies of groups. However, the stories people tell about themselves are the best indications of how they think they have been influenced by their networks. In Mrs. Akhtar's story, for instance, she states clearly that it was beneficial to have had friends and that it was valuable, given Muslim customs, for these friends to be women. Thus when they gathered, they could say they were simply going to visit some female friends. When asked more specifically about these friends, she says there were six in particular who provided the core for the Women's Network. Besides herself, one was from Sri Lanka, one was a white convert to Islam, one was an African American convert, one was Iranian, and one was Egyptian. Being from six different cultures, the women all had distinct networks and experiences, which, Mrs. Akhtar believes, helped the Network to grow, and to have greater legitimacy than if it had been associated with only one culture.

If personal narratives link individuals with social networks, they do not do so in descriptive terms alone. We cannot understand Mrs. Akhtar's story in the same way that we would assess her answer to a question in a survey asking her to list her five closest friends. Personal narratives connect the person in the story, whether that is the storyteller or another party, with *moral meanings*. The story defines its main characters as allies who are on the side of good and as antagonists who are on the opposing side. Protagonists and antagonists are goal-directed. They are engaged in activities that have moral valences—efforts to do good, secure justice, overcome evil, trump falsehood with knowledge, and inspire hope. These moral meanings may be philosophical principles that a person has read about in books. But they are personally meaningful because of the particular circumstances to which they are applied.

Personal narratives are often told to illustrate a specific transition or insight, such as a lesson that was learned or a moral that was driven home by the context in which it occurred. In retelling the story, one remembers the lesson and, in a small way, relives the process of learning it. Mrs. Akhtar learned during the course of her involvement with the Women's Network that it was sometimes important to enlist the assistance of an imam or another man, especially for help in confronting a husband who was abusing his wife. She tells the following story about how she came to this realization:

> We helped this one woman. She had already taken the step of leaving home. She had gone to this organization that is really hot on getting divorce. Once you go to them, they will say, "You're not going back

to that environment, period, and we will do everything to process your divorce." She had gone to them and she got her divorce, but her husband was still abusing her on the phone with threatening messages. She came to us and she told us her horror story of twelve years of abuse. We helped her by going to an imam at the mosque. We found out that we women cannot really do everything. We need a male, a courageous Muslim male to help us, to go talk to an abusive man. Anybody who is abusing his own wife will not talk to any other woman, and we could be in danger physically also.

We took our case to this particular imam. Three of us from our Women's Network went there formally. We made the appointment. I wrapped myself real good! We all did. We said, "We don't want to give them any excuse of us not being properly dressed." So all three of us wrapped up ourselves in hijab and we went there. I took my Qur'an with all the stickies about how a man should treat his wife. The imam treated us very nicely and he said he would help us. He actually talked to that man. The man was claiming that he had not given his wife an Islamic divorce. I call it Islamic divorce crap, because there is this belief that only a man can give a divorce. So unless he throws his trump card, the woman is not free, and many, many men in Islamic countries use that card. They say, "You can rot. You will not be able to marry anybody because I am not freeing you, and I am going to go marry three other women, but you can just sit and rot." This is a type of revenge. Very un-Islamic behavior, I would say, but they do it.

The imam contacted the man by letter and set up a meeting. The imam first had a meeting with the wife and heard her story and then called the husband and asked his story and then called both of them together. Then they had a council meeting where imams of many mosques sit together. It's a kind of Islamic court. They presented the case. The woman had kept all her husband's dirty, threatening messages on the tape, so they played the tape and listened to it, and it was obvious what the man was doing. They told him that he's not really doing anything good and threatened him with hellfire. I was impressed that they knew what method would work. "He can be threatened with hellfire, so let's threaten with hellfire." So that guy gave her a divorce. She is now happy and independent.

Narratives necessarily imply the passage of time. They typically include an opening, a middle, and an end. In Mrs. Akhtar's story about visiting the imam, the woman in trouble represents the opening part of the narrative. Her situation sets the stage by posing a problem that needs to be solved and thus explains the occasion for contacting the imam. The middle of the story provides detail about how the women dressed, what the imam did initially, and then what happened subsequently. The end of the story returns to the woman in trouble. It provides closure by showing the woman in her new state of happy independence, her problems solved. But the story is not simply a tale about one thing's leading to another. It demonstrates that action was required. The women achieved a morally desirable end, not just by believing in it as an abstract principle, but by becoming agents and enlisting a sympathetic imam in their cause. The narrative also provides the occasion for inserting a specific argument, a statement about the lesson learned, the lesson of needing a courageous Muslim male.

Personal narratives vary considerably in how personal or private they actually are. Some are easy to tell in public. They are the kinds of stories one might read in the newspaper. They reveal something about an individual, but often not much. Other stories are the kind we feel comfortable recounting only to our most intimate friends or, for that matter, to ourselves alone. These stories are truly private. Yet they are our interpretations of personal experience. They make sense of events through an inner language. Mrs. Akhtar had lost her sister a few months before the interview. She alluded to her sister's death briefly at an early point in the interview. Later, after talking for several hours and becoming more comfortable with the interviewer, she said more:

The death of my sister was so devastating in a way that nothing mattered. I came home after her funeral and I wanted to throw away everything, all my clothes. Give away every material thing, because here she was, died with a house full of her things and they were just giving it away right away. It was like I thought, "Why burden somebody else? I'm going to give away everything myself. I'm going to lighten my burden and I will give away my jewelry and I'll give away this and I'll give away that." Nothing mattered. I was totally detached from everything. It was very scary for my husband.

But slowly, it's been now three months, I am kind of coming back to reality, to the reality that I am living and I have to.

Mrs. Akhtar continues and then begins to cry. She says her faith was deeply shaken by her sister's death. Until almost the end, her sister prayed that God would perform a miracle and spare her life. When that didn't happen, Mrs. Akhtar felt like abandoning her faith entirely. "I wanted to just go away. God betrayed us."

The examples I have given thus far illustrate that personal narratives are usually organized around specific episodes. They make sense of an event by explaining what happened and why it happened or what its significance was. Narratives that have a specific focus of this kind are sometimes called *accounts*.[37] They not only provide a shorthand summary of an event that can be remembered and retold; they also justify or render legitimate the storyteller's behavior in that situation. They do so by invoking connections between the particular episode and larger values or understandings that are known to be shared in the culture, or at least by whoever the audience for the story may be. Giving an account of oneself may be an act that an outsider would judge cynically as merely an excuse or fabrication. However, an account that justifies behavior in terms of socially accepted values is an act that in a small way reaffirms the authority of those values. Other accounts serve less as justifications and more as simple narratives through which a person makes sense of a particular event by interpreting its significance. In the account of her response to her sister's death, Mrs. Akhtar begins with the categorical statement that "nothing mattered." This is the kind of statement that requires little elaboration. It points to a universal understanding that in the face of death all other concerns diminish in importance. As she continues, though, Mrs. Akhtar enters territory that requires clarification. She wants to give everything away. This could be taken as evidence that material possessions now seemed unimportant. But she also wants us to realize that she experienced this feeling in response to seeing her sister's possessions being given away and wanting to spare her family that awkward situation when her own time came to die. The other story about contacting the imam arises from a different kind of problem and thus invokes a different form of justification. Having described men as the villains in her previous account, she now needed to explain why it made sense to seek allies among them. The account introduces a kind of strategic logic. If an enemy can become a friend, then make use of that resource. The story implicitly underscores the possibility of strategic or even manipulative intervention in suggesting that the council of imams manipulated the husband by choosing an argument about hellfire that they knew would frighten him. As these examples suggest, accounts are especially important when something unusual or unexpected takes place. We do not feel it necessary to give an account of going to work at nine o'clock if that is our routine every morning. We do feel it necessary to account for a sudden urge to arrive at six o'clock, or to skip work entirely, or change jobs. The unusual or unexpected is a deviation from our normal routines, but also from our normal understandings of ourselves. Accounts weave this new event or activity into those understandings of who we are. In small ways, accounts contribute to personal empowerment by giving individuals a sense of control over events and by helping individuals to express emotion, establish order in their relationships, and gain closure.[38]

A different kind of personal narrative focuses more directly on our self-understandings and gives coherence to a larger number or longer sequence of events. These are the kinds of narratives that summarize long-term developments in one's life and that organize these developments into a story about growth, decline, or some other transition. The term *life stories* is sometimes used to describe these more encompassing narratives.[39] A life story can literally be the story of one's life, such as an autobiography that relates the significant details from one's birth to the time the story is told. More commonly, though, life stories focus on an important aspect or dimension of one's life, such as one's family or occupational history, and thus are narratives about the relationship between one's self and one's roles. Usually we do not write these stories down but relate them to our family and friends in conversation and to ourselves through the silent dialogue we carry on with ourselves all the time. They are, in the sociologist Christian Smith's apt phrase, "living narratives." We constantly revise them and invent new episodes to take account of new experiences. They consist of stories, Smith writes, "about the loss of jobs, political activism, immigration, the fairness of laws, encounters of love or violence, recovery from trauma, motherhood, organizational identities, sexual experiences, religious conversions, and more."[40] Life stories are especially important in the consideration of how people perceive themselves and how they define their responsibilities and their moral commitments. As an illustration of these narratives, we can turn to one of the more detailed stories Mrs. Akhtar tells. This is the story of her religious upbringing and subsequent religious involvements. Stories that focus on spiritual journeys are valued in many religious traditions because they serve as testimonials, showing the personal applications and benefits of abstract religious teachings. Spiritual journey stories have also become popular in recent years because of the decisions many people make to switch from one faith to another or to increase or decrease their level of religious involvement. Although she is an immigrant, Mrs. Akhtar tells a story of attachment, detachment, and reattachment that is similar to the narratives of many native-born Americans:

> When I was a child, my mother taught me how to pray, and she hired a man to come and teach me how to read the Qur'an. I was not good at reading Arabic. It was very frustrating. My brother was good at it. He was two years older than me, and he finished reading the Qur'an before me. My periods started and we cannot touch the Qur'an if we menstruate. So every month when I had to drop out for a week, my brother was after me. You don't tell your brother you have your periods. It was really hard to explain, so I dropped out.
>
> My mother used to yell a lot, "You're not up doing your prayer early in the morning," to all of us. It's like, "Why are you sleeping? It's getting late, get up and pray." So it's like fear of mother, you pray because you don't want to get yelled at. We had no idea that we should be doing it for our own selves.
>
> The moment I left home, I stopped praying. It's like, "I am on my own. I am not praying for anybody. Nobody's asking me to pray," so I took a freedom trip. Later on, when I was in America, I realized that there were these Muslim community gatherings. We have this ritual if somebody dies, you all sit and read the Qur'an. I could not read it and I was so embarrassed to tell people, here is this grown-up woman and cannot read the Qur'an. I always used to make excuses, "I have periods. I cannot touch Qur'an." I used to think, "These people must think that whenever there is a Qur'an reading, she always has periods."
>
> So I started learning on my own, finding very basic books. I wanted to teach my children. If I cannot read, how can I teach? So

I went to this imam and women went to his wife for learning to read the Qur'an. I had reached that stage where it was okay for me to admit I cannot read. I went to her and I had nail polish on. She said, "You're not pure clean because you have nail polish on. You cannot touch Qur'an." I was so ticked off I never went back to her. I lost five years with that anger.

But then I found out there are cassette tapes available of Qur'an recitation, so I can learn by those and I can listen to them. I could read, but not clearly, fluently. So I bought those and that helped me. I wanted my husband to teach the children and he always was like, "You cannot tell me to do this. I will do it when I have time." So it has to be his choice of when he wants to do it, I cannot push him to. It's always that male thing. I had this inner thing that it's my obligation, my duty to teach the children and especially that my mother didn't do it and how I have suffered. So realizing that, I say, "It is my duty. I must teach my children, and no matter what it takes." So I hired a man who came to our house. We have a little room which I call the Qur'an room. I told him that I wanted to learn with the children. He was really surprised, but he was very nice. He admired me to have the courage to admit and to learn. I sat through with my children and learned the basic method and correct pronunciation of the letters and the words and things. I learned the rhythm of reading with my children.

My husband comes from a very religious family. He knows so many good things, but he hardly has time to spend with the children. He feels like he doesn't lack this thing, so he doesn't have that hole which I had, not knowing how to. So I thought, "I don't want my children to grow up feeling that we didn't do our job," so I made sure they know how to pray. I said, "When you are on your own, it is your choice then, but it is my duty and I have done my part." So at least that burden is off.

With all that, I think teaching the children brought me closer to religion. I had to learn, and the more I learned, I became really, really spiritual. There comes a time sometimes I become so detached with worldly things that my husband says, "What is wrong with you? We have to live. Come back to the world." So I go back and forth like that. There is a Sufi woman in Chicago, she told me, "You should not even become Sufi. You should not even go to a spiritual teacher as long you have children and family because we are also told we have to do this responsibility. You cannot detach. There will be time when you have more time and become more spiritual."

As lengthy and as detailed as this narrative is, it of course emphasizes a few themes and omits a great deal. The main theme is Mrs. Akhtar's struggle to learn how to read the Qur'an in Arabic. This is a theme that makes sense in terms of the importance to Muslims of reading, reciting, and memorizing the Qur'an. In this respect, it is quite different from spiritual journeys told by evangelical Christians, in which a "born-again" experience might be central, or by someone telling about why she ceased being Catholic. It also resonates with what Mrs. Akhtar has said in her other stories about the importance of knowing the Qur'an in order to combat patriarchal misinterpretations of it. It gives coherence to her identity as a spiritual person, showing how she learned as a child the importance of praying and reading the Qur'an, why she stopped, and why the Qur'an plays such a significant role in her life as a parent and as a woman.

Coherence is vitally important to any understanding of the self. People like Sheila Larson in *Habits of the Heart* spend a great deal of time worrying about who they are, partly because the contexts in which we find ourselves are sufficiently scattered that we come away feeling that our self is scattered as well. Stories put the pieces back together. They do so by showing that there is a common biographical thread running through our experiences from early childhood to the present. Feeling inferior to the males in one's family may be such a thread. Or feeling embarrassed because one cannot read the Qur'an. Stories impose coherence by showing that one thing led to another, that events were connected not only temporally but also causally. A person's embarrassment at one stage in life becomes the motivation for her to do better at a later stage. In addition, coherence comes about through the selection process that all narratives require. There may be aspects of one's life that simply do not fit, such as the college years when people sow their wild oats, or an interval of uncertainty between jobs or spouses. These can be bracketed. The story makes sense of what it can and omits the rest. At the most basic level, narratives also create coherence because it is the self, as narrator, who occupies a central place in the story.

But we should not interpret this coherence-creating role to mean that people develop what are sometimes called "grand narratives." A grand narrative is a once-upon-a-time story that tells why humans exist, how human life began, what its purpose is, how it has changed through history, and what a person's life should mean in relation to this sweeping picture of reality.[41] I do not deny that grand narratives such as this exist. Christianity and certain formulations of Marxism are examples. So are the "cosmologies" that anthropologists write about. Nor do I question the fact that people engage in behavior that reflects the existence of these grand narratives; for instance, participating in religious rituals or studying philosophy in college. But the convenient summaries of such narratives that scholars sometimes provide are simply that—convenient summaries.[42] In real life, our narratives are usually fragments that point obliquely, if at all, to such grand narratives. This is not because we have somehow lost sight of grand narratives that supposedly governed life in earlier times. Modern life may be more complex and thus more confusing than life in the past. But I find it hard to believe that people ever lived within a single grand narrative that explained every aspect of their lives. Ordinary life is never that orderly. It is punctuated with change. The episodic nature of lived experience encourages us to tell stories about specific events. Our abbreviated attention spans and the multiple roles we play require us to live with fragments, rather than within grand narratives. The sight of a church steeple as I drive past reminds me about the grand narrative of Christianity, but even if I attend services at that church, I am more likely to make sense of my being there in terms of stories about my upbringing and my experiences with other parishioners than through a single story about "the Christian" view of the universe. The same is true if I am a working scientist wedded to the truth of science. Although I may have learned a grand narrative about science at some point in my education, that is not the sort of story I tell often or think much about in my daily work.[43] I am more likely to yearn for an account that makes sense of my day than for one that makes sense of the universe. "It was not the prospect of the Last Day which depressed him," the writer Walker Percy says of his character Billy Barrett, "but rather the prospect of living through an ordinary Wednesday morning."[44]

To say that personal narratives are fragments means there is no single narrative that makes sense of a person's life. At least not in practice. We may "believe" there is one, accepting its existence as an article of faith, but in reality the largest meanings of our lives are ones that we cannot put into so many words without doing damage to the very complexity they are meant to convey. This is why the most meaningful narratives are accounts of events, stories about memorable episodes in our lives, tales of danger or transformation, and explanations of the various roles we play. The coherence that results is not a unifying picture of ourselves and the world that puts everything into place. It is a partial coherence that makes sense of particular chains of experience. In that, there is power. This is why people claim the right to tell their own stories—why we feel diminished if someone else (parent, boss, colonizer, psychotherapist) tries to take control of our stories. It is also why good parenting involves teaching children and good psychotherapy involves helping clients to tell their own stories. Traditionally, the person who held the right to tell a community's story was accorded special status in that community. The stories themselves showed that a people claimed a distinct identity for themselves. In our time, we lay greater claim to our own stories. We want them to show that we are self-directed individuals.

The *act* of telling stories is itself a form of empowerment. A feature of Riesman's *Lonely Crowd* that recent scholarship generally overlooks is that he devoted an entire chapter to storytellers and storytelling. Riesman believed storytelling to be the primary means through which societies transmitted values. It was the telling of stories, as well as the stories themselves, that mattered. For example, a family member who tells children a story personalizes it in a way that encourages the children to identify more closely with it. The story, Riesman wrote, "can be modulated for them and indeed, since they can criticize, question, and elaborate, put into a manageable context by them."[45] Adults who tell their own stories do the same thing. They engage in what Riesman calls a "handicraft industry," piecing together bits and pieces of their experience, linking them to particular situations, and in the process become their master in the same way a craftsperson or artist does. Of course, not all storytelling functions this way. Riesman was concerned that storytelling was increasingly becoming professionalized, because of radio and television, and thus impersonal. People would lose their personal identity if they absorbed only the scripts presented, for instance, by Walt Disney. In the intervening decades, the basis for that concern has, if anything, increased. What the sociologist George Ritzer has colorfully termed the "McDonaldization" of society has resulted in greater standardization of storytelling.[46] An account of a family outing demonstrates little empowerment if it involves only a decision to eat at McDonald's and if part of the experience involves purchasing a toy character from the latest Disney movie. In more personalized contexts, adult storytelling can also elude empowerment. One can tell stories, for instance, that reinforce the idea that a person is a victim or a pawn of circumstances. Stories can be told that show how someone else was powerful, in contrast to the weak, unskilled, and ineffective storyteller. But people do tell stories that explicitly and implicitly show how strong they are and how effective they have been, and this is one of the reasons that groups in which stories are told are often associated with empowerment. In self-help groups, for instance, participants not only tell stories about their problems but also relate incidents in which they triumphed over these problems.[47] Prayer groups sometimes include storytelling of a similar kind. As prayer requests are shared and answers to prayer are discussed, the group's members articulate the belief that they can be transformed, and are motivated to work toward that transformation.[48]

Mrs. Akhtar is not one to brag, and she talks as much about what she wishes the Women's Network were able to do as about what it has done. Yet in small ways, her stories reinforce the idea that she believes she is making a difference through her efforts. Consider the following account of her interaction with a recently widowed woman:

> A friend's husband died last year and it was torture for her. Women are sometimes more cruel to other women than men are. They said, "Oh, you cannot leave home. Your husband died. For four months and ten days you have to stay home. You cannot show your head; you're a widow." I said, "My God, in all these things which I have read, there is no such thing. The only requirement is she cannot marry another man for four months and ten days." The reason was those days that pregnancy could not be detected so you had to know if the woman is pregnant and it should become obvious if she is, so you know who the father is. And that is the reason. Other than that, there is no restriction.

This is a story of power. Mrs. Akhtar uses her knowledge to contradict the counsel being given by the widow's neighbors and relatives. It is as much about motivation, though, as about power. She tells it in the context of talking about her wish list, rather than her accomplishments. She says she would like to do more to help widows. Whenever she thinks about this episode (whenever, we might say, she recounts the story to herself), she reminds herself that she wants to write a position paper about what is required and what is not required of widows. The more general point is that a strong person is, among other things, a person who can tell narratives illustrating that she or he is strong. Stories of success, of new insights, growth, and power, are rooted in actual experience, but they are also interpretations of that experience. They provide reasons for thinking that a person is strong or can become strong. In the telling and retelling of them, they become self-fulfilling prophecies. A person becomes his or her own role model. The person in the story who was powerful illustrates the possibility of being powerful again. That possibility, in turn, becomes a motivating factor. The story suggests that if one event was successful, others are possible.

In all of these examples, it is evident that personal narratives are never entirely idiosyncratic. Although they tell about a particular person with unique experiences, they employ idioms that show the narrator's embeddedness in the wider culture. Mrs. Akhtar does not speak in clichés. Yet despite her upbringing in a different culture, her language is sprinkled with idioms: "horror stories," "ego problems," "freedom trip," "divorce trap," "stickies," "trump card," "ticked off." She has not made up these phrases. She uses them without explanation, knowing that the interviewer will understand. In some cases, the use of such idioms may be strategic; for instance, to demonstrate that a person has been to college, watches television, or is assimilated. Idioms implicitly identify people with particular communities as well. Ethnic slogans, the cadence of regional dialects, words distinctive to particular religious traditions, and references to people and places known only within local communities are examples. Apart from such local idioms, there are also narratives known more widely in a society, such as stories about its founding figures or about the exploits of celebrities and public officials. These narratives serve, in the anthropologist Clifford Geertz's famous formulation, both as *models of* and as *models for* social behavior.[49] They tell what public figures have done, and they tell the rest of us to behave similarly or differently. There are also stereotypic characters whose stories resonate because they follow familiar patterns—the stranger, the newcomer, the traveler, the victim, the hero, to name a few. We recognize ourselves in these characters and pattern some of our stories after them. Like them, we embark on journeys, leave home, endure hardship, overcome obstacles, experience unexpected good fortune, earn distinction, lose our way, find ourselves, and gain new insights. These are all stories of personal change that also tell us about opportunities and obstacles in the wider society.[50]

As interpretations, as memories, and as justifications of one's behavior, narratives are the basis for self-reflection. Narratives make it possible to bring the past into juxtaposition with the present or experiences in one context with those in another. Markers of reflexivity are not uncommon in personal narratives. "I said to myself," "I went home and started thinking," and "the more I thought about it" would be examples. Narratives are marvelously flexible in permitting their characters to speak to one another or in different voices, and thus to show the internal conversations of which reflection is composed. In interviews, people often betray the extent to which their stories have been the occasions for reflection or of reflective interactions with friends. "As I told my husband" or "I chuckled about it to myself" are not just memories; they show that the story has been told before in other situations. Because narratives can be retold in our minds and among confidants, they give us ways of removing ourselves from the rush of passing events long enough to decide whether our behavior was warranted and what we might do differently next time.

Through considering personal narratives, then, we come full circle to the observation with which we began about the continuing significance of the individual. In personal narratives, the individual is central. We might say that narratives about ourselves are our primary language, the one we learned as children to express our needs, and the one that continues to mediate between the embodied life we know from the inside and the social world with which we are surrounded on the outside. It should not be surprising that we speak more easily and more often through the language of personal narratives than through any other. But these narratives also display our connections with the world around us, how we interpret that world, and the kinds of action we believe ourselves capable of taking in relation to it. They show us to be agents as well as recipients of social influences.

Strong selves, I have suggested, are persons capable of telling stories about themselves in which empowerment is involved. The capacity to tell such stories is, of course, influenced by the events people have actually experienced and by a host of other factors, including social background, education, and whether or not families encouraged storytelling. Unlike material resources, philosophical ideas, and intellectual knowledge, though, personal narratives are remarkably universal and remarkably capable of being crafted to demonstrate empowerment. These do not have to be stories about mysterious reservoirs of inner strength. The beauty of narratives, in fact, is their ability to disclose the process by which a person became empowered. Through stories, poignant encounters with mentors are remembered. Conversations that illustrate one's shortcomings or fears can be incorporated. The temptation toward presenting oneself as a hero is always there. But stories about lessons learned also serve as reminders of vulnerability and the need to continue learning. They point to goals dreamed of and not yet realized.

## CHAPTER 3

# THE JUSTICE OF PRIVILEGE

Musing as he often did about America's future, Walt Whitman predicted in 1872 that the United States would become the world's leading power and remain so for some time to come. The anguish of the Civil War, Whitman believed, would soon fade from memory, and a more optimistic spirit would take hold. The transcontinental railroad had recently been completed, commerce was growing, and an army of hardy pioneers was moving west. Whitman was inspired by these developments. More than by the prospect of military and economic dominance, though, Whitman's imagination was fired by the thought of America's becoming a *noble people*. America's role, he wrote, was "to become the grand producing land of nobler men and women—of copious races, cheerful, healthy, tolerant, free—to become the most friendly nation, (the United States indeed)—the modern composite nation, form'd from all, with room for all, welcoming all immigrants—accepting the work of our own interior development, as the work fitly filling ages and ages to come;—the leading nation of peace, but neither ignorant nor incapable of being the leading nation of war;—not the man's nation only, but the woman's nation—a land of splendid mothers, daughters, sisters, wives."[1]

More than a century and a quarter later, Whitman's vision of the United States as a great military and economic power has been fulfilled. It is harder to say whether his vision of America as a land of "nobler men and women" has been realized. The United States is a composite nation to a considerably greater degree today than it was in 1872. We have often taken pride in being a nation that welcomes immigrants. The language of peace and of waging war in the name of peace is woven tightly into the rhetoric of our national pride. During the past half century we have become "not the man's nation only, but the woman's nation" in ways that exceeded Whitman's imagination. All this and more is basis for thinking that we are *perhaps* a noble people—a people who not only enjoy a privileged place in the world, but who also make just use of these privileges. Yet we have ample reason to wonder whether these understandings of ourselves are justified.

Let us assume that Whitman's view of America is at least partly correct: we may not *be* a noble people, but we would *like to be*. If our aspiration is to be noble, what is it about our culture that keeps us from realizing this aspiration? My argument focuses on what we can learn from the stories we tell ourselves about being a nation of immigrants. These stories are rich in themselves but also illustrate the broader role that narratives play in legitimating our place in the world. With respect to immigration two prevailing narratives have helped us *think* we are a nation where privilege is not only possible but also deserved—but neither corresponded very well with reality, and both thus prevented us from attaining a clearer story about who we are. The story that emerged in the decades after the first great wave of immigration focused on privilege justified by the immigrants' having undergone an arduous ordeal. This story was sufficient to account for the modest comforts that immigrants themselves were able to attain in America. It was deficient, though, in justifying the enormous wealth that some immigrants acquired, and even more deficient in explaining the comforts of successive generations who had hardly suffered at all. In more recent years, as the suffering involved in actually coming to America has diminished, a new story has emerged. Like the earlier narrative, this one also justifies gain in terms of a corresponding loss. Yet in so doing it reinforces the idea that the immigrant must trade in home to achieve success. One must choose between the two: stay at home and give up success, or pursue success and give up home. The resulting fault line that runs through our national psyche parallels this division. But it is hard to imagine that we are a noble people if losing our homes is the price of privilege. It is difficult to feel good about ourselves if this is the bargain we have struck. It is easy to succumb to national self-doubt or to affirm doggedly in the face of criticisms from abroad that America is truly the Promised Land. It is much harder to formulate an understanding of ourselves that holds forth the possibility of achieving our aspirations—achieving them in a way that earns us the international respect that we so eagerly desire.

Following the September 11, 2001, attacks on Washington and New York, America's leaders and the American press struggled to understand the circumstances that had motivated the attack. One of the central questions in these discussions was "Why do they hate us?" President Bush posed the question in a speech to a joint session of Congress a few days after the attacks and answered that terrorists hated America because of its freedom.[2] Several days later *Newsweek* carried a lengthy cover story entitled "Why They Hate Us" about possible grievances that might have motivated the attackers.[3] In the ensuing discussion, the question gradually took on broader connotations. Pundits asked not only why nineteen terrorists hated America, but also why other groups did. Why did the Taliban hate us? Why did Muslims hate us? And why, judging from international public opinion surveys, did many people throughout the developing world hold unfavorable views of the United States? The questions themselves implied that something was wrong. Had our image in the world become tarnished? Were we not the noble people we imagined ourselves to be?

The questions about America's image in the world were less about how others saw us and more about our own understandings of America. International correspondents filed reports based on observations in foreign cities, and a few academicians wrote scholarly books about the mind-set of terrorists and their supporters. The questions, though, were not in the first instance ones that could be answered with such information. They were rather the occasion for scrutiny of the national conscience. It wasn't, as some commentators suggested, that we were surprised at not being well-liked as a nation. It was more that an attack on our homeland necessitated a new commitment to our basic values. Like a family grieving, we came together to reaffirm our identity. We needed time to mourn, but also time to think again about who we were.

In the weeks and months following the attacks the answers that emerged generally fell into three categories, two of which can be understood readily, while the third requires more careful consideration. The two answers that required little elaboration were that America's policies toward other countries sometimes generated hatred, and that the sheer fact of America's elevated standing in the world did as well. Examples of American policies resulting in problems for other countries were not hard to find. Critics pointed to a wide range of potential grievances: America's failure to uphold Palestinian rights, its stationing of troops in

Saudi Arabia, its earlier complicity with the shah's brutal regime in Iran, suspected misuse of American aid in Pakistan, and allegations of CIA involvement with the dictatorships of Brunei and Chad, to name a few. For those who believed U.S. policy was antagonistic toward Islam, the invasions of Afghanistan and Iraq and references to Iran as part of an evil axis were cases in point. Others pointed to U.S. wealth and asked why so many people in other countries were dying from malnutrition and treatable diseases. The argument about America's place in the world focused less on specific policies and more on the old saw about things' being lonely at the top. According to this argument, people around the world would inevitably be resentful of America because of our wealth and power, even if Americans did everything right.

It is easy enough to see that both arguments are credible. When an American bomb goes astray and kills children in a Muslim village, an angry response is not surprising. When American television advertises household conveniences out of the reach of 95 percent of the population in other countries, it is not hard to understand the resulting resentment. It is worth pausing, though, to consider the moral implications of these arguments. The implication of the argument about American policies is that negative effects need to be balanced by positive outcomes. We do the best we can, knowing that we cannot do everything and that we cannot do everything right. Collateral damage is, as we say, regrettable, but it is the price we pay for winning a war. If the world hates America because we sometimes fail, that means only that we need to work harder at realizing our ideals. The ideals themselves are not at fault. So, too, with the argument about the world's resenting America's place at the top of the ladder. The implication is that American power should be used responsibly, even generously.

The explanation of foreign hatred of America that requires closer consideration focuses less on America's power and status in the world and more on accusations about its self-understanding. The word that best summarizes these accusations is *arrogance*. "Overseas," writes Jon B. Alterman, a Mideast expert at the U.S. Institute of Peace, "we're seen as arrogant, we're seen as huddling behind the high walls of embassies, as supporting corrupt regimes, and as being utterly indifferent to Arab suffering."[4] And not only overseas, apparently. A CNN/Gallup Poll conducted in 2002 showed that 68 percent of the American public thought the United States was arrogant.[5] But what does it mean to level this accusation against our country?

When a person complains that another person is arrogant, the accusation can mean one of several different things. It can refer to a breach in the norms by which decisions are usually made (such as failing to take account of another party's wishes, as in the case of U.S. leaders making unilateral decisions rather than developing multilateral coalitions with allies). It can refer to a violation of etiquette (such as showing off or acting haughty, as in complaints about an American president acting "smug" or like a "cowboy"). Or it can mean that a person behaved *as if* his or her status was justified, and that the offended party was not convinced of this justification (such as making an unwarrantable claim about one's place or authority).[6] This third meaning of arrogance takes us into a more complex set of questions about how status is justified and what the consequences may be when it is not. These are questions that social theorists have discussed at great length under the heading of *legitimation*. Suffice it to say that general agreement exists on the following points: social order depends on people's feeling that whatever differences there may be in power and privilege are legitimate; legitimacy involves the cultural narratives through which people make sense of their worlds; and in the absence of such narratives people are likely to experience a sense of injustice that can result in rebellion or other expressions of malcontent.

It follows that the question "Why do they hate us?" is a question about the legitimacy of America's place in the world. In particular, it is a question about whether the United States' power and the economic privileges enjoyed by its citizens are justified. Are there good reasons for the United States to play the dominant roles it plays in world politics? Is American power rooted in American goodness? Do Americans deserve to lead privileged lifestyles?

These are important questions that focus squarely on what we think is right and good about our nation. They run deeper than questions about foreign policy or comparative advantage in the world. As important as those questions are, they do not focus directly on our basic values. Nor do the responses they evoke help very much in illuminating why we think our way of life is legitimate. Legitimacy is not something that results from the straightforward declarations of politicians and journalists about what we are doing right or could do better. Those assertions are convincing only insofar as they resonate with cultural assumptions that are largely taken for granted. Legitimacy precedes discussions about policies and values. It is grounded in the stories we hear and tell on other occasions. These stories are remote from, and seemingly disconnected from, the policies and values under consideration. It is precisely this distance that gives them power. They are the warp and woof of daily life. They do not assert specifically, but imply, that what we do is normal and natural, right and good. Our reasons for thinking that our privileges as a nation and as individuals are justified take this form. They are subtle— so subtle that something a president says or a journalist writes may ring true, but we seldom take the time to consider exactly why. When Whitman writes that we are a nation that welcomes immigrants, the implicit assertion is that there is something good about who we are. The same is true of President Bush's argument that people elsewhere are envious of our freedom. But we need to consider more carefully what these messages are. "Legitimation justifies the institutional order," the sociologists Peter L. Berger and Thomas Luckmann write, "by giving a normative dignity to its practical imperatives."[7] It is this cloak of normative dignity that we need to understand.

To anticipate my argument, I begin with a look at the way we think about privilege—whether it be the good incomes, health, or happy families many of us enjoy as individuals, or the reality that Americans and the populations of a few other countries have opportunities to experience lives of abundance and safety unknown to most of the world. Our implicit ways of understanding such privilege typically invoke notions of costs and benefits. These are unreflective calculations for the most part. The logic is merely an unexpressed notion of commensurability. Nor do I mean this in quite the narrow sense that "cost" and "benefit" may imply. I mean it rather in the sense suggested many years ago by Max Weber, who argued that we humans impose rationality of various kinds on our behavior by thinking in terms of means and ends. If we observe that something of interest has happened, we make sense of it by looking for its causes. The logic is as simple as that. View an effect, look for a cause—or, perhaps better, assume one without even having to look for it. But Weber's great insight was to realize that the perceived relationships between means and ends are also the key to whether or not we regard behavior as *legitimate*. To take a simple example: if I see that my neighbor lives in a house similar to mine and know that my neighbor earns about the same income as I do, then I am likely to figure that my neighbor's lifestyle is legitimate; if, however, my neighbor's house costs ten times as much as mine, even though our incomes are similar, I am less likely to feel that my neighbor's lifestyle is justified. In real life, of course, judgments of this kind are much more complex. I am unlikely to know my neighbor's income. I may not know my neighbor well enough to have much of an idea of his or her lifestyle. I am more likely to rely on first- and secondhand stories, on ideas I have picked up in other contexts, and on my imagination. My neighbor, for instance, may have told me a story about growing up as the son of a doctor, and from this story, I may have pieced together an interpretation of why my neighbor's house is so much more expensive than mine is. Adding to the complexity, I may or may not consider being the son of a doctor a legitimate reason for living in the lap of luxury. My values may place enough emphasis on hard work that inherited wealth does not seem justified.

My argument is that our national sense of whether or not our privilege as Americans is justified involves stories about costs and benefits, much like this imaginary story about my neighbor. I will show how these stories are constructed and how they work by considering the moral messages that are implicitly conveyed when Americans talk about what it means to "come to America." Nearly everyone has heard these stories, and many of us have told them. This is because we are a nation of immigrants, or at least a nation of the descendants of immigrants. These stories are rich with moral messages about what kind of place America is and why it is worth living here. Of course, they are not the only stories through which we justify our nation's place in the world (and I will return to some of the others). But stories about immigrants coming to America are especially interesting. Immigrants have made deliberate decisions to live in America. In contrast with native-born Americans, they have had more of an opportunity to think about why it does or does not make sense to live in America. The stories of immigrants who have achieved success in America are particularly revealing. Of all immigrants, they have special reason to think that America is a good place, and their stories are popular because they reinforce positive images of our country. Indeed, it is singularly striking to a native-born American to hear such familiar values being expressed by those who have only recently arrived. There is an interesting connection with the recent concern about foreign hatred of America, too. "America is the great international kidnapper," one observer writes, meaning that America attracts immigrants whose parents and loved ones are left behind. Those parents and loved ones, he suggests, may be left feeling demoralized and resentful.[8] They *may* be, although there is very little evidence from studies of immigrants and their families of origin to suggest this as a significant source of anti-Americanism. The point is well taken, though, if it suggests looking at how immigrants view their families and countries of origin. Do we, as immigrants and descendants of immigrants, look down on the places that our ancestors or we ourselves used to live? Does our national pride depend on these negative comparisons? Or are there more subtle connections between coming to America and believing that the privileges we enjoy here are justified?

## A NATION OF IMMIGRANTS

Whitman's vision of America as a nation of immigrants—a society distinguished by its embrace of newcomers and the cultural strength resulting from this embrace—would become a leitmotif in the United States' depiction of itself during the next century and more. Between 1870 and 1910, more than eight million immigrants flooded into the nation's harbors. They came in search of better jobs or land, to escape military conscription, and to join relatives who had already come. They were not always eagerly welcomed. Nativism and exclusion became as much a part of the story as did assimilation and inclusion. Yet when they stopped to think about it, nearly everyone was an immigrant or the son or daughter of one. It thus became fashionable to associate immigration with the core meanings of America. In 1897, Harvard president Charles William Eliot identified immigration as one of the United States' main contributions to human civilization. Typical of his contemporaries, he was interested not so much in what immigrants had contributed to the nation as in what the nation had contributed to them. America's absorption of large numbers of immigrants, he wrote, demonstrated to the world that "people who at home have been subject to every sort of aristocratic or despotic or military oppression become within less than a generation serviceable citizens of a republic." In achieving this transformation, the United States was thus a beacon to the world for freedom, happiness, and prosperity.[9] A generation later, social scientists were arguing that immigration and assimilation were evidence that America was indeed at the forefront of progress. One writer proclaimed in the *American Journal of Sociology*, "Instead of [the] race provincialism which is advocated by a few writers of doubtful scientific standing . . . , we have a gradual but continuous race assimilation which is commensurate with the advancement of the people of recent advent in this country, and the broadening of social, political, and religious sympathies which are fostered by a democratic government."[10]

There was a more sordid version of the immigration story that could have been told—a version characterized by quotas and persecution, neighborhood turf wars, and railroad tycoons sending agents to Europe with dubious promises of cheap land and abundant jobs. But it was the more idealistic version of the story that prevailed. "America as an asylum for the oppressed is one of the oldest elements of the national myth, part of the millennial meaning of the American experiment," writes Robert N. Bellah.[11] Immigration provided a compelling story about a virgin land, presumably devoid of previous inhabitants, waiting to provide sanctuary to the oppressed peoples of other nations. Bellah's mention of millennial meaning refers to the eighteenth- and nineteenth-century understandings in popular theology of America as the fulfillment of a divine plan for the earth. In these understandings, America served a redemptive role in human history. By welcoming the oppressed, it redeemed the human race from the sins of monarchs and tyrants. In the more secular versions of this millennial vision that gained popularity at the end of the nineteenth century, one of which is evident in Eliot's remark, American democracy stood for enlightenment and progress, and immigration stood for democracy.

Other elements of the national myth have certainly played an important role in justifying America's privileged place in the world and the privileged lifestyles of its citizens. But it is hard to identify any element that has been more important than the idealistic telling and retelling of stories about immigrants. In sheer visibility, few national monuments are as closely associated with American national identity as the Statue of Liberty. The millions who visit it see Emma Lazarus's famous inscription, "Give me your tired, your poor, / Your huddled masses yearning to breathe free," and millions more learn the words in school and sing them at school concerts. Immigration is readily associated in political rhetoric with statements about American freedom. It signals diversity to a greater extent and with fewer negative connotations than do statements about race or religion. If America is a land of opportunity, it is the accomplishments of immigrants that demonstrate the credibility of this claim. The stereotypical immigrant is a person who struggles, works hard, lives morally, and thus deserves whatever he or she accomplishes. The hardships experienced by immigrants are thus heroic in the same way that the sacrifices of soldiers are heroic. The Statue of Liberty points to an almost sacred tradition just as battlefields and military monuments do. In pointing to the history and mythic understandings of immigration, it is a monument to American achievement. If the Pentagon and World Trade Center symbolize American achievements that at best evoke ambivalence, immigration is a potent symbol of what we have tried to do right.

The idealized role that immigration plays in American national pride is often sharply at odds with popular attitudes toward immigrants. Many Americans view immigrants as threats to their jobs and their neighborhoods. They would just as soon roll the clock back a few decades and reimpose stricter policies against immigration. Those attitudes, however, do not diminish the continuing significance of immigration in national mythology. In a survey I conducted among a nationally representative sample of the public, for instance, 76 percent agreed that "America owes a great deal to the immigrants who came here."[12] It is in fact this sense of indebtedness that figures importantly in our justifications of national privilege. Insofar as the immigrant experience is associated with images of hardship and struggle, it is easier to believe we are a nation that deserves what we have attained, and insofar as these images are changing, we are faced with new questions about the legitimacy of privilege.

## PASSAGE TO AMERICA

For most of the immigrants who came to the United States during the nineteenth and early twentieth centuries, the passage itself was an ordeal that became a defining episode in their life story. Oscar Handlin wrote in his Pulitzer Prize–winning history of the period that "the crossing" invariably marked the pivotal episode in the life of the typical immigrant. "He who turned his back upon the village at the crossroads," Handlin observed, "began a long journey that his mind would forever mark as its most momentous experience. The crossing immediately subjected the emigrant to a succession of shattering shocks and decisively conditioned the life of every man that survived it."[13] The passage was a mark of courage, an ordeal that earned the immigrant the right to be an American.

Seymour Rechtzeit was an immigrant from Poland who came to the United States through Ellis Island in 1920 at the age of eight. Many years later, he remembered vividly the hardship of crossing the Atlantic. "Riding on a big boat across the Atlantic Ocean may sound like fun," he observed, "but it wasn't. The two-week trip was miserable!" The boat was uncomfortable and crowded, and it was beset by thunderstorms and driving rain, leaving the passengers soaked. The young Mr. Rechtzeit arrived with a bad cold, which meant having to stay at Ellis Island, separated from his father, afraid, and feeling as if he were in jail. Eventually Mr. Rechtzeit was released, went on to become a successful vaudeville performer, married, raised a family, and even met the president on one occasion. His positive feelings about life in America were richer because of the hardship he had experienced.[14]

For Mr. Rechtzeit and the millions of others who came across the Atlantic or Pacific oceans, the crossing was sufficiently arduous that simply surviving was a singular accomplishment. As many as 20 percent of those who attempted the journey died. Many more became ill and were either quarantined on Ellis Island or sent back. Thieves aboard the ships robbed unsuspecting women and children. Unscrupulous immigration officials demanded bribes, separated families for unexplained reasons, and misplaced documents. During the journey, the passengers cramped together in overcrowded steerage quarters were alone for the first time, separated from parents and siblings and thrust among strangers they did not know and who often did not speak their language. They certainly struggled with their emotions, wondering whether they would ever see loved ones again, repressing anger at being forced by economic or political circumstances to flee their ancestral homes, and fearing for their safety. Although they may have entertained high hopes for the future, they also knew from the friends and neighbors they had left behind that life in the New World would be hard, and that many who attempted it failed. Meanwhile, each moment of the crossing was so debasing that social reformers of the day believed it did serious moral damage, reducing the chances of those who made it to become responsible citizens. As one wrote, "A voyage in the steerage of many a ship is now seven days or more in an unspeakable slum, in a den wherein are herded human beasts."[15]

An arduous crossing puts one in what the anthropologist Victor Turner has famously called a state of liminality. The experience of liminality is that of being between two worlds. The reality with which we are familiar is temporarily suspended. We are neither here, where our life has always been, nor there, where we anticipate remaking our life anew. Compounding the physical danger we face, the fear that we may not survive at all, is the shock to our accustomed ways of thinking and behaving. The knowledge that helped us get along in the past is no longer as effective. We know we will have to learn new skills, but during the crossing we can only speculate about what these will entail. While the crossing is a time of danger, it is nevertheless a moment of empowerment. Especially in retrospect, when it is remembered and relived vicariously through the stories told at family and community gatherings, the crossing demonstrates that a person was strong. It is the kind of strength that comes from confronting some awesome force that is much more powerful than anything we have experienced in ordinary life. "He is a man," Durkheim wrote, "[who] feels within him more force, either to endure the trials of existence, or to conquer them."[16] As a time of empowerment, the crossing also bestows meaning that is more special or significant than the ordinary meanings of which daily life is composed. Just as dawn and dusk may be times of personal reverie for an individual, or as a major war may reshape the history of a nation, the crossing serves as a point of reference that gives meaning to that which came before or comes after. "Meaning is not in things but in between," wrote the philosopher Norman O. Brown, "in the iridescence, the interplay; in the intersections, at the crossroads."[17]

An experience of passage not only empowers a person by demonstrating that he or she was capable of surviving a difficult journey. It also justifies any rewards that follow. A passage that involves danger or sacrifice resembles what the sociologist Harold Garfinkel termed a "degradation ceremony."[18] The hazing undergone by initiates in fraternal organizations or the military is a degradation ritual. It temporarily strips away personal identity and subjects the novice to the authority of the group. The psychological transformation that takes place, Garfinkel suggests, involves an emotional identification between the victim and the source of authority, such that the victim tries all the harder to live up to the authority figure's rules. Whether or not that kind of behavior results, the mere experience of degradation shows that a person "paid the price" for the benefits he or she subsequently enjoys from participating in the group. Medical school is an example. The long hours of study, sleep deprivation, and subjection to others' orders degrade the student. They provide the student with a story to tell later about why he or she earns a high salary as a doctor. "Look what I went through to get here" is the gist of the story. The same is true of stories about hardship faced by immigrants during the passage to America. They earned their place by suffering. If America is a place of privilege, its privileges are deserved.

While the individual who has experienced liminality may be personally transformed, the stories of those who underwent the ordeal take on a larger meaning in the wider culture. Their struggle becomes a redemptive act for the whole society. They demonstrate that humanity can survive the worst and come out better for it, that a nation can be renewed by the arrival of hardy souls capable of enduring pain and loss and hardship so that future generations may succeed. It is in the telling of such stories that people remind themselves that freedoms won required that sacrifices be made. The immigrants' crossing is like the soldiers' descent into hell. Through their suffering heroes are found. It is for this reason that Americans have ritualized the telling of immigrant stories—that stories like Mr. Rechtzeit's are recounted to schoolchildren (that *his* appears on a Web site for teachers complete with instructions for students to write essays about the meaning of his ordeal). Oscar Handlin clearly recognized the salvific cultural significance of the immigrants' crossing. "With every hostile shock you bore," he wrote, "with every frantic move you made, with every lonely sacrifice, you wakened to the sense of what, long hidden in that ancient whole, you never knew you lacked."[19] The immigrant legacy, Handlin believed, was all the more poignant because it was the innocent, the simple, the naive, and even the coerced who made the crossing. Like savior figures in the great religions, Handlin's immigrants suffered more than they should have. They endured indignities, experienced hardship inflicted on them unjustly, were meanly uprooted from their secure homes, were subjected to horrible trauma, and through it all came into the Promised Land where they gained enlightenment and made it possible for their children and their children's children to realize dreams that could hardly have been imagined. These were the themes that became larger than life in such film epics as Norman Taurog's *Little Nellie Kelly* (1940), Edward Dmytryk's *Give Us This Day* (1949), and Elia Kazan's *America, America* (1963). They continued to be emphasized in such films as Joan Micklin Silver's documentary *The Long, Long Journey* (1972), in Ron Howard's *Far and Away* (1992), and in the screenplay of Amy Tan's *Joy Luck Club* (1993).[20] For Americans whose family memories of immigration had grown dim, these depictions provided nostalgic accounts of a heroic past.

There are still many immigrants for whom the crossing was sufficiently traumatic to stand out as a powerful and singularly meaningful event in their lives, and to spark the public's imagination. At an Ellis Island gathering to which President Bush spoke on July 10, 2001, the oath of citizenship was administered to the assembled immigrants by Assistant Attorney General Viet D. Dinh. Mr. Dinh was born in South Vietnam in 1968 during the Tet offensive. In 1978 he, his mother, and six siblings fled the country in a fifteen-foot boat. After losing the boat's engine during a storm and drifting for twelve days, they were fired on by a Malaysian navy ship. When they reached land that night, Mr. Dinh's mother destroyed the boat to ensure that they would not be forced out to sea again. Eventually they reached the United States—with only two hundred dollars, which they spent on used winter coats—and five years later were reunited with Mr. Dinh's father, who had been in a Communist reeducation camp.[21] In 1992, Mr. Dinh sent an essay to columnist Anthony Lewis of the *New York Times*, telling his story and mentioning a sister whose whereabouts were unknown. Mr. Lewis published the story, which was picked up by other papers in the United States and around the world. Through the publicity, the sister was found in a Hong Kong refugee camp and reunited with her family who, by this time, were running a small grocery store in Oregon.[22] Mr. Lewis wrote in 1993, "It is an American story . . . the Dinh family is doing what immigrants on the Lower East Side and so many other places did: struggling for themselves and making this country better."[23] Viet Dinh went on to graduate magna cum laude from Harvard College and Harvard Law School. He subsequently served as associate special counsel to the U.S. Senate Whitewater Committee, taught at Georgetown University Law Center, and became a principal architect of the Patriot Act and other Justice Department efforts to combat terrorism after the attacks on New York and Washington on September 11, 2001.[24] During his Senate confirmation hearing in May 2001, Mr. Dinh recalled his mother's wielding a large ax to hack a hole in the side of their boat on the Malaysian coast. "That image of my mother destroying our last link to Vietnam really stands in my mind to this day as to the courage she possesses," he said, "but also the incredible lengths which my parents, like so many other people, have gone to in order to find that promise of freedom and opportunity."[25]

Stories like Mr. Dinh's can be found often enough that native-born and immigrant Americans alike can take pride in the fact that people are willing to sacrifice so much and endure such ordeals to become Americans. The Haitian, Dominican, and Cuban refugees who arrive periodically in small boats along the Florida coast serve as the basis for this kind of American pride. Similar connotations radiate from stories of Mexicans and Central Americans risking their lives during long crossings to the border of the southwestern United States and of Asians being smuggled into American harbors in sealed shipping containers. One barely has to mention a story like this to a native-born American for a story about his or her own ancestors' perilous passage to spill forth. The sheer difficulty of getting here means that the destination was worth it. Whatever privileges Americans presently enjoy, some immigrant relative or acquaintance paid the cost. Others may hate us, thinking us undeserving of what we have; we know otherwise, that our freedom has been won through sacrifice.

But for most recent immigrants—and probably especially for those who have come as, or become, members of the educated professional elite—the crossing itself does not involve the dangers or carry the symbolic value it once did. Air transportation has made it a matter of a few hours, in most instances, rather than an ordeal of days and weeks. One no longer speaks of "crossings" or "passages" at all. While there are often delays in dealing with the Immigration and Naturalization Service or difficulties in transferring funds, the danger involved en route is not a large part of what makes the experience of immigration meaningful. "A hundred years ago," writes the anthropologist Nancy Foner, "immigrants arrived at Ellis Island dirty and bedraggled, after a long ocean journey in steerage; now they emerge from the cabin of a jet plane at John F. Kennedy International Airport, often dressed in designer jeans or fashionable attire."[26] They probably boarded at an airport not far from where they lived and flew only a few hours before arriving at JFK. The ones unable to dress fashionably probably still find it relatively inexpensive to pay for their ticket. In my New Elites Project, hardly anyone mentioned the actual trip at all.[27] Most of their stories about coming to

America focused on what they hoped to achieve when they arrived, not on the difficulties involved in transit. Many had already traveled to the United States or to another country as tourists or students. The decision to emigrate was seldom easy, but the passage itself typically was. One young man, for instance, spoke volumes in describing how friends in Chicago had secured him a job. "I got the job one day and three days later I was in the United States."[28]

The fact that travel has become easier takes nothing away from the emotional trauma involved in leaving one's country behind and moving to another. It does, however, change the valence attached to immigration by the wider public. It is harder now than in the past to believe that America is somehow redeemed through the hardship endured by those who come as immigrants. "In story, film, and family lore, turn-of-the-century immigrants are often recalled as noble sufferers and heroes who weathered hardships in Europe and a traumatic ocean crossing to make it to America," Foner writes.[29] Today, the occasional story of immigrants surviving a difficult journey is diminished by the public perception that these are people coming illegally and for no good reason. And when others arrive at international airports in designer jeans, it is again difficult to connect the cultural dots between these images and the idea that privilege in America is won through hardship.

What has replaced the story of an arduous crossing to America is now an account of difficult *psychological* adjustment. There is still a period of liminality, but it occurs after the immigrant arrives, rather than during the journey itself. These stories seldom involve physical trauma or the risk of death and thus may convey weaker messages of heroic struggle to the culture at large. They are nevertheless quite real to the immigrants who experience them, and to their families. The hardship of adjusting to a new society continues to serve as a powerful element in immigrant narratives about the meaning of America. Rob Nixon, an immigrant from Scotland, writes of this adjustment as a feeling of being an alien and of being suspended between two worlds. "I moved through my first two American years—spent in Iowa—with a certain spectral insubstantiality," he writes. "I lived as an extraterrestrial, an 'immigrant alien' in the full sense of the phrase. I probably won't ever feel so otherworldly again, this side of the grave."[30] In my interviews, people spoke less poetically but often remembered how they or their parents were "scared," "worried," and disoriented. A man from El Salvador remembers his first months in the United States as so difficult that he went to church every day and prayed, "My God, please help me; I don't like this life!" A woman from Vietnam characterized her first years in the United States as a time of overwhelming "uncertainty." A man from Indonesia remembers feeling completely powerless. An immigrant from India says he temporarily lost his identity. Another immigrant from India remembers "crying a lot." A man whose parents came from Mexico remembers they were very unhappy and considered themselves failures for having had to move. A man whose parents fled Vietnam in 1975 says they just seemed to be detached from everything. In these accounts, it was a mark of courage to have survived the shock of moving to a new culture. The children of immigrants typically saw this courage in their parents as a sign of character and as a kind of investment, a sacrifice, that they, as the beneficiaries of their parents' courage, were required to repay.

An arduous passage or a difficult period of adjustment as a kind of liminal experience, though, is only one source of stories about immigration and what it contributes to our understanding of America. It is the fact of coming to America, of leaving one place behind and assuming residence in a new one, that now provides an even more significant chapter in the immigrant story. The hardship is not so much the physical journey, as it was for Mr. Dinh, as it is the act of giving up one's home. For those who make the sacrifice, the logic is that they give up one thing that is valued in order to obtain something else that is valued more. There is a clear break, a transition from "before" to "after," and this break is a pivotal moment in one's understanding of what it took to become successful. In the larger stories that emerge from these individual narratives, the move to America is also symbolically rich. It shows what Americans must be willing to lose if they are to gain entry into the privileged elite, and the values that must be carried along if the journey is to be completed successfully. A significant way in which we justify the privilege we enjoy as Americans is through these stories about leaving home.

## THE MEANINGS OF LEAVING HOME

Immigrants' stories of leaving home and coming to America are similar, at first glance, to what students of religion refer to as *conversion narratives*.[31] Minus the part about the particular moment of conversion (which is a liminal state like an immigrant's "crossing"), a conversion narrative tells of life before, when things were bad, and life after, when things were better. The narrative may unfold slowly and in excruciating detail or may describe an almost instant transformation, but the essential logic is binary. Whatever was wrong before the conversion is healed by the conversion, and the more one casts the first phase as a time of darkness and despair, the more the second phase appears as a time of illumination and rejoicing. If immigrants' stories really corresponded to this simple binary logic, it would not be hard to see in them a source of the world's misgivings about America. Just as the unrepentant see the righteous convert as insufferably arrogant, so might non-Americans view a nation of immigrants whose stories described all but their new land as places of darkness.

But I want to suggest that immigrant stories are more complicated than this binary depiction suggests. It is not so much that immigrants valorize America by contrasting it with the deficits of other countries. Narratives of that nature might implicitly justify our sense that America is a place in which all privileges are deserved, while leaving people elsewhere feeling that Americans regard them as backward and inferior. It is rather that immigrants' stories are more nuanced in how they describe the virtues of America and of their countries of origin. Their narratives are accurately described not as stories about leaving something undesirable but as accounts of giving up much that they continue to cherish. What they leave behind is also a gift that, in a sense, remains with them—a gift of powerful memories, good upbringing, and values. In these stories, America emerges as a nation that is to a degree appealing as a place to live. The privileges Americans enjoy are purchased by the genuine loss that immigrants experience, and, in this sense, these privileges are earned. Yet America is also found wanting. It is a place of deficits as well as of benefits. The advantages of living in America can only partly outweigh the costs. America is no longer the Promised Land—or at least no longer the unambiguously utopian land of milk and honey.

The one thing my interviewees mentioned most often when asked what they or their parents hoped for in coming to America is the opportunity to be successful. Not only had they attained success in their respective professions; they said explicitly that becoming successful was one of their most important goals in life. They viewed the United States as a place where success could be pursued and attained. A typical remark comes from a young man whose parents emigrated from Hong Kong when he was a child. "My mom had relatives here in the Southwest, particularly in Arizona, and I think they saw the United States as a chance to break free of some of the struggles that they were experiencing and to also give us some opportunities." A man whose parents moved to the United States from Chile said almost the same thing. "They wanted to come here for an opportunity to get a better job that would also then allow them to provide for their families. They came here looking for an opportunity, looking for an opportunity to work, to work hard." Other remarks include such reasons for coming to the United States as "to achieve good status," "have a better life," "stability in economics," "make a lot of money," "opportunities for personal success and wealth," and simply "better opportunity." In comparison with the United States, countries of origin in these accounts offer fewer opportunities to be successful. The man whose parents came from Hong Kong, for instance, says, "Jobs and access to education, especially to college and universities, are severely limited in Hong Kong, very highly competitive and highly expensive." A man who moved to the United States from Mexico says it is very hard to be successful in Mexico. He remembers being frequently depressed before he came because of repeated financial setbacks. Once in the United States, he was able to launch a successful chain of restaurants. A Pakistani man says Pakistan is an "extremely poor" country where people "live hand to mouth." He feels very lucky to have left.

In the self-perceptions of these upwardly mobile immigrants, there is thus a strong connection between "America" and "success." We shall need to look more carefully at what exactly success means (in chapter 4), but for now it will suffice simply to observe the connection. America is a special place because people can pursue their dreams of becoming successful. To a person, these successful immigrants believe that they have in fact become more successful in America than they would have in their native countries. America is *better* in this respect. It is a privileged place and a place where privilege can be attained. The way success is described frequently points to other favorable aspects of America, too, and not just to economic opportunities. For instance, the son of a Korean immigrant says his dad came to America because Korea at the time was ruled by a dictator, and that meant not being able to import the goods that would have been most profitable to his father's business. Economic opportunity in the United States and democracy were thus linked. A doctor who had emigrated from Syria drew a similar connection between economic opportunity and American science: "It is no secret that the U.S. is a big power, not militarily but a big power in science, and it's the leading country in the world, and for physicians you always want to offer your patients the best possible option in medicine." Coming to the United States was thus a way for this doctor to excel in his field.

Where immigrant stories become more complicated is in their depiction of what was lost in the departure from their countries of origin. The specific contrast between their old life in another country and their new life in America is not simply between one country and another. What they have left behind is *home*. What they have attained is not home but something less, something that leaves them unsatisfied. Home means parents and siblings, aunts and uncles, and grandparents. But it means much more than this. Homes are places of warmth and love that evoke nostalgic memories. They are familiar places in which a person's identity is taken for granted. They are secure places that provide comfort, but also nurturing places that make one strong. To leave them behind is thus to experience an acute sense of loss. What is lost may be as specific as a mother's smile or a father's whiskery face. It is often more diffuse. Home connotes not only one's immediate family but one's friends, the street on which one lived, a familiar shop or school, religious or ethnic customs, the convictions one learned as a child, and of course one's native language. It may never have been experienced quite the way it is remembered, but the sense of a place elsewhere that has been lost is preserved in memory through the telling of stories.

Amjad Masali is president and CEO of a software company that creates systems for searching and organizing electronics components. Mr. Masali was born in Jordan and moved to the United States in 1978 at the age of eighteen. His family lived in Palestine before they moved to Jordan. The sense of loss is acute in Mr. Masali's understanding of his family history and of himself. It is a familiar story among Palestinians. In 1948, Mr. Masali's parents were expelled from their homeland when the state of Israel was founded. Leaving behind a successful grocery store, they fled to a village on the West Bank where during the summer they sought shelter under some trees and in the winter lived in a cave. They lived there for three years, caring for two small children. On one occasion his father tried to return to his native village only to be captured and shot, which left him partially disabled. Another four years passed, and the family moved to a newly established UN refugee camp near

Amman, Jordan. They lived in a two-room duplex, and Mr. Masali's father once again was able to run a grocery store. Mr. Masali says his parents' experience of being refugees profoundly influenced his outlook on life. One effect was to make him frugal and appreciative of everything he had. "Even a small piece of bread, we were not allowed to throw it away." He especially remembers his father's telling him not to take anything for granted, and always being prepared for the worst. "There will always be a bad day in your life and you have to prepare for that bad day. Don't be caught off guard." The other thing was remembering their homeland and keeping alive the hope of returning. Mr. Masali recalls his father's telling him "everything about his homeland, even the names of the streets." He says he can remember "all the stories he told me about his life in the village before he was expelled from Palestine. It was like a dreamland to me. It was like something that is out of this world that I want to go back to one day."

This awareness of a beloved place that has been lost and that cannot possibly be regained, Mr. Masali says, has been an important factor in his own efforts to succeed. He learned growing up in the refugee camp that it is necessary to work harder than everyone else if one is to succeed. "Life is difficult in the refugee camp. People who want to make it there really have to go the extra mile. It was a challenge to walk three miles in mud to get to school in the early morning. To do that every day taught me I have to work hard all the time." He applied that lesson especially to getting an education. He earned high enough grades in high school to be accepted to several universities in Europe and the United States. He came to the United States because he knew he could support himself by working on the side, and he figured there would be good jobs when he graduated. For him, it was the opportunity "to start a new life." He also thinks education will be the way for the Palestinian people in general to overcome the loss they experienced in 1948. "Without education and without being successful, the Palestinian people will never get back their homeland. Education is the number one goal Palestinians should aspire to. They should get the highest education possible and be as successful as they can be."

Such stories of acute loss are especially common among immigrants who have come to the United States as refugees. There is a sense of injustice about the loss they have experienced. Not only their home, but also their *homeland* has been lost. "The thing about being in exile," a refugee from Vietnam remarks, "is that you live the rest of your life longing for a place that you cannot return to." That is a severe form of displacement. A similar sense of loss, though, is common among immigrants who are not refugees. The hardest thing about coming to America, they say, is losing the familiarity and warmth of their original home. Home is most tangibly the house in which one was raised and the immediate family who lived there. But it is the *meaning* of these places and people that matters most. Words like "safety," "security," and "support" are common in immigrant narratives. A woman from Mexico says her parents' coming to America involved giving up the "safety of the family" and the "support system" it provided. A second-generation immigrant from Puerto Rico still feels that home is where his parents lived, rather than anywhere in the United States. "When I go to my parents' hometown," he says, "there's a particular rock on the mountain that I stand beside late at night. I look up at the stars and I say, 'I belong. I come from somewhere. I come from this spot. I am connected to a culture. I am connected to a people. This is who I am.' " He says that when you are an immigrant, you leave all of that behind.

The image of the United States in these accounts is one in which home is lacking or at least devalued. If home connotes succor and warmth, the United States is a place of rationality and cold calculation. Life may be richer here financially, but the emotional ambience is flat. Instrumental thinking replaces expressive attachments. Before leaving, one had deep and lasting friendships; now one's relationships are superficial. Home was a place of attachments; America is a place of freedom. A woman from Argentina says that leaving her family behind was the hardest part of coming to America, but if Argentina still connotes family for her, the United States offers "adventure," the challenge of "doing it on my own," and the opportunity of "succeeding on my own." There is a kind of symmetry in the meanings of America that such remarks imply. Home is positively valued, and it is a collectivity in which one holds membership and with which one identifies. It is also distant, located elsewhere than in the United States. Against its loss, one gains other things that are positively valued. These things are not collectivities. They are personal attributes. Being "on my own" is what one gains from the loss of home. The loss of home need not be either literal or enforced: America is seen as a place where people leave home voluntarily. This is a cultural norm that immigrants see clearly in the United States because it often contrasts so sharply with the customs in their native countries. A woman from India makes this point especially well in describing the differences between growing up there and in the United States. "In India we had a very protected life. The girl will stay home until she's married, even if she's twenty-three. Boys stay home when they're going to college. And at home, you are totally obedient to your parents. Here, when you are fifteen or sixteen, you are not sitting at home. If you stay home, people will look at you."

The home one leaves behind may be warm, but it is ultimately not a good place to stay. The emotional attachments it involves connote childish feelings that must be transcended when one becomes an adult. A woman from Mexico says she misses the good old days when she could see her grandparents and eat frijoles. But it was "absolute clarity of mind" that led her to leave. It is as if she believes her earlier memories had been clouded by irrational emotions. A doctor who grew up in Syria makes a similar comparison between his homeland and the United States. He fondly remembers the town where his ancestors had lived for a thousand years and where he could say "Hi" to half the people on the street. But he also associates home with being so immature and lazy that he seldom made his own bed. Coming to America was a good move that taught him how to rely on himself. For many, home also has gendered connotations. It was a place, one woman explains, where she and her sisters, mother, and aunts all cooked dinner together and talked. Home is mentally associated with one's mother, more than with one's father. It evokes memories of mother-love, but also of domestic duties, housework, and staying at home. Leaving home involves making the hard decision to depart from this comforting place. The person who leaves home is a male or a woman who behaves like a male. She makes the difficult choice to be a responsible person in the wider world, rather than to stay at home like her mother.

## FEELING GOOD ABOUT AMERICA

In our national mythology, America is a nation of immigrants who have worked hard and sacrificed much to gain the privileges they and their descendants enjoy. One does not have to be a recent immigrant to participate in these narratives. Culture is not always personal, not always about oneself; it is also symbolic, referential, and about the way we understand things to be in our society in general. Culture is composed of stories that make us feel good *vicariously*. It warms our hearts to watch a film in which the townspeople band together to help one another. We identify with the goodness portrayed. Whether we are immigrants or not, it makes us feel good about America to believe that people come here seeking a better life and achieve it by working hard. But America's mythology is also more complex. It is layered with meanings that are powerful because they are seldom examined critically. Some of these meanings carry inadvertent messages.

The inadvertent messages conveyed in our narratives about immigration are that one must *leave home* in order to earn the benefits America has to offer. Home is somewhere else, far away, in a place that had to be left behind. It is warm and comforting, but it is also gone. The places that provided succor are not the rationally minded places in which one can expect to succeed. They were alluring, and it would have been easy to stay there, but in the harsh light of reality, it was necessary to move on. Home was not something a person could bring along on the journey. It was too much baggage. There were customs that would have tied one down. Coming to America made it possible to break from these restrictions. The new life would be different from the old one. A person might still have family and friends, be a good parent, and raise a family. But these new roles would not be the same as what one knew at home. The new life would be freer and more focused on achieving success, even if the price of that success was loss of home. As home is lost, striving for individual success becomes all the more important as recompense.

The motif of leaving home is a powerful element of American culture. Immigrants leave home, but so does the aspiring young person who goes off to college. He or she leaves home in order to learn new skills and, more important, to become a new person—a person with a unique identity forged from exposure to new ideas and a mobile set of friends who enter and leave one's life as one's interests change. The home of one's childhood may be an anchor, a refuge, but it is differentiated in cultural understandings from the real world in which careers are made. The real world requires sacrifice as well as hard work, and home is the sacrificial offering. A person is likely to be guided by emotion, passion, and deep values at home; those should be left at home, not carried to the office or the boardroom. Life in those nonhome contexts should be governed by rational thought and by self-interested calculations. The two realms are too far apart to be easily joined.

All this is ironic in view of many Americans' belief that their chances for success were available because of the gifts they received from their families of origin. Home is not only a place to escape from. It is never completely left behind in the psychological sense that wanting to escape implies. The baggage is inescapable. Home is a place where others sacrificed in order to give one a gift. The people there endured hardship, they sacrificed their own dreams, they spent extra hours on the job, and they devoted extra energy to instilling good values in their children. These are the gifts the children carried with them when they left home. The parental sacrifices incurred debts that need to be repaid. The values learned at a mother's knee are resources that one must respect and use wisely. Yet the culturally accepted way to repay these debts is to succeed professionally and financially, not somehow to remain at home. The society provides ladders to climb that have little to do with home itself. Climbing these ladders requires abandoning strong attachments to home. The resources for climbing them must be internalized by the individual. Only the individual can succeed.

As a nation, we are thus an ambitious people, willing to leave home, and in that willingness to embark on our own journeys we are a people who believe we deserve the privileges we may attain. The cost is that we then find ourselves without the places of warmth and security that we once cherished. The cost is in broken homes, in weak extended families, and in declining community attachments that might otherwise have been sustained by those networks of relatives and friends. The cost lies not only in a sense of rootlessness, but in truly being a people without deep or nurturing roots. A society like this will always fall short of its aspirations, for our highest aspirations involve having a home, too, in which our values and convictions can be nurtured. These shortcomings may be only a small source of the antipathy projected toward America from abroad. But they are surely an important source of our own ambivalence about who we are and who we would like to be.

CHAPTER 4

SELF-MADE MEN AND WOMEN

On November 2, 1913, the *New York Times* devoted a full-page article to penniless immigrants who became unbelievably successful through little more than their own efforts. They included "coffee king" Herman Sielcken, "lumber king" Frederick Weyerhaeuser, "telephone king" Michael Idvorsky Pupin, and "king of the kitchens" Jules Weber. Each had come to America in steerage class, started at the bottom, and worked his way to the top. Weyerhaeuser's story was typical. He immigrated at the age of eighteen, worked at a lumberyard in Illinois, saved enough money to buy a small lumber mill of his own, managed it prudently, and within fifteen years turned it into the largest lumber business in the Mississippi Valley. The other stories were similar. Sielcken began as a shipping clerk, became an itinerant wool buyer, made his way to New York where he joined a coffee importing business, and soon became so successful at soliciting contracts that the firm made him a partner. Pupin was the son of Serbian peasants. He worked as a farmhand in Maryland, moved to New York, and eventually invented several profitable devices for the telephone industry. Weber worked as an egg boy at the Astor House, moved up to assistant cook, saved his money, opened his own restaurant, and made a fortune in real estate. "Hundreds of immigrants" like these, the article reported, "came to America with little more than energy and hope, and today are kings of industry, many of them with wealth greater than that of any hereditary monarch."[1]

Stories of self-made men whose hard work and common sense took them from rags to riches are a prominent thread in the American mythos. During the nineteenth century these stories circulated widely in textbooks and popular literature. McGuffey Readers included stories of orphans and paupers who came to America and became heads of businesses. More than one hundred million schoolchildren were reared on these standard schoolbooks.[2] Other texts instructed pupils about such self-made men as Benjamin Franklin, Daniel Boone, and Abraham Lincoln. The early twentieth century provided more grist for these stories. Andrew Carnegie and Theodore Roosevelt became new models of the self-made man. In popular literature, few stories sold as widely as those of Horatio Alger. The oldest son of a New England minister, Alger grew up in a debt-ridden family, was small for his age, and suffered from bronchial asthma, but he overcame these difficulties, graduating Phi Beta Kappa from Harvard and going on to become one of the most successful writers of his era. He produced 118 novels in book form, another 280 novels in magazines, and more than 500 short stories. After his death in 1899, his books continued to sell, totaling as many as 250 million copies over the next half century.[3] His protagonists were mostly boys who, like himself, overcame adversity and became rich or famous. Their success typically resulted from a lucky break, such as being in the right place at the right time. But these lucky breaks were deserved. The boys who experienced them were, in a sense, being rewarded by fate for working hard and living clean moral lives.

The broader significance of the self-made man has not been lost on observers of American history and culture. "The legendary hero of America," wrote the historian Irvin G. Wyllie in 1954, "is the self-made man." It is the accomplishments of this figure, however fictional, that singularly reinforce Americans' patriotic pride, Wyllie argued. The message of the self-made man is that America is a good and just society. "Where but in America is there such an abundance of opportunity? Where, except under our institutions, is the individual so free to work out his economic destiny? Where has the nobody so often become somebody on the strength of his personal powers?"[4] It was this same self-made man whose apparent decline worried David Riesman and, a generation later, the historian Christopher Lasch in his jeremiad against the narcissism of the 1980s. And it is the same image that more recent scholars have returned to repeatedly for insights about the changing character of American self-understanding.[5]

## RAGS TO RICHES

Rags-to-riches stories continue to emerge from the experiences of America's recent immigrants. One is that of Linda Alvarado, founding president and CEO of Alvarado Construction and part owner of the Colorado Rockies baseball team in Denver. In April 2001, she received the Horatio Alger Award at a ceremony in Washington sponsored by the Horatio Alger Association, an organization that honors the achievements of outstanding individuals "who have succeeded in spite of adversity."[6] Ms. Alvarado considers herself a second-generation Hispanic American. Her grandfather was a migrant laborer and itinerant Protestant minister who lived in Baja and worked seasonally in California and New Mexico. Her parents settled in New Mexico, where she was born. Some accounts of her upbringing say she was raised in a three-room adobe home without indoor plumbing and only a wood stove for heat.[7] Neither of her parents had attended college, and with six children money was never plentiful. All of the children, though, managed to earn scholarships and attended college. Ms. Alvarado went to Pomona College in Claremont, California, where she majored in economics. Through college, she was undecided about a career, knowing only that she wanted to have one and thinking she might be an artist or teacher. She credits a part-time job during college with launching her career in the construction industry. "I obviously needed to work," she recalls, "and I got a job at the new botanical gardens. I thought, wow, this is pretty cool, I get to wear Levis to work and get a tan. I showed up for the interview and they told me, 'No, no, you don't understand. Girls work in the cafeteria, boys work in the botanical gardens.' I said, 'Well, where does it say that?' Over time they relented and said, 'Okay, come on, you can water the plants.' " Ms. Alvarado returned to this job each summer and then got a position with the company that had constructed the botanical garden. She worked there on mixed-use projects for several years as a contract administrator. After taking classes to gain a better background in construction, she changed jobs and worked on a retail housing and commercial development project processing subcontractor applications and billing, monitoring payrolls, and doing other administrative tasks. She was the only woman doing this kind of work.

Ms. Alvarado remembers that after a few years she began thinking she was smarter than her boss. She says this tongue in cheek, noting that she had a fierce competitive streak that came from growing up with five brothers (all of whom were athletes) and being somewhat of a tomboy herself. "I started to have these wild dreams that I could build things on my own—something small, maybe a duplex or a 7-11 store." In 1974 she moved to Colorado and a year later started her own business. Only twenty-four years old and one of the few women in the construction business, she found it difficult to persuade banks to loan her money. But after six failed attempts, she succeeded in borrowing $20,000 and was on her way.[8] Her first project, which she recalls with pride, was building small bus shelters for people to stand in to get out of the rain. By the early 1990s, Alvarado Construction was doing more than $50 million in business annually and specializing in high-rises and other large commercial buildings and public projects. One of Ms. Alvarado's projects was a $30 million contract to build a large maximum security prison for the state of Colorado. Other large projects have included the Colorado Convention Center, the Navy and Marine Training Facility in Aurora, Colorado, and the High Energy Research Laboratory. With her husband, she has built and operates approximately 150 KFC, Taco Bell, and Pizza Hut restaurants. In 1995, *Hispanic Business* magazine profiled her and her husband, placing them among the nation's seventy wealthiest Hispanic families with an estimated net worth of $35 million.[9] Ms. Alvarado is a corporate director for several Fortune 500 companies—including 3M, Pepsi, Lennox International, Pitney Bowes, Cyprus Amax Minerals, and Engelhard—and she has served as chair of the board of the Denver Hispanic Chamber of Commerce and as commissioner of the White House Initiative for Hispanic Excellence in Education.[10]

The great difference between stories of self-made Americans at the start of the twentieth century and those of a century later is that the recent ones are more inclusive. They show the paths to success of Latina women like Linda Alvarado or of women of color, like Oprah Winfrey. They are no longer exclusively about the self-made *man*. And they are more likely than in the past to include Asian Americans, or others of non-European descent, and thus to reflect the greater diversity of contemporary society.[11] Yet there are similarities between the recent and the earlier narratives as well. Rags-to-riches stories have always included narratives of outsiders. It was young Benjamin Franklin, the outsider from Boston, who came to Philadelphia and made it there, and it was Andrew Carnegie, the Irish-Catholic immigrant, who succeeded in Protestant America. The stories do not reflect statistical realities as much as they tell of possibilities. They show that strangers and immigrants can make it; they suggest equally that America is an open society, a place where all can succeed. While current stories of self-made Americans are about women and people of color and new immigrants, this is no indication of widespread belief that these groups have achieved parity with men and whites and native-born Americans. Rather it indicates that we—collectively, as a people—believe it is still possible for any hard-working, talented, morally upright individual to win big.

The question is whether the *moral meanings* attached to success in these stories are still the same as they were in the past. Do we in fact believe that hard work, talent, and good character are the reasons some Americans win big? Or have the stories changed so that they convey a different message? We are, after all, a much different society from what we were in 1913 when the *New York Times* wrote about the achievements of penniless immigrants. For one thing, we are more culturally diverse. It is not just a few tutored elites who write stories about the presumptive reasons for others' success. The women and people of color and new immigrants who are the subjects of these stories are also their own chroniclers. Historians typically characterize the mythologies of self-made Americans as distinctly American—as somehow part of the core culture shared by insiders. But is it possible that this core culture is so powerful that new immigrants from all over the world come quickly to share it? Is it possible that these assumptions about American success are not so distinctly American after all? Perhaps they are part of what is sometimes euphemistically described as the "globalization" of culture, meaning that they may be assumptions either universalized through U.S. dominance of the world media or already a part of the way many elites and aspiring elites throughout the world view their own pathways to success.

As intriguing as these questions are, there is another possibility that is even more interesting. The realities governing the achievement of success have clearly shifted during the course of the last century. It may still be possible for a stock clerk or a field hand to strike it rich. But the road to wealth and power is much less likely to start there now than it was in the past. Do the stories we tell ourselves and our children about making it big take account of these new realities? Do they seek to inspire by telling at least partial truths about what is now required to become rich and famous? Or do the stories of self-made men and women function at some other level? Are they moral tales that encourage good behavior, preserving timeworn understandings of desirable traits, even if these traits misidentify some of the major realities of our time?

We must be careful about how we approach these questions. Stories of the successful few are never accurate depictions of the many. They are not meant to be the unvarnished truth, even for their principal protagonists. Understanding the role of these stories in the past is a matter of "intellectual history," Wyllie cautioned, not of economic or social history.[12] As intellectual history, they are among the ideas of which our collective cultural understandings are composed. We can examine them as we do popular literature, and, indeed, what we know about them usually does come from literature. Yet these stories would clearly be of less interest if they were *only* literature. They are of greater interest because they somehow *reflect* how we think about ourselves and, for that matter, not only reflect but also *influence* our thinking. But therein is the rub. What *is* the relationship between these stories and life?

Stories are imaginary constructions or selective reconstructions of life; as such, they hold the potential to shape the behavior of those who consume them. A person who reads about a self-made man or woman may, in this sense, be inspired to model his or her life after that man or woman in hopes of also becoming successful. However, thinking about the influence of stories this way is too simple. When I was growing up, I spent the better part of one summer reading a series of popular biographies about such people as Benjamin Franklin, Thomas Edison, and Amelia Earhart. Even though I am sure these books influenced me, I am quite sure that I never imagined myself following in the footsteps of any of the figures portrayed. I did not view them as role models, and by no means did they change the way I led my boyish life. In fact, I quickly grew tired of these books and turned to more entertaining literature (such as detective stories). How then do we think about the influence of such stories?

Roland Barthes's observations about "mythologies" are a useful starting point for thinking about the influence of stories. Although Barthes's most important work dates from the 1950s, it continues to have a significant impact on contemporary thinking about literature and culture. Barthes insists that narratives play a mythologizing role by transforming ideas and beliefs into the taken-for-granted or "natural."[13] The power of narratives lies in the fact that they establish the frame in which thought and behavior take place, more so than in the specific messages they convey. The implied or signified meanings are typically multivalent, suggesting possibilities that do not become explicit enough to be examined critically. This is how stories of self-made men and women are culturally influential. They are part of the background culture, the shared meanings, the "known." The "legendary hero" is, in fact, legendary, meaning that he or she is commonly known, either in the sense of being specifically recognizable (as in the case of Benjamin Franklin) or through his or her representativeness of a generally recognizable trajectory of success (as in the case of Linda Alvarado). Although the individuals portrayed are rare in the degree of success they achieve, they also stand for the common person who experiences life as a series of hopes and ambitions. The stories of rare success demonstrate that such possibilities do exist, even for common people. They are stories with the potential to inspire hope, just as a lottery ticket does. At another level, the self-made man or woman serves as a symbol of legitimacy. In the individual case, people deserve what they get because their success is earned. It is achieved through hard work and right living. For the society, whatever system of rewards and punishments is in place is also legitimate. There is a relationship between input and output. The self-made person does not die suddenly or unexpectedly, but lives to reap the fruits of his or her labor. The uncertainties and tragedies of life, from which it may be impossible to recover, are not the stuff of which these stories are made. They are rather stories about the possibility of personal transformation. A person may not realistically hope to become wealthy but can see in the self-made person the possibility of recovering from a lost job or broken marriage. The hard work on the job that leads the indigent immigrant to become the owner of a multimillion-dollar business serves symbolically for the hard work it may take to recover from an addiction or stay on a diet. Good or bad luck is ultimately denied, as is randomness. Behavior follows a rational course, driven by the intervention of responsible individuals. Barthes describes this as the "buttonholing" character of myth.[14] It is the individual person who takes action in the story. The self-made person rises from his or her social context and, in this fashion, becomes decontextualized. The narrative invites its audiences to think of themselves as individuals and to behave as individuals, believing in the efficacy of their own behavior.

The stories of self-made men and women are a continuing part of our cultural heritage, made public in novels and children's books, and increasingly through television and political rhetoric. At a White House ceremony held on April 6, 2001, to honor the recipients of that year's Horatio Alger awards, for instance, President Bush commended Ms. Alvarado as "a young woman who mortgaged the family house for money to start her business, and now runs a major construction company." (He also quipped that as a fellow managing partner of a baseball team he knew how much she suffered.) A ceremony of this kind is one of the ways in which the nation reminds itself of its values. The president's speech referred to self-made men who had occupied the White House: Harry S. Truman ("a small Missouri farmer who never graduated from college and spent his best years working on the farm"), Herbert Hoover ("a poor boy from Iowa, orphaned at age nine, who as a man would save millions in Europe from starvation after two world wars"), and Abraham Lincoln ("a child of the frontier who would become a land surveyor, a store clerk, a lawyer, a legislator and one day helped to free slaves and save the Union"). Lest anyone miss the larger significance of these narratives, he concluded: "In America, we believe in the possibilities of every person. It doesn't matter how you start out in life; what really matters is how you live your life. That has always been our creed. It has always given hope to those who dream of a better life. And that hope has always been the source of our nation's greatness."[15]

It is hard to imagine that large numbers of Americans paid attention to the president's remarks on this occasion. Yet occasions like this are not infrequent, and they often have spillover effects. The Horatio Alger Association, for instance, provides more than a hundred scholarships each year to high school students, ensuring that these hundred are paying attention when the Distinguished American awards are given, and that thousands of other applicants may be as well. Ms. Alvarado is an example of someone whose symbolic significance has multiplied in other ways. In 1995, she founded the Denver Hispanic Chamber of Commerce Fiesta Colorado, an annual black-tie gala that pays tribute to other successful Hispanics. Those honored have included Christine Arguello, the first Hispanic Colorado chief deputy attorney general; Betty Benavidez, the first Hispanic woman elected as a Colorado state representative; and Rich Gonzales, Denver's first Hispanic fire chief. At the 2001 gala, Ms. Alvarado explained, "This event is a way of highlighting the people and their stories that are an inspiration to kids about how to be successful as positive role models."[16] She has also been a featured speaker at motivational seminars sponsored by American Dreams, a Las Vegas–based organization that produces books, seminars, television programs, and online stories about successful Americans. At one of these seminars, Alvarado gave her definition of the American Dream: "I think the American Dream is a genderless and raceless dream. It is a changing vision and a changing dream as well. It is looking forward. It is saying, at least in my own case, that there will be a balance between the spiritual side as well as with the business and intellectual side."[17]

The stories of self-made men and women are autobiographical as well as biographical. They are part of the self-understanding of people who have attained success. Self-understanding is never created in a cultural vacuum. The stories we hear provide templates for telling our own stories. In our heart of hearts, we may know that our stories are more complex than is usually conveyed. Our stories can be told in many ways and with different implications. Yet there are also acceptable norms about how to tell these stories in public. These norms mold the content of success stories into predictable shapes. This is evident in the accounts successful immigrants currently give of their achievements. Despite the differences that continue to reflect their diverse ethnic and national origins, there are also striking similarities.

What we see in the success stories of highly accomplished recent immigrants to the United States is clear evidence of America's changing position in the global economy, especially its prominence in international education and commerce. Yet these stories also bear the residues of nineteenth-century individualism, especially in their emphasis on hard work, personal sacrifice, and unrivaled moral virtue. As cultural tropes, these success stories convey messages about the possibilities open to all who try hard, and they present role models that young people are sometimes explicitly encouraged to emulate. More than that, they define the meanings of success in our society and demonstrate that success is generally deserved because it results from personal effort. These are powerful stories. They collectively reinforce the idea that America is still a land of opportunity, that it is a place where newcomers from diverse backgrounds are not only welcomed but given the freedom to fulfill their highest dreams. They further reinforce the assumption that success essentially means gaining distinction through one's career, and doing so by devoting oneself 110 percent to that goal, all the while denying that lucky breaks or social factors had much to do with one's success. Powerful as they are, these stories nevertheless ring hollow at the end of the day because they illuminate only a fraction of what it means to achieve distinction. They leave out most of the factors that researchers find predictive of educational and occupational success. In so doing, they also leave us as a society with a skewed understanding of the differences between those who are privileged and those who are not.

## MAKING IT TO THE TOP

The men and women in my New Elites Project provide an exceptionally candid look at what it takes for immigrants and children of immigrants to become self-made Americans today—and the narratives through which these achievements are publicly portrayed. Everyone in this study had attained distinction within his or her field. The interviewees included presidents and CEOs of companies, self-employed businesspeople, attorneys, doctors, college presidents, heads of other nonprofit organizations, actors, musicians, professional athletes, journalists, scientists, and government officials. Two-thirds (67 percent) were men, and one-third (33 percent) women. Two-thirds (66 percent) had been born abroad; the other 34 percent were children of immigrants. Of the first-generation immigrants, half had arrived in the United States after 1977; only 16 percent had come before 1965. The first-generation immigrants had been born in thirty-eight different countries, and the second-generation immigrants' parents had lived in twenty different countries. The most common countries of origin were Mexico, China, India, Pakistan, and Taiwan.

Higher education was the principal avenue of career success for these first- and second-generation immigrants. Ninety-one percent had graduated from college. Almost two-thirds (65 percent) had earned a graduate degree of some kind. Twenty percent had an M.A. or M.S. degree, 13 percent had an M.D., 10 percent had a Ph.D., 9 percent had a J.D., and 8 percent had an M.B.A. *First-generation* immigrants were slightly more likely than second-generation immigrants to have earned a graduate degree (67 percent compared with 60 percent). The major ethnoreligious groups in the study varied in this respect, too, but a *majority* of all the groups had earned graduate degrees: 77 percent among Hindus, 72 percent among Muslims, 60 percent among Buddhists, 55 percent among Asian American Christians, and 53 percent among Latino Christians. A great many of these immigrants and children of immigrants had received at least some of their education in the United States. Whereas only 34 percent had been born in the United States, for instance, 71 percent had received either an undergraduate or a graduate degree in the United States. In most cases, levels of education among these immigrants and children of immigrants were also higher than among their parents. For instance, only 23 percent of the men said their fathers had postgraduate degrees, and only 14 percent of the women said this about their mothers.

If higher education was the path to success, *hard work* was the means of progressing along that path. Most said they had been hard workers in school, and most still worked long hours at their jobs. When asked about their current schedules, 91 percent said they sometimes work late at their jobs. Seventy percent said they typically work late at least one day a week; 42 percent said they work late more than one day a week. More than half (58 percent) said they "fairly often" work on Saturdays, and almost half (46 percent) said they "fairly often" work on Sundays. The median number of hours worked per week was 60. A quarter reported working more than 75 hours a week. Ms. Alvarado, for instance, usually arrives at work by 6:30 in the morning and stays until 7:00 in the evening. She works every Saturday. Others report similar schedules. A man from Bangladesh who runs an engineering company starts work at 7:30, leaves the office at 6:30, meets with a customer or investor over dinner almost every evening, works at the office until midafternoon on Saturdays, and is connected by cell phone to the company twenty-four hours a day seven days a week. A research scientist from Laos says she works from 8:30 to 6:30 every day, takes home several hours of reading each evening, and works about two Saturdays a month. A surgeon from Syria usually begins his workday at 7 a.m., finishes at 7 or 8 p.m., sometimes works until 10 or 11 p.m., and almost always works on Saturdays and Sundays. These are clearly longer work weeks than those of the average American, and they even exceed estimates for people who work in the professions or as executives.[18]

When asked how they learned to work hard, these immigrants and children of immigrants typically credit their upbringing. "A strong work ethic in our family" was the way one put it. "Both my parents were very, very hard workers," said another. One woman remarked, "It has a lot to do with my upbringing; failure was not an option." Sometimes one parent or the other was singled out: "I have the example of my father," "I'd have to go back to my dad," or "My mother had an incredible work ethic." Occasionally a grandparent or older sibling who played a parental role was mentioned. In a few cases, learning to work hard grew from another parental figure, such as a high school teacher or a family physician. But usually the story revolved around a self-sacrificing parent who put in long hours just to pay the bills. A man who grew up in Pakistan remembered his father's working exceptionally long hours. "He used to work twenty hours a day, twenty-two hours sometimes. He'd sleep two hours and then go back to work again. He was forced to work that hard. He had four younger brothers he was responsible for. Their father had died and left nobody to take care of them." The family was still poor when this man was growing up. His father hoped he would quit school after the eighth grade and get a job. Instead the man hunkered down and got a scholarship so he could stay in school.

The typical parent not only worked long hours at his or her own job but also made it a point to instruct the children about hard work. Some parents' admonitions still ring in their children's ears. A woman in her late fifties, for instance, remembers her father's saying, "Do something constructive. You cannot just sit and watch television." She says these words still motivate her. "My father is behind my mind all the time." The children of such parents apparently learned by doing as much as by observing. Eighty-six percent remember doing household chores while growing up, and 52 percent held jobs outside their homes while they were in school. Almost half (44 percent) felt they worked harder than their classmates in school. "From day one, I had to put in double hours compared to everybody else," recalled one man who became a doctor. For many, working hard was a necessity. Another man, for instance, remembers that everything depended on the national exam that students took in high school. "You have one shot at it, you cannot repeat it, that's it." A woman raised in India recalls that her family was so poor that her mother supplemented her father's meager salary by taking in sewing. As a child, the woman helped her mother with the sewing. "I think these things helped me to understand that life is very precious and that you just don't waste time," she observes.

But whether it was a necessity or was learned from parents, these men and women came to understand their work ethic as something intrinsic to themselves. It was not a set of values they were exposed to by virtue of living in a particular culture or ethnic group, but a pattern of behavior that they had deliberately chosen. It was something they *internalized*. One man said working hard was just part of him, rather than something he had learned. Another man explained his orientation toward work as his desire to "make sure you accomplish something at the end of the day." Yet another man attributed his working hard to the fact that "I've come to trust myself more than anybody else," and another noted that his motivation came from inside. "You can achieve as long as you depend only on yourself for motivation," he explained. "Don't go looking for it elsewhere." A woman said she learned to work hard just because it gave her pleasure. Another woman explained, "I learned to work hard because I loved what I did." Yet another said, "I thrive on success," and another remarked, "I wanted to be the best." Working hard was thus a feature of their personal identity. It was a drive that appeared to come entirely from within, and that defined who they were.

There was also a strong connection in their minds between working hard and being successful. Some, such as the woman who said she loves what she does, viewed hard work as a source of personal pleasure; indeed, most talked animatedly about the aspects of their work that they enjoyed. But it was even more evident that they regarded hard work in instrumental terms. It was not an end in itself but a means to an end, and that end was success. "I want to be a success. I want to show my family that I'm a successful father. I don't want to be a loser. I'm a competer. I just want to be successful," explained a man from Cambodia. A man from Vietnam said much the same thing, attributing his hard work to his "inclination to excel." It was thus not surprising that most of these people regarded their occupational success as the result of hard work. They were in this important sense self-made. They had set their sights on being successful and were, quite literally, the product of their own labor.

From other remarks, it was clear that these men and women thought of themselves as highly autonomous individuals. Not that they were alone. Most cherished their families of origin, and many had children of their own, as well as coworkers, clients, students, and customers. Autonomy meant that they were different from other people and had often deliberately gone their own way. For instance, 86 percent felt they had had to "go it alone" or "do things differently" while they were growing up. They were out of step with the crowd because they worked harder, carried different burdens (including the burden of being exceptionally talented and energetic), and had different goals in life. Autonomy also meant increased control over their lives. They worked long hours because they wanted to. Their schedules were their own. They also insisted that they were guided by their own internal compasses—morally, spiritually, and emotionally. When the going is difficult, they look inside themselves, and when they need strength, they find it within. "I have my goal, my vision, I want to do something with my life, and I never give up," said a man from China. "Everything comes from myself," said another. Others spoke of "a belief in me," "a trust in myself," "confidence in my abilities," "believing in myself," "my makeup," "a positive attitude," and "pride in myself." Being guided from within did not mean making up their own rules; it meant doing what they were sure was right, even when others behaved differently. "I have a really good sense that I'm doing things right," said a man raised in Mexico. He meant *morally* right. He pays his taxes, surrounds himself with honest people, and behaves honestly himself. Being successful was thus not the result of cutting corners but the reward for being a moral person. "Good actions will receive good reactions," said one. "Hard work and honesty always pay off," said another.

Autonomous individuals suffer setbacks. Although these men and women are highly successful, they have endured adversity—not just as children, but along the way—and their success has been sweeter because of this adversity. It proved their mettle. They may have drawn strength from the example of their parents or from their faith in God. Yet there was no sense of their having felt powerless or dependent during these times. It was rather that *they* chose to persevere. *They* were self-determined enough to pick themselves up and move on. *They* made decisions, drew on their inner reserves, and did things—listened to music, prayed or meditated, exercised, thought positive thoughts, read something— that helped them. Even those whose faith helped them through rough times had a highly personalized view of faith. It was *their* faith that gave them courage. "There's a God up there who has a plan for *me*," said one man. "*My* God is with me all the time," remarked another.

These are common themes in American self-help literature. Despite growing up in more than three dozen different countries, these immigrants articulate the familiar idioms of American self-determination. Success is not something to be ashamed of but a goal to be pursued actively and aggressively. The best way to attain success is to work hard and be a good, moral person. It may be necessary to go against the grain. Always do what you know is right. Rely on no one but yourself. Be assured that good behavior will result in winning. These idioms are sometimes described as distinctly American. But if that is so, it hasn't taken long for America's new immigrants to learn them, either since their arrival or before it. "You remember the movie *Grapes of Wrath?*" asked a man who had grown up in Taiwan. "I saw the movie when I was in my early teens. Henry Fonda told his mother, 'If there's hunger, I'll be there. If there's injustice, I'll be there.' Once you believe it, you'll make it happen. All my life I remembered that. I never give up."

The idea that hard work and self-determination lead to success is not only a stock tenet of American fiction. It is a fundamental conviction of the American public. In one national survey, 74 percent of the public responded that "being wealthy" is mostly "a matter of hard work," while only 21 percent thought it was "a matter of luck."[19] A second survey tried framing the issue differently to see whether responses would be different: when asked whether "Hard work offers little guarantee of success," 68 percent disagreed, while only 30 percent agreed.[20] In yet another survey, respondents were offered a somewhat more complex set of options, but 64 percent felt that "people get ahead by their own hard work," while only 10 percent saw "lucky breaks or help from other people" as the reasons people get ahead, and 24 percent attributed personal success to a combination of the two.[21] It is not only that we think this is how the world is. It is how we think reality *should be.* Thus when asked what should matter in "deciding how much people ought to earn," 85 percent of the public in the survey just mentioned said "how hard he or she works" should be an "essential" or "very important" consideration (only 2 percent said it should not be very important).

Of course it may be easier for people at the top than for those at the bottom to believe that success is the result of hard work. But surveys show few differences of this kind. For instance, among the top quarter on a standard measure of social status, 66 percent in the survey under consideration attributed getting ahead to hard work, while among those in the bottom quarter, 65 percent did. Only slightly more of the latter than of the former (12 percent versus 9 percent) thought getting ahead was chiefly the result of luck or social connections.[22] In short, we are a society that believes fairly uniformly in the efficacy of hard work. We are not disposed to think that people with more are on top because of lucky breaks. The world, we are persuaded, is more rational than that. What we put in determines what we take out. This is an implicit mental calculation that affirms our faith in our own efforts. It is a faith that also applies to our society. There is a kind of justice about how our system works. Believing that hard work is the source of success means also believing that people of various ranks *deserve* what they get. For instance, among those in the survey just mentioned who attributed getting ahead to hard work, only 13 percent thought people "at the top in America today" were corrupt, whereas 30 percent of those who attributed getting ahead to luck believed in pervasive corruption in high places. Similarly, only 18 percent of those who associated getting ahead with hard work thought "coming from a wealthy family" was essential or very important to achievement, compared with 36 percent of those who associated getting ahead with luck. Indeed, this was the pattern on a whole range of issues. People who believed in the efficacy of hard work were more likely to think that America rewards people for their intelligence and skills, that they and their family have a good chance of improving their standard of living, and that inequality does *not* exist mainly because it benefits the wealthy and powerful.[23] We simply feel better about ourselves and our society if we believe our successes in life are not the result of some random or unjust forces—which means that stories about self-made men and women fit well with how we believe, and how we want to believe, the world works.

## THE MISSING PIECES

The fear that some observers expressed about America a century ago—that it would become a closed oligarchy of the rich and powerful, incapable of incorporating newcomers—appears to be belied by the successes of newcomers from many different ethnic and national backgrounds. Their success suggests not only that it has been possible for newcomers to be incorporated but that others will also be able to follow in their footsteps. The power elite that was once upwards of 90 percent concentrated among white, Anglo-Saxon, Protestant males has clearly become more diverse. While the oligarchy has shown itself to be inclusive, it has nevertheless distanced itself further from the ranks of ordinary Americans, including the foreign born. More of the nation's wealth is now concentrated among the 1 percent at the top than was true even a few decades ago.

The narratives of success mask this growing inequality. The successful person is depicted in these narratives as having been no different at the start from any number of people in the same age group. The one who becomes successful does so through his or her own efforts, perhaps with the help of parents, but certainly without the assistance of anyone else. The narratives teach us to admire successful people and to believe that the wealth and power they achieve are deserved. These stories are meant to inspire, not to provide an accurate analysis of why some people succeed and others do not. Comparisons of that sort are not included. The sibling who fails to achieve the same success is usually left out of the story entirely. Few people, for instance, have ever heard about Emma Mae Martin, a struggling welfare mother who happens to be the sister of Supreme Court justice Clarence Thomas. Few would know that Emma Mae Martin was on welfare because her husband abandoned her, leaving her to support four children by herself on two minimum-wage jobs.[24] When unsuccessful siblings *are* noticed, the lesson is that it was indeed the hard work and determination of one that led to greater success than the other attained, since both presumably had the same genetic heritage and family environment. Stories of self-made men and woman bracket these specific comparisons from view and, in so doing, lead away from questions about the larger sources of social inequality.

The reality is that hard work and success generally do go together— but not for everyone, and usually not to the degree suggested in the stories of wildly successful self-made men and women. For instance, data compiled by the Bureau of Labor Statistics in 1997 showed that men employed as executives or managers earned an average of $1,039 a week if they worked 45 hours a week or more, compared to only $747 if they worked between 35 and 44 hours a week, or an earnings advantage of 1.39 per week or 1.06 per hour. Among men employed in the professions, those who worked more averaged $982 per week while those who worked less averaged $824, which was again an earnings advantage on a weekly basis (of 1.19), but not on an hourly basis (0.95). The results for women were almost exactly the same, although average earnings in all categories were lower than for men. Among all occupations, the largest gains from longer hours were in sales, which yielded higher earnings on both a weekly and an hourly basis. In some occupations, though, there was no net gain; for instance, teachers who worked longer hours earned the same on a weekly basis as teachers who worked shorter hours, which meant that the latter actually earned *more* on an hourly basis than the former. Moreover, the differences in earnings attributable to longer or shorter hours within occupational categories were seldom as significant as those *between* occupational categories (such as between professionals or managers and service or farm workers).[25] It should go without saying, too, that no differential in hours worked could account for someone's earning 50 to 100 times the amount of the average worker.

An even more significant bias in success narratives stems from the fact that protagonists in these stories are *decontextualized*. What I mean by this is that the self-made person achieves success in these stories *alone*. It is the individual person's efforts that matter. He or she works hard, makes the right decisions at the right moment, has fortitude, and demonstrates good character. Even when the self-made person benefits from having good parents, those benefits are individual moral values that become part of the person's internal makeup. The values learned are about work and determination. They apply equally in any situation. They do not involve the ambience of a particular place, cultural tradition, or set of lived family and ethnic practices. The success narrative is thus linear. It tells of overcoming adversity, of one good decision's leading to another, and of the present's being better than the past.

The decontextualized protagonist of the past was typically a character who marched to his own beat while the crowd blindly followed the time-worn patterns of tradition. The protagonist succeeded through inner resolve, not by seeking advice from others or by working cooperatively with them. The "little engine that could" was the stereotypic protagonist of the past. The full story demonstrated success stemming from positive thinking. The self-made protagonist of today is even more likely to be decontextualized. In popular self-help books, authors cultivate an individual relationship between themselves as authorities and readers as apprentices. Few self-help books encourage people to draw support from their families or community organizations. The self-made person is supposed to lose weight or overcome some other personal problem by *individually* following a set of instructions supplied by the author. The aspiring self-made person is thus a consumer, an isolated individual who watches the latest television guru alone and goes alone to the bookstore or health food shop.

Whereas the self-made protagonist of the past might be the subject of a novel or newspaper account, the protagonist of today is further decontextualized by virtue of changes in the media. The contemporary self-made person is, as some critics have pointed out, more likely than past counterparts to be a media personality, such as a movie star or popular television figure. Being self-made is thus a matter of cultivating one's image, or of inventing and reinventing oneself, and not necessarily being a person of long-standing moral virtue. Even more than that, though, the media now encourage us to think about success and its determinants in short sound bytes and in brief visualizations, rather than in full narrative accounts. Perhaps the best example of this new approach is a recent national billboard campaign called "Pass It On." The campaign encourages people to strive for something better by showing a picture of a well-known entity, captioned with a single word or a short phrase. Examples include Kermit the Frog ("Live your dreams"), Shaquille O'Neal ("Perseverance"), Whoopi Goldberg ("Hard Work"), and Christopher Reeve ("Strength"). The campaign's purpose, according to one spokesperson, is to "inspire good people to do more good things."[26] The implicit message is that being successful results from applying the specified virtue.

The problem with decontextualized stories is that they pay little attention to the social factors that contribute to the successes achieved. The published accounts of Ms. Alvarado's rise in the construction industry, for example, do not pause to ask who may have suggested that she start building bus shelters in the first place, or whether there was a mentor in college who played a supporting role or an acquaintance later who offered advice about how to bid on government contracts. It is not that these social factors are absent in reality, only that the cultural framework in which success stories are told discourages their being emphasized. The more common pattern of storytelling focuses on the protagonists' efforts to gain *distance* from social influences. The protagonist in McGuffey Readers and Horatio Alger tales refuses to cheat and steal like his co-workers, reads his Bible when other boys at the orphanage poke fun, and studies hard while others play. The contemporary self-made men and women behave similarly. They become restive in their work, realize that they could manage better on their own, quit their jobs, and start their own companies. They are also *moral outsiders*. Others at work cut corners; they do not. Their personal honesty and integrity shine in contrast with others' lax standards. It is a corrupt boss who makes them realize the need to leave the company. They struggle against the moral failings that get others in trouble, but eventually succeed.

Research on immigrant success consistently demonstrates that, however much hard work and determination matter, *social factors* are also important. Immigrants do better if their families already have good educations and decent incomes, their businesses depend on social networks, and they typically receive help from family and friends in getting settled and finding initial employment.[27] For instance, when asked whether there was anyone in the United States who helped them or their parents get settled, 80 percent said there was, only 9 percent denied there being any assistance of this kind, and 11 percent were unsure. Not surprisingly, the largest category of people mentioned as sources of assistance was kin. In all, 25 percent mentioned immediate and extended family members as their most significant source of assistance in getting settled in America. As with previous waves of immigration, these family members were typically brothers or sisters, cousins, aunts or uncles, or in-laws who had already come to the United States. The next most frequently mentioned source of assistance comprised people the immigrant had met through school or work. Fifteen percent said these contacts had been most significant in their getting settled, and among this number, school ties outnumbered workplace ties by a margin of two to one. Respondents were equally likely to mention fellow students as they were to name professors or administrators. The other sources of assistance identified with any frequency were churches and ethnic associations. These were mentioned by about 10 percent of those interviewed.

## DECONTEXTUALIZED MORALITY

I am more interested, though, in how the neglect of social factors affects prevailing understandings of *moral responsibility*. People who have ostensibly achieved success "on their own" are morally accountable to no one but themselves. They have no obligation to pay anyone back for

helping them. Whatever they achieved, they earned. The moral investment was paid in the process; for instance, hard work and distancing
oneself from one's peers demonstrate one's worth. An affluent lifestyle
is simply the reward for being a good person. Once a person has risen
to the top, the main priority can be paying back *oneself* by buying luxury goods, taking vacations, and the like. If such a person decides to do
volunteer work or become a philanthropist, as many do, those activities
further demonstrate the goodwill of the individual, rather than an understanding of social obligation. Philanthropy is *voluntary*, a choice
freely made by an autonomous individual who happens to be moved to
help others.

An example that illustrates the decontextualization of morality comes
from the story of another winner of the Horatio Alger Award, Philip
Anschutz. Mr. Anschutz received the award in 2000, a year before Linda
Alvarado. According to Horatio Alger Association publicity, his was a
typical rags-to-riches story. He "entered the work world at an early age,
working in a variety of jobs as a yard boy, grocery sacker, messenger,
and bank teller." Early in life Mr. Anschutz hoped to attend law school
but "was instead needed to run the family business, which was experiencing difficulties." Like earlier Alger protagonists, Mr. Anschutz soon
proved to be a successful businessman. He started his own company,
built up its assets, and eventually expanded his holdings. When he received the Alger Award, he was the largest individual shareholder of the
Union Pacific Railroad and of Qwest Communications, the third largest
long-distance provider in the nation. "It is only by sticking to an objective through adversity that a goal can ever be realized," Mr. Anschutz is
reported to have said at the award ceremony.[28] True to this conviction, his
is the foundation that has spent millions on the "Pass It On" campaign
encouraging Americans to pursue their dreams through perseverance
and hard work.

The rise from adversity was only part of the story. Mr. Anschutz did
start working early (other accounts tell of his selling Kool-aid as a fourth
grader), and the family business was experiencing difficulties (his father
fell ill). But, like other self-made men, Mr. Anschutz received a college
education and did so at a time when a majority of people his age did not.
There *was* a family business capable of providing considerable backing
and opportunities not open to most Americans. At the time Mr. Anschutz took control of it, the Anschutz Land and Livestock Company of

Denver owned extensive holdings in Colorado, Wyoming, and Utah.[29] The business included oil drilling, which was always fraught with uncertainty, but Mr. Anschutz struck it rich within a few years on a ranch in Wyoming and bought up surrounding leases. Within little more than a decade, his holdings were worth $500 million. He then invested in railroads, taking control of Southern Pacific a few years before it was sold to Union Pacific, which brought Mr. Anschutz additional wealth. Controlling this much railroad right-of-way also gave him a foothold in the fiber-optics business that was being developed at the time. By 1999, his net worth in Union Pacific and Qwest totaled approximately $10 billion.[30] That year *Fortune* portrayed him as "the richest American you've never heard of."[31]

Three years later, *Fortune* described Mr. Anschutz quite differently. In an article about corporate greed, *Fortune* observed that "top execs were cashing in stock even as their companies were tanking," and concluded that the average stockholder had been left holding the bag in the wake of such "rapacious" and "infectious greed."[32] In that context, the article named Mr. Anschutz as the greediest executive in America. The magazine determined this dubious distinction by selecting the twenty-five large corporations whose stocks had dropped 75 percent or more from their boom-time peak, and then identifying the ones where officers and directors took out the most money via stock sales from January 1999 through May 2002. Mr. Anschutz headed the list, having profitably sold $1.57 billion in stock during the period under examination. Subsequent inquiries proved no wrongdoing on Mr. Anschutz's part, although a lawsuit was brought against several top Qwest executives accusing them of fraudulent accounting, and congressional investigators opened an examination into whether Mr. Anschutz had advance knowledge of the company's looming financial problems when he sold his holdings.[33] Other inquiries showed that Mr. Anschutz had made money from Union Pacific at a time when its shareholders and customers were experiencing a financial nightmare from the company's operations. At the time, the Anschutz Corporation was also under attack by environmentalists and American Indians concerned about drilling in Indian burial grounds.[34]

Being named the "greediest man in America" may simply be the price of being one of the richest. There was no hint in *Fortune*'s story that Mr. Anschutz had acted illegally or, for that matter, in any way differently from other business leaders with massive assets. In fact, it would be easy to interpret Mr. Anschutz's decision to sell at an opportune moment as nothing other than shrewd business, which is how company spokespersons responded to the story.[35] There is, however, a larger implication of the story that shifts the focus from possible wrongdoing on the part of one individual to the broader question I raised earlier about the *cultural* decontextualization of morality. This question surfaces when we consider how a self-made man from a small town who goes to church, contributes to charitable causes, and is described by friends as a person with deep family values could come to be depicted (even if wrongly) as the greediest man in America.

The key lies in recognizing that self-made people do not earn their fortunes entirely by themselves; they necessarily exist within particular social contexts. Mr. Anschutz spent much of his childhood in a small farming town in Kansas.[36] Had Mr. Anschutz stayed there, earning his living, say, as a merchant or banker, arguably he might still have been the greediest man in town (what village doesn't have one?), but there would have been more community pressure against amassing great wealth at the expense of one's friends and neighbors. The greediest man in town would have had to face friends and neighbors at the post office and in church or when they came to do business in person. Instead, Mr. Anschutz lives on a five-acre estate in suburban Denver with a guardhouse that straddles the driveway; he has insisted on such extreme privacy that journalists writing about his achievements have seldom been able to secure photographs or interviews.[37] Associates have been quoted as saying that his personal seclusion stems from shyness and concerns about security. They defend his behavior by arguing that at least prior to his becoming a major investor in the Los Angeles sports and entertainment industry, his business had nothing to do with the public. Yet it is hard to deny credibly that anybody so powerful in transportation, communication, utilities, and agriculture has nothing to do with the public. Such a marked split between private and public means that an individual known for hard work and personal morality can engage in public behavior that is questionable.

Stories of self-made men and women whose wealth and power reflect only high moral standards perpetuate the idea that morality can be separated from public life. According to this view, individuals behave morally or immorally, but social entities such as corporations do not. As long as a CEO upholds "family values," the corporation can conduct business however it chooses short of breaking the law. The corporation may or may not behave unethically. But it is the nameless and faceless entity from which the ordinary citizen feels alienated. Namelessness and facelessness imply a lack of moral consideration. The antidote is to associate names and faces with those collective entities. Morality is never sufficiently understood if it means "to thine own self be true," and nothing more. In the fullest sense, morality always implies responsibility to some social entity, whether that be one's family, one's shareholders, or one's nation. This is the sense in which morality is contextual—not that morality is thus relativized, as critics of "situational" morality have charged, but that it becomes concretized in relation to the real social contexts in which a person is embedded. Morality is always collective because of these obligations. It is a response to the indebtedness a person perceives as a result of the benefits and opportunities supplied by those social contexts. To understand oneself as purely self-made and without any such obligations is as cynical as believing oneself merely the beneficiary of luck.

The further difficulty with such understandings of personal morality is that even well-intentioned efforts to be a good citizen cease with individual acts of charity. The son of a wildcat oil driller may have a keen understanding of what it means to enjoy good luck. With religious overtones, the same understanding of good luck can be interpreted as divine intervention. But how does one repay such unconditional and unmerited good fortune? By helping others lead the same morally upright, hard-working life that presumably led to one's own good fortune. The self-made American is unlikely to perceive any *systemic* ways in which the society might be improved, other than calling for individuals to be better persons. The irony then is not that the poor are overlooked; it is rather that their condition is misunderstood. Instead of supporting measures aimed at reducing inequality, self-made persons place their bets on helping the few whose lives may with time emulate their own. The very individualism that worried Tocqueville continues to threaten democracy by focusing power in the hands of those few.

CHAPTER 5

# IN AMERICA,

# ALL RELIGIONS ARE TRUE

Throughout our nation's history, the relationship between America's places of worship and its democratic form of government has been peculiar. On the one hand, we have insisted on strict separation of church and state, meaning that religious organizations cannot participate directly in government and that government must refrain from actively promoting religion or doing anything to favor one religion over another. On the other hand, religion has long been regarded as one of the mainstays of American democracy. Tocqueville's observation is no less true today than it was in the early nineteenth century: Americans gather at their houses of worship, discuss matters of common interest, form associations, and engage in service projects through these associations that otherwise would be accomplished only through government agencies.[1] American religion has inspired many of our best efforts to be a better nation. It played an important role in legitimating the American War of Independence, fueling the abolitionist movement in the 1830s and 1840s, and more recently mobilizing the drive for civil rights in the 1960s. But American religion has also been a significant factor in some of our darkest hours. If it inspired abolitionism, it also served up arguments for slavery, and it has often been a source of bigotry and conflict.

Until the 1950s, the relationship between American religion and democracy was a story that could be told largely in terms of Protestantism. Protestant denominations accounted for a majority of the churchgoing public, and to a large degree their members held the most influential positions in government, business, and higher education. That dominance was of course as much rooted in myth as it was in reality. Catholics were in fact the single largest religious body in the United States. During the century following the Civil War they had constituted the largest share of immigrants and had gained considerable power of their own. So also with the Jewish population whose numbers had swelled during the 1920s and 1930s as a result of pogroms and the rise of fascism in Europe. The new reality was expressed appropriately in Will Herberg's book, *Protestant-Catholic-Jew,* in which he argued that each of the three main branches of the Judeo-Christian tradition was now a respected way in which its adherents could consider themselves "American."[2] In that era, religious participation reached a historic high and the threat of "godless communism" brought American religion and American democracy into a closer alliance than ever before. The 1950s were in retrospect a time of unparalleled growth in American religion. New houses of worship were constructed and older ones were renovated on an unprecedented scale. The religious optimism of the period was reflected in the political climate as well. Leaders of the major Protestant denominations could with some justification believe that what they had to say would be heard by influential members of their congregations and would be reported in influential newspapers. The more conservative of their members felt enfranchised by the conservative Republican Dwight Eisenhower, even if his theological views did not always square with theirs. In rural America, where religious conservatism was firmly grounded, there was a sense of still mattering. Despite the fact that population and political clout had already migrated to the cities, agriculture flourished better than it had at any time since World War I. Protestants and Catholics could each in their own way feel confident they were doing the right thing in rooting out red sympathizers at universities and in the motion picture industry. Quietly, there were also deep divisions between them, giving each faith community reason to be vigilant against the other. Protestants and Catholics warned their respective offspring against dating each other. They spent money supporting and upholding the integrity of their respective colleges. Protestants formed clergy alliances in local communities and held Reformation Day services that warned against the incursions of papism. In some predominantly Protestant communities, temperance campaigns were still as popular as fund-raisers to combat polio. White Protestants and Catholics had little to do with African Americans. There was also an undercurrent of anti-Semitism that continued to find expression in quotas at elite colleges and universities and in periodic desecration of synagogues.[3]

A half century later, the religious landscape looks quite different. The traditional Protestant denominations that once thought of themselves as "mainstream" have lost members, both in absolute terms and relative to the rest of the population. These denominations have also undergone what some historians have termed a process of "disestablishment." They have ceased taking for granted that theirs would be the most influential voices in their communities. Disestablishment has meant, among other things, that Protestant denominations no longer control the nation's elite colleges and universities. Public funding and a more diverse faculty and student population have dramatically changed the face of higher education. The mainstream Protestant denominations still maintain offices in Washington to lobby for various causes, but these offices are understaffed. It is more common for staff to describe themselves as voices in the wilderness than as influential insiders. Catholics have remained a strong presence and have gained especially in such modes of common respectability as achieving higher education and entering the more prestigious professions. Yet Catholic churches and schools are quite different in many communities from what they were a half century ago. Clergy shortages, scandals among the priesthood, and restive members have unsettled Catholic traditions in the same ways that disestablishment has affected mainline Protestants. The Jewish minority has remained small. Anti-Semitic bigotry—sometimes quite virulent in earlier periods—has apparently diminished, but as the boundaries separating Christians and Jews have weakened, so have the traditions that encouraged religiously homogeneous marriages and lifelong loyalty to religious organizations. African American churches have continued to be important centers of social and political activity in their communities, but the communities themselves are more divided economically than they were in the past. Evangelical Protestants have become more numerous and, though also internally divided, have repeatedly drawn attention to themselves through political endeavors. But the most far-reaching changes in American religion have come about as a result of immigration. No longer simply an aggregation of Protestants, Catholics, and Jews, we are now a society better described, writes the comparative religion scholar Diana Eck, by "our jazz and *qawwali* music, our Haitian drums and Bengali tablas, our hip-hop and *bhangra* dances, our mariachis and gamelans, our Islamic minarets and Hindu temple towers, our Mormon temple spires and golden gurdwara domes."[4]

The impact of immigration on American religion is evident in the fact that a significantly larger number of Americans now participate in religions other than Christianity or Judaism than was true even a few years ago. According to a national study conducted in 2000, there were more than 1,200 mosques in the United States with total adherents of approximately 2 million Americans. Thirty percent of these mosques had been established in the 1990s and another 32 percent dated only to the 1980s. Eighty-seven percent had been founded since 1970. Seventy-seven percent of the mosques studied reported an increase in participation during the five years prior to the study; only 5 percent reported declining participation.[5] In another national study, data collected in the mid-1990s showed that there were at least 200 Hindu temples or meditation centers, 100 Sikh temples, and 60 Jain temples. These temples and meditation centers were most heavily concentrated in several metropolitan areas, especially southern California, but were also located in every state.[6] By 2003, a more comprehensive study conducted by the Harvard Pluralism Project had located 680 Hindu temples and centers, 219 Sikh temples, and 89 Jain temples. Approximately 1.5 million Americans were thought to be participants at these various temples and centers.[7] The number of Buddhists in the United States has been estimated at between 2.5 and 4 million.[8] A study conducted in 1998 among more than a thousand Buddhist meditation centers found that 70 percent had been established since 1985.[9] The majority of participants at these mosques, temples, and meditation centers are immigrants or children of immigrants, but a substantial minority are converts. For instance, the mosque study estimated that 29 percent of regular participants were converts. At least that percentage of American Buddhists are thought to be converts.

As a proportion of the religiously active population, Muslims and Hindus or Buddhists and Jains are still arguably little more than a token presence. Their numbers are small compared to the large proportion of the public—some 80 percent—who identify themselves as Christians. The cultural impact of this new religious diversity is far greater than the numbers of adherents would suggest, however. In part, this is because a much larger proportion of the population has had opportunities to make personal contacts with the members of non-Western religions through their work or in their neighborhoods, or to hear about these religions through the mass media. In the Religion and Diversity Survey I conducted in 2003, nearly half (48 percent) of the American public said they had had at least a little personal contact with Muslims. Thirty-five percent said they had had at least a little personal contact with Hindus, and 34 percent said this about Buddhists. Merely having contact with people from religious traditions other than one's own, of course, does not mean that one becomes familiar with those traditions, especially if religion is never actually discussed. A substantial minority of Americans do feel, however, that they have gained some familiarity with non-Western religious traditions, either through personal contacts or through reading and travel. In the Religion and Diversity Survey, 33 percent claimed they were at least somewhat familiar with the basic teachings of Islam, 29 percent with the basic teachings of Buddhism, and 22 percent with the basic teachings of Hinduism.

Another reason for the larger-than-anticipated impact of the new religious diversity is that it occurred at the same time that Americans were becoming more interested in tolerance and inclusiveness. Gallup polls showed that as many as half of the nation's people had been unwilling in the 1940s to vote for a well-qualified person for president if that person was Catholic or Jewish. By the late 1950s, that proportion was still close to a third. However, it dropped significantly during the 1960s, and in polls conducted since then, hardly anyone holds that view.[10] In the Religion and Diversity Survey, Americans were clearly divided in their opinions toward newcomers whose religious orientations differed from theirs, but positive opinions generally outweighed negative ones. For instance, 59 percent of those surveyed said they would welcome Buddhists' becoming a stronger presence in the United States in the next few years, while only 32 percent said they would not welcome this development. Almost the same proportion (58 percent) said they would welcome Hindus' becoming a stronger presence (33 percent said they would not). And 51 percent said they would welcome Muslims' becoming a stronger presence (42 percent said they would not). An even larger proportion recognized the value of cooperation and greater understanding among the leaders and followers of the various religions. For instance, 78 percent of those surveyed said that increased cooperation among the leaders of the various religions in the United States was somewhat or very desirable, and 74 percent thought it was desirable to have greater understanding among the followers of different religions.

Besides the growing impact of non-Western religions, American religion has also become significantly more diverse as a result of new immigrant congregations among Catholics and Protestants. A national study of immigrants conducted in 1996 showed that 42 percent identified themselves as Catholics and 19 percent as Protestants.[11] A study of Latinos living in the United States in 2000 showed that 70 percent were Catholic and 23 percent Protestant.[12] As the Latino population has grown, Latinos represent a larger proportion of the overall membership of the various faith communities. Among Catholics, for example, between 30 and 38 percent nationally are estimated to be Latinos. Although fewer than 4 percent of Catholic priests are Latino, 40 percent of Catholic dioceses include Latino ministries.[13] Latino Protestants, of whom there are an estimated 7 million nationally, also contribute increasing diversity to many Protestant denominations. Two-thirds of this number are affiliated with Pentecostal or charismatic denominations, and another 15 percent are affiliated with mainline denominations.[14] Even in denominations with relatively few Latinos, new ministries have been initiated in significant numbers. For instance, among United Methodists 75 new Latino congregations had been founded between 1995 and 2000, and 900 outreach ministries involving Hispanic members had been initiated.[15] In the Evangelical Lutheran Church of America, 168 ministries had been established with Spanish-language worship services by 2000. Asian American congregations are also increasingly prevalent, especially among Presbyterians, Baptists, and Catholics. According to one study, there are at least 3,000 Korean, 700 Chinese, and 200 Japanese Christian congregations nationally.[16]

These profound changes in American religion are developments we must consider carefully if we are to understand how America has tried to become a better nation and yet has fallen short. Inclusiveness toward new religious groups has been one of the significant ways in which we collectively tried to reinvent ourselves during the last third of the twentieth century. For the most part we saw diversity as a good thing, and that included religious diversity. We tried to become a better nation than we had been in the past by being more tolerant of religious diversity. When historians reminded us of the bigotry that Protestants had once expressed toward Catholics or that Christians had once felt toward Jews, we increasingly found ourselves embarrassed by that history. We knew at some level that civil rights meant the right to worship freely, and that included people whose worship stemmed from quite different religious traditions from those of the majority.

One of the more telling indications of this attitude was the way Americans responded to Muslims in the weeks and months following the attacks on New York and Washington in 2001. As word spread of scattered acts of violence against Muslims, public leaders denounced these acts and called on the public to distinguish between Islam and terrorism. Polls taken after the attacks showed an unusual pattern of responses. Some Americans who had not previously thought much about Muslims said they now held negative opinions. But an even larger number said their views toward Muslims were now positive. Other polls showed that there was indeed a reservoir of misgiving toward Muslims. For instance, in the Religion and Diversity Survey, 47 percent of the public said they considered the Muslim religion "fanatical," and 40 percent thought it was "violent." Yet the prevailing attitude—the view expressed by a large majority of the public—was that we needed to live and let live. No longer could we ignore the fact that some share of almost any community of any size would worship differently from the ways most Americans had worshiped throughout most of the country's history.

As a result of these changes, American religion, perhaps more than any other major social institution, has had to reinvent itself. Protestant denominations that could at one time count on growth largely by retaining the children reared in these denominations have had to realize that much of their growth was coming from the founding of new congregations for Latinos, Korean Americans, or Hmong refugees. Catholic dioceses faced the need for Spanish-speaking priests and for resettlement programs that would bring Cubans and Haitians together, or Italians and Salvadorans. And for Christians who may have considered their teachings the only source of divine truth, it now became necessary to rethink whether that was the case, and, if so, what their relationships should be with Muslim or Hindu neighbors.

These changes in American religion have raised important questions about their possible implications for American democracy. In the population at large, religious participation appears to have remained fairly constant since the early 1970s (although at lower levels than in the 1950s). For instance, in Gallup polls between 40 and 42 percent of the adult public reports having attended religious services during the past seven days.[17] Researchers question whether these figures may be inflated, but there has thus far been only limited evidence that attendance may have declined. Whatever the actual numbers, religious involvement also appears to be higher in the United States than in many other countries. There are nevertheless concerns about other ways in which religion is changing. Evangelical Protestants and conservative Catholics sometimes argue that religion is increasingly excluded from the public sphere. They worry that important values are thus being ignored (for instance, freedom to worship or protection of the right to life). Some social observers worry that new immigrants belong to religions that encourage religious nationalism or theocratic movements, rather than democracy. Others are concerned that greater religious diversity makes it harder to achieve consensus and therefore harder to govern.

The most important question, however, has to do with the impact of immigration on the character and vitality of American religion itself. If immigration encourages recent immigrants and their children to be more actively involved in their houses of worship and in their communities (as immigration appears to have done in the past), then its main impact will be to increase the vitality of American religion and presumably whatever positive benefits religion has for democracy as well. This impact may extend well beyond immigrant communities themselves. New vitality in these communities may enliven the activities of older congregations or stimulate religious leaders to plan new multiethnic congregations better suited for multiethnic populations. And if religious vitality increases, then Americans will be more likely to do volunteer work, form service organizations, discuss social and political issues at their houses of worship, and think of themselves as Americans who have a legitimate stake in their communities and in their governing institutions. The prospect of religion's playing a more active role in the society is, in this view, not one that secularists should fear, either. The very diversity of American religion will prevent any particular sect from gaining too much power. There will be a healthy competition for members, but no force monolithic enough to carry the nation into some fit of theocratic passion. Democracy will be strengthened in the best possible way. Religious communities will be active, but not so active that America would try to become an imperial power in the name of religion as so many dominant powers have sought to do in the past.

In this chapter I want to look more closely at these arguments about American religion and democracy. They are rooted in ideas about markets, competition, and rational-choice economics. These are very powerful ideas. They have proven attractive to many observers of American religion because they are, on the surface, more compatible with the existing evidence than were earlier ideas that emphasized secularization and the gradual decline of religion. However, as with any new arguments, these need to be examined critically. Indeed, my reading of the evidence persuades me that these arguments need to be refined quite considerably if we are to arrive at a good understanding of how American religion has been changing and how those changes will in turn affect religion's relationship with American democracy. I will suggest that the heightened diversity bred by recent immigration has probably stimulated religious involvement in the ways that have been argued, but that diversity also breeds privatization of religious beliefs and practices, and that privatization is at best a worrisome development for American democracy. In short, my argument is that American religion has changed during the past half century, and that these changes have helped our nation become more inclusive—in that sense, we have become a better nation; however, the privatization of religion has continued, and this privatization has severely limited whatever potential American religion may have had for making us a better society.

## A CLOSER LOOK AT RELIGIOUS MARKETS

During the 1970s, nearly every journalist and academic commentator who wrote about American religion observed that something peculiar was taking place. Religion seemed to be flourishing. Hare Krishnas were dancing on street corners and followers of the Reverend Sun Myung Moon were collecting money in airports. On campuses, new yoga groups and Jesus-centered ministries were springing up. People were joining religiously oriented communes and practicing meditation in corporate boardrooms. At first, observers assumed that all of this was youthful exuberance, an outgrowth of the unrest associated with the Vietnam War or the drug culture, and that it would fade as quickly as it had appeared. After all, Protestant churches seemed to be losing members, and things were not much better in Catholic parishes. As the decade came to a close, the mass suicide in Guyana among the Jim Jones cult suggested that the religious excesses of the 1970s were surely at an end. At almost the same time, however, an Islamic revolution in Iran pointed to the possibility that religion in other parts of the world was more politically energetic than ever. It was interesting to note that in the United States President Jimmy Carter was a devout Southern Baptist who regarded himself as a born-again evangelical Christian. It was even more interesting that another Baptist, the Reverend Jerry Falwell, was attracting large numbers of conservative Christians to a new movement he called the Moral Majority. All this was peculiar because academics had been predicting for at least a century that religion would gradually become less and less important. The United States may have had reasons historically to be a highly religious nation, but as time went by, it would, according to the prevailing view, become more and more like Western Europe—where hardly anybody took religion seriously.

The evidence of continuing, and even increasing, religious activity in the United States required academics to do some soul-searching of their own. If religion was not declining, what could account for its vitality? A bold "new paradigm" was set forth in a paper by the sociologist R. Stephen Warner that circulated privately for several years and was then published in the *American Journal of Sociology*.[18] Warner argued that the idea of gradually declining religion—or secularization theory, as it was called—had been formulated by European scholars (such as the German political economist Max Weber and the French sociologist Émile Durkheim) who drew insights from their own Western European contexts and were, for that reason, wrong. Religion had declined in those contexts, Warner wrote, because of the particular configuration of state-sponsored churches that had grown up following the Protestant Reformation. State funding meant that each religion enjoyed a monopoly within its own territory and thus grew lazy for lack of competition. The United States, in contrast, had always experienced competition among religious groups that had to work hard to secure their own funding. That competition was the reason for religious vitality in America. Of course this argument was not new. Historians and religion scholars had long argued that separation of church and state was the key to America's religious vitality, and that separation had in fact encouraged competition or at least given Americans more incentive to be religious because they could pick and choose from a wide variety of religious options. Whereas this observation had been considered an account of "American exceptionalism," though, Warner argued that the United States was actually the rule, and Western Europe the exception. All over the world (from India to Japan and from Latin America to New Zealand), societies were becoming more diverse. Competitive religious markets were emerging in religion, just as they were in free market economies.

At about the same time, the idea that religion could be understood in the same terms as economic behavior was being explored by the sociologist Rodney Stark, along with several coauthors including Roger Finke. In *The Churching of America*, Finke and Stark argued that it was useful to think of something they called "religious economies," which were very much like competitive religious markets.[19] In these religious economies, religious organizations competed with one another for scarce resources, particularly members and their contributions of time and money that made it possible to pay clergy salaries, construct buildings, and launch new congregations. The key insight was that some religious organizations seemed to be better competitors than others in such markets. For instance, during much of the nineteenth century Methodists and Baptists had attracted new members and built new churches at a much faster pace than had Congregationalists or Presbyterians. To explain these differences, Finke and Stark borrowed an idea from a book published in the 1970s by Dean M. Kelley that linked church growth with theological conservatism. Kelley had shown that the denominations with the highest growth rates during the 1960s and early 1970s were Southern Baptists, Assemblies of God, and a few other conservative organizations, and he speculated that the reason was these denominations' requirement of greater commitment among their members.[20] Finke and Stark reformulated Kelley's observation in economic terms, suggesting that conservative churches offered a more rewarding product, namely, assurance about eternal salvation, and thus were able to persuade people to pay more for that product in terms of time and money. This argument was then further refined by the economist Laurence Iannaccone, who identified *strictness*—in terms of distinctive dress, morals, beliefs, and lifestyle, resulting in a clear and persuasive sense of personal identity— as the secret to success in any competitive religious market.[21]

The idea of religious markets carries strong normative implications that help to illuminate how religion contributes to the good of society. Although it is a perspective that helps make sense of the vitality of American religion, the idea of religious markets often conveys an implicit statement about what is good about American society as well. That statement derives from the assumption that religion is generally beneficial. Its benefits may or may not involve saving souls, as some religious leaders themselves would argue. From a purely secular perspective, religion is beneficial because it empowers people. It gives them an identity, which is often hard to find elsewhere amid the complexity and chaos of the contemporary world. Religion brings people together, forging ties among them that they can use to attain political power, find jobs, or address their communities' needs. Naturally, there are exceptions to the rule, such as the occasional cult leader who exploits his or her followers, or the terrorists who use religion to rationalize violence. But for the most part, religion is arguably beneficial in these ways. Consequently, whatever helps religion to flourish is also good. In the American case, open markets encourage religious flourishing, just as they do business. We are a good society because we have found the secret to religious flourishing. If we have managed in recent years to accommodate greater religious diversity, then we are an even better society. Whatever religious vitality we may see among new immigrants, or among gays or college students, in small charismatic congregations or in large megachurches, is all evidence that we are doing it right.

With respect to new immigrants, the open markets argument makes possible at least two important predictions. First, that immigrants themselves will become more religiously active, once they are situated in the context of the competitive religious environment in the United States, than they were in their countries of origin. For instance, a Muslim from Turkey who took his or her faith for granted there because everyone was Muslim would probably start participating more actively at the masjid (mosque) and at home in America. Not all immigrants will follow this path, but the religious market will surely encourage them to do so. As new Buddhist temples or Latino fellowships spring up, we can be confident that the religious market is working. Warner, for instance, sees the vitality of new immigrant congregations as one of the clearest indications that religion in America is flourishing. These immigrant communities are also better for it. Instead of encountering the isolation they would experience as solitary individuals, and instead of simply being assimilated into some faceless Americanism, they find the strength to preserve their distinctive heritage but also gradually make successes of themselves. In brief, the religious market works well to incorporate new immigrants into the society. The second prediction is that these religiously active immigrants then ratchet up the competition, so to speak, in a way that encourages other religious groups to expend more energy and become more competitive. The lively masjid down the road, for example, sparks more interest at the Presbyterian or Catholic church in the neighborhood as well. In both ways, then, the influx of new immigrants over the past four decades has been good for American religion. The religious market has expanded, and concurrently the vitality of religion and democracy has increased.

Of course there will be differences among immigrants because they come from countries with vastly different cultural and religious traditions. As a consequence, some become more religiously active in the United States, while others do not. Warner notes that Korean immigrants seem to have started churches in large numbers, whereas immigrants from Iran tended to distance themselves from Islam. This difference stems from the fact that Korean immigrants were often Christians already, and many had fled North Korea earlier to escape communism, whereas Iranian immigrants were more likely to have been "modern" or "secular" members of the professions who had enjoyed favor under the shah and feared persecution under a more militant Muslim regime. Immigrants are also influenced by the general religious climate of their countries of origin. For instance, a national survey conducted in Taiwan in the late 1990s showed that only 11 percent of its population attended religious services every week. At the same time, a comparable survey estimated that 32 percent of the U.S. population attended services every week.[22] Thus Taiwanese immigrants could easily be more religiously active in the United States than in Taiwan yet at the same time be *less* active than native-born Americans. The same would be true for immigrants who have come from Russia or from other former Soviet countries, such as Azerbaijan, Belarus, Croatia, Estonia, Serbia, Slovenia, and Ukraine.[23]

These caveats notwithstanding, most of what we know now from numerous studies of new immigrant and ethnic congregations suggests that American religion has in fact reinvented itself in the favorable ways suggested by arguments about religious markets.[24] A study of immigrants from Taiwan by the sociologist Carolyn Chen is especially revealing. Chen found that Taiwanese immigrants in southern California were considerably more religiously active than they had been in Taiwan. Some converted to evangelical Christianity, while others became more engaged at Buddhist temples and meditation centers. Their religious involvement was an acceptable way of being American *and* preserving their ethnic heritage. Southern California was a vibrant religious market. The various immigrant groups started their own congregations and then, as communities grew, started more. Among the Christians and Buddhists in Chen's research, there was a healthy competition for members.[25]

Another interesting study was conducted in Philadelphia and Boston by the sociologist Wendy Cadge. In Philadelphia, Thai immigrants gravitated to a Theravada temple. The temple offered children's classes in Thai and was a place for people to meet and stay in contact with others from their homeland. In Boston, the Buddhist meditation center Cadge studied was populated by native-born Americans who found Buddhism an attractive alternative to the Christianity or Judaism in which they had been raised. Rather than dropping out of religion entirely, they were able, because of the religious market, to find a devotional practice that suited them.[26]

Yet another study focused on immigrants from India. The sociologist Prema Kurien, herself of Indian background, found that Indian immigrants often identified more closely with Hinduism in the United States than they had in India. Hindu temples served as community centers as well as places of worship. Outsiders largely left these immigrants alone to practice as they wished. It was legitimate for people to build houses of worship, even if these buildings bore little resemblance to churches or synagogues. The immigrants and their children, Kurien argued, found an acceptable way to be Americans.[27]

The best conclusion from the evidence currently available, then, is that there is, as ethnographers have shown, considerable religious vitality among new immigrants. This vitality may not have been enough to raise all boats, as it were, at least judging from surveys. But the idea of religious markets is not just about overall rates of religious participation. Newcomers quickly discover that religion is one of the ways in which Americans band together and express their identity. Religious competition encourages new immigrants to start their own congregations. America has benefited from the "ingenuity of grass roots religion," as Warner puts it.[28] The native-born population probably should not take much credit for this religious efflorescence—not, at any rate, if its religion has been what Warner describes as "the top-down codes of ecclesiastics." But Americans can take heart in the fact that good old-fashioned ingenuity is still very much alive. The same pioneering spirit that populated the frontier with churches and synagogues is now burgeoning in the Muslim sections of Dearborn and the Latino neighborhoods of Jersey City. It is abundantly clear, too, that new immigrant congregations are doing well in the United States because they have adopted many of the customs and practices of more established religions. Imams refer to the people associated with their mosques as *congregations*, a term that would not be used in Indonesia or the Middle East. American mosques are typically governed by a lay board of directors, another practice unknown in most Muslim countries. At the Buddhist temple Wendy Cadge studied in Philadelphia, worship services were held at the same Sunday morning hour as were church services in the area, and temple lunches bore similarities to church potlucks. Korean preaching and Latino masses are increasingly conducted in English because fewer of the congregants speak Korean or Spanish. Although some Hindu temples are large structures modeled after temples in India, many are small buildings that blend as easily into their suburban neighborhoods as would a Masonic lodge or an academy for the martial arts. To be sure, there is a segment of the larger population who think it illegitimate for people to be meeting at Muslim mosques or Hindu temples. This segment, however, is not the majority. And its presence is itself part of the competitive process that encourages people to initiate different religious organizations of their own.

## WHEN ALL RELIGIONS ARE TRUE

I suggested earlier that religion in the United States has not just expanded in beneficial ways, as the religious markets perspective helps us see; religion has also become increasingly privatized. To understand what privatization means and how it inhibits religion's potential for social betterment, we must look at something that proponents of the religious markets perspective seldom consider: religious belief. Religious organizations do not compete simply because one leader wants a following larger than another leader's, although that may certainly be part of the story. They compete because they have different beliefs—different understandings about how divine truth is revealed, about how to worship, and about what to do to gain divine favor in this life or the next. The religions people were willing to die for throughout many centuries of human history were ones believed to be ultimately true and, for that reason, infinitely better than any of the competing religions that were no more than purveyors of falsehood. This was the kind of religion that prompted crusades and religious wars or large-scale efforts to convert other populations. To be sure, there were additional matters at stake, such as power and wealth, but if religion mattered at all, it was because one group believed it knew the truth and thus knew also that the other group's religion was false.

Among the various religious traditions, the followers of monotheistic religions such as Christianity, Judaism, and Islam have been more militant than, say, Buddhists or Hindus in defending themselves as God's chosen people or true disciples. Christianity, as the dominant religion in the United States, has also been subject to claims and counterclaims put forth by particular denominations and sects that *theirs* was the only true interpretation of the faith. The religious market that spread so widely during the nineteenth century can hardly be understood without recognition of these claims and counterclaims. Baptist congregations did not grow simply because they encouraged strict lifestyles or had more entrepreneurial leaders. They grew because their members believed souls were at stake and that Congregationalists and Catholics were going about it—the pursuit of salvation—wrong.

At present, there is still a sizable share of the American public who believe that Christianity alone is a true religion. For instance, in the Religion and Diversity Survey, 31 percent of the public said they agreed strongly that "Christianity is the only way to have a true personal relationship with God," and another 13 percent agreed somewhat. Given the long history of Christian teaching about the necessity of believing in the Bible and in following Jesus, it is not difficult to understand why this large a segment of the population would believe that only Christianity is true. What is more interesting is the fact that so many people, even among those who consider themselves Christian, do not.

The extent to which Americans think all religions are true is evident in national surveys. In the Religion and Diversity Survey, 74 percent of the public agreed that "All major religions, such as Christianity, Hinduism, Buddhism, and Islam, contain some truth about God." A majority of the public (54 percent) also agreed that "All major religions, such as Christianity, Hinduism, Buddhism, and Islam, are *equally good* ways of knowing about God." Other studies have drawn similar conclusions. For instance, in a national study of churchgoing Protestants who defined themselves as evangelicals, the sociologist Christian Smith found that evangelicals generally believe the Bible to be divine truth and regard Jesus as their savior; however, these evangelicals were reluctant to say that the followers of other religions might not also be saved.[29] Drawing on surveys and qualitative interviews, the sociologist Wade Clark Roof found that baby boomers especially took a relativistic stance toward religious truth. They became spiritual seekers, shopping around for bits and pieces of religious wisdom from various traditions. In the process, they often drew a distinction between religion and spirituality, arguing that religions were at best culturally constructed ideas about truth, whereas spirituality was what they knew personally to be true from their own experience.[30] In a book drawing insights from research conducted by ethnographers, the sociologist Alan Wolfe has also argued that Americans generally take a live-and-let-live approach when it comes to religion. Even if they think their own religion is uniquely true, they make few efforts to convert others to it. Studies of evangelicals, Wolfe notes, suggest that they are committed to the *idea* of winning souls, but in practice they are restrained by not wanting to seem rude or offensive, by valuing consensus more than persuasion, and by feeling ill-prepared to talk about their faith with strangers.[31]

In any era, there have been Americans who either believed that all religions were true or who cared little one way or the other. It is unlikely that as many people thought that way in the past as do at present, however. At least in the heartland, where Christianity was practiced almost exclusively, it was easy to think that it was indeed exclusively true. One of the clearest indications of how this attitude has changed comes from Muncie, Indiana, which the anthropologists Robert and Helen Lynd chose to study in the 1920s as a typical Midwestern town, and to which sociologists returned for a follow-up study in the 1970s. In Muncie, or "Middletown," as it was dubbed by the researchers, 94 percent of the 1920s respondents said they believed that "Christianity is the one true religion and everyone should be converted to it"; by the 1970s, that figure had dropped to 41 percent.[32]

The reasons *why* so many Americans believe all religions are true have not been rigorously investigated but can be adduced from some of the arguments that the scholars just mentioned (and others) have put forth. One of the more interesting arguments is that believing in the exclusive truth of one's religion depends not only on convincing theological teachings, but also on being surrounded by like-minded believers and isolated from people who believe differently. If that argument is correct, it may help us understand why people in remote corners of the world who had never been in contact with other societies believed the way they did. Or it might explain why the members of a cult who cut themselves off from the world and spend all their time in the presence of a cult leader would believe that only that leader's teachings were true. But it also helps us understand why most Americans would *not* at some deep level believe that their religion was the only truth. The communities—or *plausibility structures*, as Peter L. Berger has called them—in which Americans live are hardly ever that hermetically sealed.[33] Through their personal contacts, and if not those, through reading and watching television, Americans are exposed to people who hold beliefs different from their own. They know about atheists if they are believers, or about Hindus if they are Christians, and so on. They may even have been challenged to regard their beliefs as less than absolutely true by interacting with other Christians who held different interpretations. Americans who have traveled internationally or who have been exposed over longer periods to higher education are even more likely to have been influenced in these ways. Exposure of this kind involves direct encounters with people from different cultures and different religious traditions; it also specifically encourages people to consider different points of view and to believe that we more closely approximate truth by entertaining multiple perspectives than by clinging to only one. Such thinking fits well with living in a market-oriented society. The good consumer is one who considers several different products and chooses the one that seems best.

In adopting the view that all religions are true, Americans have also been encouraged by several prevailing assumptions in our culture. One is the idea that all people are capable of determining what is right and what is wrong. This commonsense understanding of morality was actually rooted in Christian teachings, early in our nation's history, about the presence of God's grace and the ability of people everywhere to understand something about God because God had created them and the world around them. Commonsense morality was further reinforced during the early nineteenth century as religious and political leaders struggled with the question of how a democracy based on popular sovereignty could possibly function. The answer was that everyone, not just devout Christians, shared the ability to distinguish right from wrong and thus could arrive at good judgments through the political process. In more recent years, this same assumption is evident in the way the majority culture treats newcomers. We do not worry that Muslims or Hindus are incapable of arriving at the same moral judgments that Christians or Jews do. In fact, we assume that there are probably teachings within those religious traditions that encourage commonsense morality and are thus true to at least that extent. Another widespread idea is that divine truth, by virtue of being different from human truth, is ultimately a mystery. It cannot be known fully, only approximated. This means that it may be approximated by religions other than mine, and that even mine is not entirely accurate. Yet another assumption is that religion is not so much about truth anyway, but about practical results and good experiences. American religion is in this respect decidedly focused on the present life, more than on whatever happens after death. Although a large majority of Americans report believing in life after death, they are confident that they will reap heavenly rewards as long as they lead good lives. For this reason, religion is true if it helps one to be happy and if it sometimes yields moments of transcendence. For all these reasons, then, it is common for Americans to believe that all religions are to some extent true.

For our purposes, the more important question is what the implications are of believing that all religions are true. The implication that is most relevant to our understanding of the relation between religion and democracy is that religion becomes *privatized*. It becomes a matter, not of divine truth, not of principle, but of personal opinion. This way of understanding religion has often been noted in qualitative studies, where people hedge their statements with phrases such as "in my experience" or "that's just my personal view." We can see it in survey responses, too. In the Religion and Diversity Survey, for instance, 58 percent of the public agreed that "Christianity is the best way to understand God," but only 25 percent said it was best for everybody—the remainder said it was best just for them personally or that it depended on the situation. Another way that religion becomes privatized is by people's not talking about it. Not only is it their personal opinion, it is an opinion too personal to share. This reluctance is especially evident when Americans who identify themselves as Christians are asked whether they have "talked specifically with anyone who was not a Christian to persuade them to become a Christian." Only three in ten have done so more than once or twice, and hardly anybody has actually tried to persuade someone who belonged to a different religion. For instance, only 4 percent said they had tried to persuade a Muslim, and only 2 percent had tried to persuade a Hindu.

There are strong norms in the United States against making too much of a public display of one's religion. Of course there are lavish buildings that loudly proclaim themselves as houses of worship, and occasional road signs provide terse messages about God or Jesus. Preachers appear on television and public officials sometimes testify about their faith. There are special reasons for these exceptions, which we will come to later. But for the average American, it remains best to be quiet. Appearing too sure of one's convictions puts one in jeopardy of being branded a zealot. We know that politics and religion are not suitable topics for polite conversation at dinner parties. It may be acceptable for political candidates to talk about their faith, but, judging from surveys, we prefer they not do so too often. In the same way, we worry when pulpits are used for political purposes. As large megachurches spring up in suburban communities, their buildings can sometimes be seen from miles away. But these religious buildings are no longer adjacent to the town square like the churches in seventeenth-century New England or even the churches built in Midwestern towns at the end of the nineteenth century. Some of the mosques and Hindu temples that have been built in recent years have cost tens of millions of dollars and make a public statement simply by being there. It is more common, though, for new immigrants to meet in buildings that offer few clues about their use. The Hindus Prema Kurien studied in southern California met more often in private homes than at a temple. Another researcher reported having trouble locating an Islamic center because it was a plain white house with no sign. She had a similar experience finding a Buddhist temple, driving past it twice before noticing the small wooden sign stationed near the road in front of a plain brick dwelling. New immigrants may be reluctant to announce their presence for fear of animosity from the neighbors. But there are also ideas in the culture at large that discourage flaunting one's faith. In some contexts, such as schoolrooms and public buildings, laws prohibit saying much about religion. We have religious teachings such as the ones I mentioned previously—about

God's being a mystery and religion's being more a matter of personal experience than one of truth—that discourage us from being more public about our convictions.

Just how powerful these norms of privacy are is especially evident in the remarks of new immigrants. Even among those who are deeply devout, the prevalence of these norms is readily apparent. The responses of the men and women interviewed for the New Elites Project are revealing. Seventy-five percent of these first- or second-generation immigrants say they pray or meditate regularly, 80 percent report belief in a soul that lives on after death, and 86 percent say religion is a source of strength in their work life.[34] All but 20 percent attend religious services, although regular attendance varies considerably by tradition (whereas a majority of Asian American and Hispanic Christians say they attend services weekly, Muslims, Hindus, and Buddhists are more likely to attend on special holidays or no more than once a month). Nearly all also talk articulately about their religious beliefs and why these are important in their lives. Yet two-thirds (67 percent) acknowledge that their religion has been influenced by their lifestyle, their education, and their work. *How* it has been influenced is especially notable in responses to questions about what it means to be a true practitioner of their particular faith. Most say something about following the *teachings* of their tradition. But when asked for specifics about these teachings, they focus more on beliefs than on behavior. "I am a good Christian," a woman who grew up in Hong Kong says. "I truly believe there is a God [and] that Jesus Christ is the son of God." She adds that she does not go to church every week or "follow certain rituals." A man from India says his understanding of Hinduism is to grow spiritually as an individual. "There are different types of truth that work for different people," he explains. Some of these immigrants say their beliefs are even too private to describe in an interview. An immigrant from Japan, for example, explains, "Everything I do is so inside me that it's difficult to pinpoint and isolate something and verbalize it." Others insist that beliefs need to be put into practice, and many mention activities that are rooted in their faith: they work hard, try to be honest, are good parents, participate in religious services, and donate money to charity. Yet it is still one's *attitude* toward life that seems to matter more than doing anything that might distinguish a person as a practitioner of a particular faith. For instance, an immigrant from Korea says that "giving 100 percent of yourself up and totally [relying] on God" is the mark of a "true Christian or true Buddhist or true what-ever." A Muslim man who grew up in Syria makes a similar point. His view is that one's relationship with God is "a personal thing," and that's more important than whether or not he prays five times a day.

The exceptions—those who clearly make their faith public—are the ones who wear distinctive clothing or a distinctive hairstyle. Sikhs are easily identified by their turbans and beards or flowing white dresses. Hindu women are sometimes identifiable by their dressing in a sari. A Muslim woman says she wears "loose dresses," which she interprets as being Muslim because they are modest and hide the outline of her body. But in other cases, distinctive clothing that makes a statement about one's religion has become a matter of choice. A person wears such cloth-ing, not because it is commanded, but because it is a way of dressing up for a holiday or some other special occasion. A Muslim man from Jordan who works in the computer industry, for instance, explains that "the outfit from there really doesn't work here," but he does have "some clothes from there" that he and his children wear "on special occasions." Another Muslim man insists that he is "American" so there is "abso-lutely no reason to dress differently from anyone else." Those who occa-sionally wear distinctive dress also make a point of saying that what they do is optional and reflects a conscious decision they have made. For instance, a woman from India says she sometimes wears a sari—but never at work and only if the weather is good. Another woman from India says she wears distinctive garb "when I feel like I want to."

These immigrants are obviously drawing on language they have heard in the United States. Like their Christian or Jewish coworkers, they em-phasize that religion is more a matter of the heart than anything else. But this view is also reinforced by their experience of having lived in one culture and then moving to another. Cross-cultural exposure of this kind makes them more aware that religion is influenced by its cultural setting. Particular styles of worship or teachings about dress and moral behavior are as much about culture as about religion. A person may choose to worship in that manner or follow those customs because they are familiar and remind one of home. But they are still matters of *choice*. It thus becomes important to distill from all the habits and customs what one thinks of as the pure essence of one's religion. A devout person can hang on to that essence, while discarding many of the cultural trappings that no longer seem as important. And that essence, given the culturally diverse context in which the person now lives, is very likely to be regarded as something highly personal. The Syrian man I quoted previously, for instance, says he has come to realize that there is a big difference between "true religion" and that which is "actually tradition and practice." He mentions the practice in some Muslim societies of women's wearing black burkas (dresses covering head to toe). He thinks this probably came from the "dark ages of Islam" and is not essential to Muslim teachings. He sees no reason why Western Muslims should dress that way. Having a *personal* relationship with God makes more sense to him. His view is very similar to that of a Sikh woman who says she has learned "not to look down" on anybody else's religion. She connects that view with the assertion that her own religion gives her "inner strength." As long as it continues to "fulfill that inner need," she is content with it.

When religion functions mainly to fulfill personal needs, it loses its authority to make claims in the public arena in behalf of *specific* teachings or traditions. All religions are true as long as they prove personally useful, and any religion may work some of the time for some people. Thus religion needs to be protected as a kind of generic social good, and people can even promote it (as we sometimes see public officials doing) on grounds that it does more good than harm. This is an arrangement that nearly everyone can buy into fairly easily. For public officials or secularists, it prevents having to deal with religion on grounds other than utilitarian ones. For religious leaders who no longer claim to speak with special authority, it offers a way to escape having to debate what constitutes religious truth. The Christian majority can believe Christianity to be true, not through scriptural warrant, but because all religions are true. Individual believers, whether Christian or adherents of various new immigrant religions, can posit that their own religion is true *for them* because it gives them inner peace or inner strength, and by implication other religions must be true in the same way. The historian William P. Hutchison describes this kind of pluralism as the pluralism of "tolerance" and "inclusivity." It is, he says, "intrinsic to the social covenant," meaning that we not only take it for granted but also find that it works well to preserve the status quo. Hutchison writes that we have developed a kind of national pride in this manifestation of pluralism. As America has become more diverse, we have managed with seeming ease to accommodate this diversity, even to the point of engaging in what Hutchison calls a patronizing form of triumphal pluralism ("I'm more pluralistic than you are").[35] And yet that pluralism is not as great an accomplishment as we would like to think, given that religion has become so private and inward in the process.

To say only that contemporary religion is privatized, though, is to make too sweeping a generalization. Although many Americans emphasize the highly personal nature of their beliefs and say little about them in public, others seem intent on influencing the public arena now more than ever. Fundamentalist preachers who fill their airwaves with warnings about America's need for repentance may be the best example. But public officials have increasingly taken the view that disclosing stories about their experiences with God is a good way of winning elections. And if many immigrants seem to have adopted a privatized kind of faith, others have formed advocacy organizations to fight for their interests locally and nationally. The sociologist José Casanova terms this apparent reentry of religion into the public sphere "deprivatization."[36] We have the curious situation, then, of religion's seeming to run in two opposing directions at the same time.

## DIFFERENT STAKES IN RELIGIOUS ADVOCACY

The principal reason for this difficulty is that scholars of American religion seldom pay attention to the fact that religious communities are never internally monolithic. They have been treated as if they were monolithic largely because studies have dealt with the topic of religious markets either by looking at raw membership statistics or by rendering secondary interpretations of historical figures without paying much attention to the history underlying those figures. In either case, the important question has been simply whether some religious organizations grew (that is, gained adherents) more rapidly than others. However, if we are interested in the larger relationships between religion and society, such discussions focusing on raw membership figures simply will not do. We must instead recognize that religious communities are internally divided. They are always divided between clergy or other elites and the rank-and-file membership. And both the leaders and the followers may be divided along other lines as well (such as social class, ideology, or where they regard their self-interests to lie).

It will be helpful to borrow an idea from the historian R. Laurance Moore, who argues that nearly all religious communities in the United States have at one time or another thought of themselves as outsiders.[37] Catholics, Episcopalians, Methodists, Baptists, Mormons—all have histories as religious outsiders. They were sometimes overtly persecuted and in other cases felt simply that their beliefs and practices were not those of the majority population or its leaders. Outsiders, Moore argues, often do a good job of keeping their members and threatening them if they are disloyal. Religious outsiders are, in this sense, "strict," and they proliferate for some of the reasons suggested by the proponents of rational choice economics. To speak of outsiders is again too broad, though. We need to remember that the leaders and the followers in an outsider community may have different stakes in how they relate to the wider society. The leaders may need to show that they are powerful enough to make people in the wider society listen to them. The followers may find it more comfortable to go quietly about their business, not letting on that they are outsiders any more than they have to (even though they firmly believe themselves to be right). Recent research among American evangelicals, for instance, has shown precisely this pattern. Leaders rail against American culture and argue that the nation is divinely condemned because of abortion, divorce, and immorality; rank-and-file evangelicals pretty much live like their nonevangelical neighbors. There may also be differences among the followers. Those who have become successful in terms of education, occupation, or income may feel like insiders part of the time while remaining outsiders in terms of their religious identity. These relatively successful outsiders are probably the ones who have the most reason to keep quiet about their beliefs. In contrast, followers who are marginalized economically as well as religiously may be more militant about their beliefs and practices. If nothing else, they have principles to live by and to stand for.

The relevance of these distinctions to our considerations about religion and democracy is that immigrants, as religious outsiders, have different stakes in bringing the weight of their religious convictions to bear on the political process. Elites who claim to speak on behalf of some constituency will be likely to present themselves in terms of their religious identity—especially if religious bodies are important sources of support, as, for instance, in the case of African American clergy. For some of the rank-and-file immigrant population religion will also be an important part of their identity. They will attend services regularly, do volunteer work at their house of worship, and allow their views on social issues to be influenced by what their leaders say. Others, though, will find it embarrassing to say much about their religious loyalties outside of their immediate group. Especially if they are successful business or professional leaders, they may find it easier to keep quiet about their religious beliefs.

Studies of immigrant congregations show how these dynamics affect the expression of religious beliefs. One of the more telling of these studies was conducted by the sociologist Elaine Howard Ecklund among Korean Americans who were actively involved in their congregations. Ecklund's study is particularly interesting because she examined whether these Korean Americans—most of whom were successful younger second-generation immigrants—were politically active, voted, took part in advocacy efforts, and in other ways participated actively in their communities, either on behalf of their churches or as individual citizens. Like other Americans, many of Ecklund's respondents did volunteer work at their churches and were involved in service activities in their neighborhoods. However, they were less likely than other Americans to vote, to participate in political activities, or even to deem it valuable to form or join in political advocacy efforts. The exceptions to this pattern were a few of the respondents who regarded African American churches as a model, and who, for this reason, considered it important to speak out on behalf of their communities. The others found numerous reasons to keep quiet about their faith. They felt there was enough to do at church without expending effort on communitywide endeavors. They identified with a current of thinking in the larger evangelical Protestant community that said political activities were less important than trying to save souls. Or their church involvement so strongly reinforced their sense of being outsiders to the wider society that they felt incapable of launching advocacy efforts or even knowing how to cast their votes.[38]

If Ecklund's observations hold true in other contexts, they suggest that the new religious diversity stemming from immigration may be repeating established patterns, rather than significantly contributing to the vitality of American democracy. An immigrant congregation, mosque, or temple may well perform the kinds of civic functions that Tocqueville identified at a time when America was much different from what it is today. These religious communities take care of their own.

They provide a safe space in which ethnic traditions can be affirmed. There may be efforts to mobilize volunteers to help the needy. The members nevertheless remain outsiders to the political process. When they go to work, vote, and send their children to school, they do so as individual citizens, not as representatives of a religious community. It is the political operative, the elite whose job it is to represent the community, who assumes a more public role. That role may be occupied by a local member of the clergy but is more likely to be fulfilled by a special purpose organization, such as a group devoted to protecting Muslims from discrimination or a Korean American business association. The rank-and-file member can keep quiet about his or her religious convictions because a more public religious identity would be risky.

The New Elites Project provides an even more vivid sense of how being an immigrant who is also a successful professional or businessperson generates tensions in religious beliefs and practices. Although few of these immigrants have abandoned the religion in which they were raised, they nearly always identify a progression away from the more public practices or distinctive customs of those religious traditions. This progression involves what might best be characterized as *individuation*. Their faith has become *theirs* and thus different from the teachings and practices of any religious organization. They consider themselves more tolerant, less committed to being distinctly associated with one particular tradition, and more willing to blend in with people from different backgrounds. A Korean immigrant who has been quite successful in his business is particularly candid in explaining why he no longer follows the religious teachings of his church as rigorously as he once did. "I like socializing with people. I like meeting new people. I like entertaining people. Sometimes if you follow strict Christian beliefs and procedures, it's difficult." A man who grew up in Cuba says he is deeply religious even though he no longer goes to mass and disagrees with many of the teachings of the Catholic Church. He mostly "keeps quiet" about what he believes or does not believe. Being in a more pluralistic environment has encouraged him to "look at other philosophies and religions and try to come up with my own." He has decided that "the Egyptians, the Buddhists, the Christians, the Jews, all of them have certain common denominators." For a person like this, then, adapting to a new world composed of very diverse religions and lifestyles involves retaining one's conviction that there is truth in religion by deciding that there is truth in all religions. That being the case, it makes little sense to argue about religion or to wear one's particular religion on one's sleeve.

It is hardly surprising that immigrants who are highly educated and successful in their chosen professions—or who desperately want their children to achieve success—feel acute pressures to keep their religious convictions under wraps. The norms that quietly guide such behavior are often subtle, such as the raised eyebrows some Muslims and Sikhs report seeing when they wear religious garb in public. But these norms are also reinforced in more overt ways. After the 9/11 attacks, street gangs retaliated by ripping head scarves from Muslim women. The media condemned these attacks, but in interviews immigrants reported that they had started encouraging their children to wear Western-style clothing. Journalists play a powerful role in formulating public opinion, and their views about religion are often curiously mixed. Because of their own stake in free expression, journalists generally line up in favor of court rulings that permit people to speak or dress according to religious customs. Yet there is often an undercurrent of suspicion toward religion that comes through much more loudly than the rudimentary refrains about freedom of religion. A *New York Times* editorial about Muslim girls wearing scarves in French and German schools is a good example. The editorial argued that following the dress or dietary codes of one's faith is an exercise of freedom of conscience. Much of the editorial, however, pointed out why reasonable people might be concerned about such expressions of conscience. It might in some cases "amount to proselytizing or otherwise infringing on the freedoms of others." These freedoms had been won only after a "long a bitter struggle" between church and state. Wearing scarves might be a legitimate concern to feminists "who see the scarf as a symbol of women's subjugation." Readers should also be wary of "the pressures and taboos of sectarians and ideologues." Referring to "the battle with extremism," the editorial went on to suggest that "wearing a head scarf may well be a political statement, and it may even inspire schoolmates to explore radical Islam."[39]

What would a Muslim parent conclude from reading an editorial like this? Only the foolhardy would risk sending a daughter to school wearing a *hijab*. She might be permitted to wear it. If a court case resulted, she might win and her victory would be lauded by the media. Meanwhile, though, her parents would know that intelligent, well-placed, influential, politically liberal opinion was hardly on their side. The very people who were willing to defend their freedom to dress in keeping with their faith were concerned about that faith's becoming a "political statement" and encouraging the subjugation of women, if not sectarian extremism as well.

But it is not only the better-educated reader of the *New York Times* who comes to understand that religion is best left at home. Despite the fact that as many as a quarter of American adults attend religious services every week, the vast majority of Americans do not participate very regularly at religious organizations, even though nearly everyone claims to believe in God. For this majority, faith is not something to be practiced but a kind of experience one may have had during some dark hour when it seemed better to think there was a God in the universe than that there was not. There is widespread skepticism about the necessity of being active in a religious organization and even more concern about people who too loudly proclaim their convictions outside of those organizations. In a national survey conducted in 1999 I was able to examine the extent to which Americans manifested some of these signs of religious privatization. In the public at large, 72 percent agreed with the statement "My religious beliefs are very personal and private," and 70 percent agreed that "My spirituality does not depend on being involved in a religious organization." Younger and older people were equally likely to agree with each statement, and there were few differences between those with higher and with lower levels of education. Of greatest interest, immigrants were *more* likely than native-born Americans to agree with the first statement, and almost as likely to agree with the second. The only category in the wider public who disagreed disproportionately with these statements comprised self-defined "religious conservatives," and even in that category a majority agreed.[40] Judging from these data, then, religious privatism is widespread in the American public. It is not present just among elites, and it is prevalent among immigrants. If immigrants have been able to express their religious beliefs freely in the religious marketplace, they have also found that considering them private may be the best means of expression of all.

## PRIVATIZATION AND DEMOCRACY

I come finally, then, to the question of what difference it makes if religion has become a matter of personal experience and private opinion.

Theologians and biblical scholars, or even religious historians, might consider this development regrettable because it appears to relegate religious doctrine to the dustbin of history. From the standpoint of what benefits a functioning democracy, though, we might worry less about this development; we might even celebrate it. Surely there are benefits when religious people no longer believe they know the mind of God, and are willing to acknowledge that their religious opinions are just that. Alan Wolfe, for instance, suggests that the essential question is whether democracy is "safe from religion." He believes it is because religion has been "transformed" to the point that nobody, not even evangelical Protestants, takes doctrine very seriously. Instead, Wolfe argues, religious believers live by a code of civic decorum that deters them from standing very firmly on such issues as abortion or school prayer.[41]

From one perspective, privatization can be a very significant way of rendering religious beliefs and practices more compatible with democracy. Privatization makes religious differences easier to deal with. It means I leave my beliefs at home when I go to work or when I vote or run for public office. If I happen to mention them in public, I describe them as happenstance views associated with the particularities of my upbringing. I do not cause trouble by arguing about them with people who happen to hold different views. I focus instead on the issues at hand, pondering them on their merits, rather than in relation to my beliefs and values. I try to be rational in presenting arguments, and I know that an argument based simply on my personal opinion is weak. What I will get testy about is someone's telling me I am not entitled to my opinion. Or that I cannot write a letter to the editor expressing my opinion. I know that I have a right to do this, whether or not I choose to exercise that right. The democratic system works well for me as long as it protects that right. The democratic system may even encourage me to regard my religious beliefs as private opinions. After all, I learned to keep them to myself when I was in school. My employer does not want me to talk about them at work. And the only contexts in which I see others expressing them in public are op-ed columns and television talk shows.

Yet there is clearly a cost to democracy when traditions and the values rooted in these traditions are excluded from public debate. We can talk about policies in terms of whether or not they are fair, but it becomes harder to discuss them in terms of what is right or wrong. Right and wrong, in fact, become matters of personal opinion and of behaving one way if we are not under surveillance and another if there is a chance of being caught. Having some principles on which to make decisions is especially important when these decisions are complex, as most decisions currently are. Without principles, complex decisions end up being made in terms of whatever seems most workable or in terms of that part of the problem that happens to grab our attention. If we are guided in our thinking about religious matters by regarding them as personal opinions, then we may approach other decisions the same way. An event, an emotional appeal, or the charismatic personality of a public official carries more weight than it should. We may hope, of course, that rational people are having rational discussions somewhere about what is best for our nation. In a democracy, those rational decisions still have to be sold to the public, however. Or, more accurately, the public needs ways to mobilize to ensure that its voice is heard. Faith communities with long traditions and deep loyalties have been effective ways of mobilizing the public in the past. But when faith becomes my private opinion, it is hard to see how that faith could become a basis for democratic mobilization. "Pluralism goes beyond mere tolerance," Diana Eck writes. It requires participation of the kind that bridges between one's own faith community and the larger society. That means being willing to express one's religious convictions somewhere other than in one's private prayer chamber. "I would argue that pluralism is engagement with, not abdication of, differences and particularities," Eck argues.[42] It should not result in the kind of relativism that holds all beliefs to be interchangeable, or that says my faith is true only for me.

The irony is that when all religions are true, those who still believe theirs to be distinctly true are more likely to mobilize and thus gain the upper hand. Their constituents will be more incensed than anyone else if they are asked to compromise their principles, and for this reason will take action to uphold those principles. This is why the religious right has been as effective as it has. Its leaders can send out mass mailings proclaiming that immigration is threatening the Christian fabric of our society or that the United Nations is doing so. Religious bullies raise money for themselves and their ministries by threatening believers that the truth will not be upheld unless they send in checks. The only redeeming aspect of privatization is that the most strident religious bullies have a difficult time mobilizing enough support to make much of a difference. Their followings are limited by the fact that fundamentalism also becomes a matter of personal opinion. And that prevents the nation from becoming a theocracy or mounting its imperial designs very persuasively in the name of religion.

But privatization also defeats the efforts of many others who try to engage in advocacy or who voice criticisms in the name of religious principles. Think how ineffective Dr. Martin Luther King Jr. would have been had he expressed his arguments about civil rights simply as personal opinions that he happened to hold by virtue of being African American. That would have relativized his arguments to the point that opponents of civil rights could have simply said they held different opinions. This in fact is very much what has happened to most religious groups other than fundamentalists. Mainline Protestants have taken stands on such issues as poverty, affirmative action, or gay rights on grounds that civil rights were at stake. They could frame these arguments in terms of fairness or individual freedom. Yet it has been more difficult for them to make compelling statements in terms of divine truth. The same has been true among American Catholics. Although the pope routinely makes declarations about social and moral issues, it has become popular to regard these as the pope's personal opinions, rather than as statements having any special authority. Religion writer Kenneth Richard Samples calls this current perspective the "politically correct" approach to religion.[43] It applies the same relativistic criteria to religion that one practices toward soft drinks or tastes in music. People get along with one another because it matters little whether they choose one soft drink or another. The prophetic voice of religion is muted.

The muting of those plural prophetic religious voices is particularly troubling at a time when the United States seems intent on widening its influence in international affairs to the point that phrases such as *American empire, new world order*, and *globalization of the U.S. economy* appear increasingly in our leaders' rhetoric. When multiple prophetic voices are engaged in serious debate, the ones that call for imperial wars have to contend with others demanding world peace, and those begging for open markets are confronted with arguments about such principles as human rights and social justice. Those voices are simply not heard when everyone regards his or her religion as a matter only of personal inspiration. The present climate, writes the sociologist Robert N. Bellah, is a "culture of mass consumerism and [an] ideology of privatized self-fulfillment." A climate of this kind, he argues, is not well-suited to extending American democracy to other parts of the world because it lacks the higher-order principles that serve as the foundation for morality, decency, and the resolve to sacrifice self-interest for the good of others. "Consumerism and privatization undermine the very institutional basis of democracy," Bellah observes. "It is a strange time for America to take on the responsibilities of empire—a time when our own society, from the family to the corporation, shows signs of deep inner incoherence."[44]

One may not care very much about the pros or cons of religious truth, but when religious truth is widely viewed as religious opinion, it becomes easier for understandings of truth in other realms to follow suit. Politics takes on the character of personal opinion and thus becomes increasingly a matter of personal charisma and carefully orchestrated sound bytes or photo ops, rather than an arena for serious debate about values and principles. About the only consensus that spans the political spectrum is that everyone should have the right to his or her own opinion. Political conservatives cast their arguments in terms of freedom from government. Political liberals do so in the name of diversity and the right to choose. But neither has much success in framing arguments about what we should do with our freedom. In this respect, fundamentalists and evangelicals who believe in absolute truth do the larger society a favor when they argue that absolute truth should be taken into account. They at least force their opponents to come up with better arguments themselves.

We need to remember that arguments about divine truth are seldom as erratic or individualistic as critics like to think. It isn't that Jerry Falwell or Pat Robertson receives a direct communication from God and marches accordingly, anymore than this is what happened to Martin Luther or John Calvin. That view is a caricature popularized by the media and secular academics. It turns divine revelation into another form of personal opinion—only an opinion that its foolish bearers take too seriously. Quite the contrary. What drives fundamentalists and evangelicals is not so much private revelation as an entire worldview, one that was worked out over many years through the work of biblical scholars and in countless debates at church meetings. It is this worldview that persuades religious leaders to seek answers to social questions through literal readings of the Bible. It may well be wrong, and it is certainly a product of the history and social context in which it developed. But it is no more a private, personal opinion than the kind of worldview that emerges in supposedly rational, secular contexts.

Once we understand that claims about divine truth emerge through collective, deliberative processes and are subject to modification by those processes, then there is no reason to exclude them from the wider discussions through which democratic decisions are made. To be sure, it becomes more difficult to have these discussions when some of the parties refuse to budge because their truth is God's truth. Yet their very presence should encourage others to defend their own arguments in terms of principle, rather than presenting them simply as personal opinions.

These considerations lead me to conclude that much of the academic wrangling about religion that has taken place of late is on the wrong track. The trouble is not, as many academics seem to believe, that advances toward greater religious and cultural inclusiveness have been hindered mainly by bigots on the religious right. Of course it is easy to demonize groups with whom one disagrees. But American religion has not just been a struggle in recent years between those who wanted to reinvent it and those who wanted to keep it the way it was. The difficulty in moving toward a more inclusive society in which democracy is actually informed by competing religious principles has been deeper and harder to identify because it is ingrained in our culture. Culture is always powerful, and it changes much more slowly than we might think in this fast-paced world of ours. American culture has influenced new immigrant religions in obvious and rather superficial ways: they may hold services in English and may model themselves as churches. But there have also been deeper and more powerful influences. The new is very much like the old in discouraging anyone from arguing in public about religious truth. Doctrines and beliefs are not absent from the lived religions that have always appealed to Americans at the grass roots. There are so many pressures against discussing them, though, that it is sometimes easy to imagine that religion is nothing more than some personal need surrounded by arbitrary customs.

The greater religious diversity that now characterizes the United States would be truly beneficial to American democracy if the various religious communities represented were willing to bring deeply held values that stem from their various traditions to the table for public consideration. Some of these values will be common and will evoke fairly easy agreement; others will be more hotly contested, requiring more debate. If all religious traditions become so highly personalized that each person's faith is purely his or her own, though, the new diversity will not have added much. We will have expanded our cultural borders but encouraged everything within them to look the same.

## CHAPTER 6

# ETHNIC TIES THAT BIND (LOOSELY)

America's collective efforts to become a better nation have in no small measure been concerned with achieving full inclusion for marginalized racial and ethnic groups. These efforts reflect a growing awareness that we must accord greater respect to the distinctive cultural traditions and lifestyles of minority groups. In recent decades, programs focusing on racial and ethnic inclusion have sought not only to overcome discrimination and provide equal opportunities, but also to move beyond older "melting pot" notions that assumed everyone would be like the white Anglo majority. The guiding vision of inclusion has been to supersede the old model of immigration that emphasized *Americanization* with a new model focused on ethnic *pluralism*. Just as we have sought to overcome the view that Catholics were inferior to Protestants, and Jews to Christians, we have moved haltingly toward greater understanding of the cultural integrity and contributions of African Americans and of the many nationalities represented among Latinos and Asian Americans. In this shift of perspectives, ethnicity no longer connotes backwardness or a refusal to fit in. It is assumed to provide personal identity and strength in the face of an uncertain world; ethnicity is a valuable source of community solidarity and social capital. Ethnic organizations help transmit values to children and younger adults, ethnic associations contribute to the well-being of their communities, and ethnic loyalties are an important part of the cultural diversity that we believe enhances learning and makes America an interesting place.

Like the quest for greater understanding of religious differences, the move toward greater appreciation of ethnic diversity has not progressed as far in reality as the ideal of ethnic pluralism would suggest. The culprits inhibiting ethnic pluralism are sometimes identified as white supremacists and political conservatives of all stripes who dig in their heels and resist change; if only these people's prejudices could be overcome, the argument goes, we would be much closer to achieving an equitable, pluralist society. But if that were true, all we would have to do is press on with the fight against prejudice and discrimination. We know there is more to it than that. The forces that have inhibited America from becoming a society in which ethnic diversity is truly valued, I shall argue, are rooted in deep cultural understandings about the priority of individual freedom. These understandings are in turn reinforced by corporate, educational, and political arrangements. To see how powerful those assumptions are, we will need to look more closely at recent ideas about what a pluralist society should be, at evidence concerning the largely symbolic meanings of ethnicity, and at how these interpretations have prevented us from achieving the ideals of community and cultural diversity to which we aspire.

## THE VISION OF A PLURALIST SOCIETY

The ideal of genuine pluralism holds in part that America should be a place where newcomers can find a home and, more than that, be treated as full citizens with all the rights and privileges citizenship bestows. This much of the ideal is deeply ingrained in our national consciousness. It is a principle that has not changed very much from the beginning. The part of this ideal that has received increased emphasis in recent decades is that the members of America's diverse ethnic groups should not have to abandon their distinctive ethnic traditions in order to achieve these rights and privileges. Rather than having to assimilate to the point that they think and behave like white Anglo-Saxon Protestants, the various racial and nationality groups of which the nation is composed are understood to have traditions of their own that should be respected and preserved. The individual citizen is, in this view, not simply an autonomous being with rights bestowed by the Constitution but is a *social* creature whose hopes and aspirations are grounded in families, neighborhoods, congregations, ethnic organizations, and other communities of memory and association. Democracy is thus more than a system for representing the interests of isolated individuals. It is composed of group interests that influence the governing process and that must be given due recognition and protection within this process. More than their formal place in the political process, though, the various groups and organizations of which ethnic subcultures are composed contribute to the enrichment of their members and, collectively, to the well-being of the society as a whole. They do so by giving people a sense of personal identity that links them to traditions and values that transcend their individual lives. They provide social networks on which people can draw for support and to which they can contribute. None of these networks and organizations are coercive. Their members have the right to disengage from them if they so choose. But these ethnic communities do exercise moral influence over their members, creating obligations that are both constraining and rewarding. In principle, ethnically diverse subcultures also provide a safeguard against the society's being overtaken, as it were, by a monolithic cluster of values that might be in the interest of one dominant social class or group, such as the corporate elite or leaders of a particular political party. Moreover, just as with religious diversity, strong cultural representation of diverse ethnic traditions and nationalities is arguably in the nation's political and economic interest insofar as these diverse traditions and nationalities serve as bridges between the United States and the rest of the world. The vision of a pluralist society is thus one in which no single subculture exercises control over the others; in place of hegemony, there is healthy disagreement and cross-communication reflecting the distinctive customs and practices of the diverse communities with which citizens identify.

Putting this ideal into practice has always been difficult. Ethnic and racial minorities continue to be the targets of prejudice and discrimination. Recent statistics compiled by the FBI (which are at best incomplete) show, for instance, that more than four thousand race-based hate crimes and more than two thousand ethnicity- or nationality-based hate crimes are committed each year.[1] Hate crimes may represent an extreme, but surveys show that public opinion toward immigrants is typically fraught with misgiving. In a poll conducted for Fox News, 38 percent of the public thought that "immigrants who come to the United States today help the country and make it a better place to live," while 33 percent said they "hurt the country and make it a worse place to live."[2] My Religion and Diversity Survey showed that 22 percent of the public would *not welcome* Asians' becoming a stronger presence in the United States, and 21 percent said the same about Hispanics—a minority, but notably higher than the 12 percent who gave the same response about African Americans.[3] Judging from the same survey, there is a fairly widespread feeling that immigrants should blend in rather than retaining distinctive customs; for instance, 46 percent of those polled agreed that "foreigners who come to live in America should give up their foreign ways and learn to be like other Americans."

Progress in combating intolerance *has* been made, though. A national study documented a significant reduction between 1990 and 2000 alone in the percentage of white Americans who opposed "living in a neighborhood where half of your neighbors were black" (from 48 percent to 31 percent).[4] Over a longer period, changes in such attitudes have been quite substantial. For instance, 68 percent of white Americans in the early 1940s felt that black and white school children should attend separate schools; by 1995, fewer than 4 percent still felt that way.[5] Polls measuring attitudes toward housing, transportation, and interracial marriage have revealed similar shifts. "The single clearest trend shown in studies of racial attitudes," writes the sociologist Lawrence D. Bobo, is "a steady and sweeping movement toward general endorsement of the principles of racial equality and integration."[6] The factor most responsible for these changes was the civil rights movement and the broader change in cultural climate that accompanied it. The significance of this change is evident in studies comparing the attitudes of older and younger Americans. In one of the most comprehensive of such studies, the sociologist Thomas C. Wilson found that white Americans who came of age after the civil rights movement (after about 1960) were significantly less prejudiced against African Americans than were white Americans who came of age before the civil rights movement. The younger cohorts were also significantly less prejudiced against Hispanics and Asians.[7] Another reason for greater tolerance is familiarity. Although the *prospect* of large numbers of immigrants is perceived as a threat by many native-born Americans, studies show that personal contact with diverse ethnic groups and with immigrants typically reduces intolerance.[8] As intolerance has diminished, gains in ethnic and racial inclusion have also been made, although the pace has often been slow and uneven.

Besides movement toward greater inclusion, the past three decades have witnessed a sharp redefinition of the very terms in which inclusion is discussed. The language of assimilation is no longer as fashionable as it was, while interest in pluralism has grown. Scholars of a previous

generation who wrote about assimilation often described it as an evolu-
tionary process through which immigrants gave up inferior lifestyles
and learned the superior values of American civilization.[9] More recent
defenders of assimilation take a softer approach. They point out that
assimilation is not a one-way street. Immigrants sometimes bring new
ideas that nonimmigrants find attractive; for instance, German beer and
Irish folktales. Soft assimilationists also argue that immigrants happily
go along with being assimilated. They *choose* to marry outside their
ethnic group and raise their children with little exposure to ethnic traditions.[10] Assimilation has been promoted by ethnic leaders as a way of
circumventing the ill effects of discrimination. If Jews and Italians who
lived in ethnic enclaves could easily be identified and thus subjected to
gang warfare, slurs, job discrimination, and political gerrymandering,
then the way to avoid such abuses was to break up these enclaves, scat-
tering their members, and encouraging them to become invisible. Pluralists do not deny that immigrants have been forced to make choices of
these kinds. The pluralist view, however, stresses the costs of assimilation, as well as its benefits, and argues for the added advantages of cultural diversity. For instance, pluralists are less likely than assimilationists to believe that interethnic marriage and moving away from ethnic
communities are simply good ways to achieve better jobs; they worry
about the attendant strains on families and breakdown of communities.
Pluralists, therefore, disagree with assimilationists about the *means*
through which immigrants and other ethnic groups achieve equal rights
and opportunities. For instance, pluralists are more likely to envision
colleges and universities that teach about the accomplishments of various ethnic traditions, whereas assimilationists are more likely to favor a
single core curriculum. In so doing, pluralists argue that knowledge is
constructed by and embedded within cultural traditions. What appears
to an assimilationist as simply a universal truth may appear to a pluralist
as a white, Western European way of thinking.

Pluralists have by no means won these arguments, but they have increasingly set the terms of debate and put old-style assimilationists on
the defensive. Controversies in recent years about curricula in schools
and affirmative action in the workplace have been more about the specific policies through which diversity is to be achieved than about the
principle of diversity itself. The sociologist Nathan Glazer's book *We
Are All Multiculturalists Now* is an apt characterization of the present

situation.[11] Without endorsing many of the specific programs associated with multiculturalism, Glazer argues that the basic premises of cultural pluralism are now widely accepted. As a nation, we officially embrace the value of ethnic and racial diversity. We doubt that it is possible, let alone desirable, to have a society in which everyone is a carbon copy of everyone else. Skin color, gender, and other physical characteristics continue to matter more than we may have imagined they would, and so it becomes necessary to recognize them instead of attempting to live as if they did not exist. In all of this, the continuing significance of racial discrimination against African Americans has been an enormous cultural influence. If race is so deeply implicated in American culture, then it is difficult to conceive of new immigrant groups, such as Asian Americans and Latinos, without racial categories' coming into play—and, indeed, studies show this to be the case, both in how immigrant groups perceive themselves and in how they are perceived. Of course pluralism, especially under the rubric of multiculturalism, has often been oversold and has thus been an easy target for its critics.[12] In some versions, militant multiculturalists argue for total revamping of high school history texts or English department curricula, leading critics to worry that Shakespeare and Milton will no longer be taught. In others, multiculturalism is associated with relativistic views of truth and with agendas that strike even sympathetic critics as paying too much attention to culture and not enough to the harsh realities of employment and housing. "Multiculturalism will not lead to better jobs," the political theorist Jean Bethke Elshtain writes, nor to "higher achievement, decent neighborhoods, safer streets. That demands a political project, not the articulation of racial fantasies."[13] And yet a political project that seeks fair employment and decent housing takes account of racial and ethnic diversity through its very existence.

Where assimilationists and pluralists most clearly part company is on the question of individual freedom. Assimilationists write about people's escaping the bonds of ethnic communities and struggling to break free of parochial and ethnocentric obligations. They believe firmly in a classical liberal view of democracy that emphasizes the rights of individuals to choose their own destinies. Pluralists urge against a watered-down form of ethnicity that gives individuals some of the ceremonial trappings of an ethnic past without encumbering them in any serious way with social obligations. The pluralist perspective is more congruent with associationalist and communitarian views of democracy. It reminds us that we need groups and organizations even to accomplish our most self-interested objectives. Meaningful ethnicity for this reason must be more than an occasional nod of one's ethnic head toward some fond memory of quaint family customs. The idea of pluralism points to the possibility of multiple *cultures* existing in the same society—meaning that groups and organizations need to be present to uphold these cultures. The assimilationist view, to its credit, recognized that such groups and organizations had often existed in the past from sheer necessity. Ethnic communities faced with discrimination and prejudice were forced in on themselves, forming their own organizations in order to defend themselves. But when those external threats diminished, the reason for these organizations also gave way. Finding a way past assimilation to a more authentic form of democratic pluralism has thus meant rethinking the role of ethnic organizations, networks, and other structures capable of maintaining distinctive ethnic cultures.

The desideratum for such structures is their ability to monitor the behavior of individuals in a way that encourages conformity to the norms and values of a particular ethnic tradition. The sociologists Alejandro Portes and Julia Sensenbrenner call this *enforceable trust*.[14] People within ethnic communities trust one another and do so freely and voluntarily, rather than from fear. They trust one another to share the same basic values. At the same time, those who seek benefits from the community without conforming to its expectations can be monitored and encouraged to change their ways. A family member who benefits from his or her parents' sacrifices and then moves away and fails to help his or her parents when they are in need is unlikely to be welcomed warmly at family gatherings. A young person who marries someone against the family's wishes is likely to find it harder to get a job at a cousin's business. A child who skips school may come home to find out that a store owner told a family friend who told the priest who told his or her parents. Through networks of this kind, ethnic identity carries weight.

## THE REALITIES OF SYMBOLIC ETHNICITY

The chief difficulty in realizing the pluralist vision is that achieving success in the wider society often compromises the very networks and organizations through which ethnic loyalties are maintained. Going to college and being an attractive employee of an international corporation require leaving one's parents and neighborhood behind. A person on that trajectory is likely to marry someone from a different ethnic background along the way, and to have no desire to work in a cousin's business. The child who misses school may be doing so to take science lessons with her parents' approval and in direct violation of neighborhood customs. The result is that for the very people who have enough power and wealth to be leaders in their community, ethnicity ceases to be effective in maintaining itself. To the extent that people try to preserve their ethnic heritage, they often do so halfheartedly. Part of them wants to remember the ethnic cooking they loved when they visited their grandparents, while another part would just as soon eat fast food. They may attend an ethnic festival once every few years but would not spend time serving as an officer in an ethnic association. The sociologist Herbert Gans terms this selective appropriation of one's heritage "symbolic ethnicity."[15] It involves preserving the accoutrements of an ethnic tradition without in any way compromising one's personal freedom. Acculturation and assimilation into the mainstream society continue unabated. Symbolic ethnicity is "cost free," Gans writes, in that little time and energy are devoted to maintaining it, and few sacrifices are required in terms of decisions about marriage, where to live, or choice of careers. The fact that ethnic traditions can be maintained in these ways bears testimony to the wider acceptance of pluralistic norms. There is, in a word, latitude for diversity of this kind. If symbolic ethnicity seems shallow, it is nevertheless significant in the lives of those who practice it. They take pride in their ethnic heritage instead of shunning it. Ethnic pride is deeply associated with how people think of themselves and how they relate, in some instances, with others. One's personal identity is more distinctly grounded in family traditions than if one were simply an individual American. A person who practices symbolic ethnicity is not ashamed to belong to an ethnic association or to describe his or her ancestry to friends; at the same time, symbolic ethnicity discourages one from making too much of these personal identities. One would not, for instance, want to feel that a job promotion had been received—or denied—because of one's ethnic identity. In this sense, ethnicity becomes optional; people choose their ethnic identities, sometimes selecting among several ethnicities.[16] The matter of whether or not to identify strongly with an ethnic group is more intentional and less ascriptive. Ethnic organizations resemble other voluntary associations, rather than being necessities of life.

When Gans wrote about symbolic ethnicity in the 1970s, the examples that most readily illustrated it were third- and fourth-generation Jews and Catholics. Those groups' parents had fully assimilated to the point of having lost most of their ethnic identity. Among middle-class third- and fourth-generation Americans, symbolic ethnicity was about all that could be hoped for. It was a way to rediscover one's roots, although the process might involve as little as visiting Ellis Island or constructing one's family tree. Whether the idea of symbolic ethnicity remains applicable in the very different ethnic climate a generation later requires closer consideration. The present period is sufficiently different to suggest that ethnic loyalties among first- and second-generation immigrants should be deeper than they were among third- and fourth-generation immigrants in the 1970s. Like African Americans, Hispanics and Asian Americans experience discrimination based on skin color and other physical features. For this reason alone, ethnic boundaries may be more real than symbolic. At the same time, greater cultural acceptance of diversity opens possibilities for ethnicity to be grounded in behavior and organizations. Studies of ethnic businesses, for instance, show that success is often related to maintaining strong ties with ethnic customers and clients.[17] Research also shows distinct ethnic neighborhood clustering in cities with large immigrant populations, such as Los Angeles, Houston, and Miami—often because of language barriers and low-wage jobs. Another reason for thinking that ethnic identities are easier to maintain now is the ease with which immigrants can return to their countries of origin. Rather than making a clean break with the past, they can be genuinely bicultural. Yet the question that has not been sufficiently addressed is what the ethnic practices are like among immigrants who assimilate into the middle class. Do these immigrants practice symbolic ethnicity, or are they assuming leadership roles in strong ethnic organizations and communities? If their ethnic identity is already mostly symbolic, we might conclude that the pressures associated with assimilation may be stronger and even more quickly encroaching than earlier research suggested.

The New Elites Project has provided an opportunity to examine ethnic practices among an influential, upper-middle-class segment of the immigrant population who, in theory, have the potential to be leaders in promoting ethnic pluralism. Nearly all of these people say they take their ethnic background very seriously. They are proud of it and want it to be respected and preserved. One of the clearest indications of these values is that 87 percent say they want their children to preserve their ethnic heritage. This figure is significantly higher than the 57 percent who say they want their children to have the same religion as they do—an interesting difference in view of a long-held belief among social scientists that religious identities are somehow more acceptable than ethnic ones to maintain over time. The only exception to this pattern, moreover, is the Muslim community, among whom nearly as many want their children to preserve their religious heritage (70 percent) as their ethnic heritage (74 percent). For each of the other major groups—Hindus, Buddhists, Asian Americans, and Hispanics—ethnic heritage matters to a larger number than does religious identity. "I want them to know who they are," says a young mother who grew up in Hong Kong. "It's who they are. Their ancestors. I want them to know their lineage." She hopes her children will grow up liking Chinese food and will one day learn about Chinese history. People are less adamant about wanting their children to preserve religious tradition, in contrast to ethnic tradition, because they believe religion to be guided by a kind of inner light. As I suggested in the previous chapter, religion is privatized. A person can have an inward conviction that leads him or her to change religions. Marrying someone of another faith can lead to an inward conviction of this kind. If that happens, parents understand, perhaps reluctantly, that each person must find God in his or her own way. Ethnicity is not so easily changed. It is deeply connected with parents' hopes that their children will be *like them* and share their values—one of the fundamental principles in pluralist arguments.[18] "I want them to enjoy the things that I grew up enjoying," says a woman of Mexican descent, "like beans and rice and tortillas." Ethnicity is thus about lifestyles and (literally) taste. As pluralists argue, ethnicity is a cluster of preferences that cannot easily be separated from the smells and flavors and sounds of a distinctive ethnic community.

Another indication of the role of ethnicity in contemporary life is how people identify themselves when asked about ethnic labels. The U.S. Census Bureau has acknowledged the importance of such labels in asking more complex census questions about ancestry and race. In the New Elites Project only three people offered responses that denied a distinct ethnic identity of one kind or another: "I don't like the concept [of ethnicity]." "I feel as a human." "Typical American." In view of the assimilationist argument that everyone wants, above all, to be considered *American*, it is interesting that fewer than a third (31 percent) volunteered a phrase that included the word American. Some of these phrases are the ones heard on television or seen in newspapers, such as "Asian American," "Hispanic American," "Korean American," and "Mexican American." Notably, though, these labels more often focus on specific ethnic origins: phrases such as "Pakistani American," "Muslim Egyptian American," "Laotian American," "Sikh American," and "Syrian American" are more typical. The majority who do not include any reference to America simply refer to country of origin or to some other specific ethnic designation. "Argentinean," "Burmese," "Chinese," "Korean," "Mexican," and "Pakistani" are among the labels referring to countries of origin, while more specific labels include "Puerto Rican–Chinese," "Taiwanese-Chinese," and "Buddhist Vietnamese." Both their own identity and what they value for their children, then, suggest that ethnicity is an important dimension of these immigrants' lives.[19]

If preserving one's ethnic heritage is something parents aspire to for their children, though, other values and interests often conflict with what it would take to preserve that heritage. When asked to talk about the values they have tried hardest to instill in their children, these parents seldom mention anything that is distinctly ethnic. "I just want them to be happy," says one parent. "To be fair, open-minded, passionate," says another. Other values that are commonly mentioned include honesty, respect, hard work, and compassion. Only rarely do these people allude to something that might be construed as ethnic loyalty, such as "their heritage," as one person says, or "obeying your elders," in the words of another. What we would probably consider generic or universal values are much more common. "Respect others." "Be fair-minded." "Be honest, friendly, and work hard." This is not to deny the possibility that values such as honesty and respect have ethnic connotations. But if such connotations exist, they are probably communicated more by example than by explicit instruction. The single value that parents emphasize most often when talking about their children—being successful—is also the one that may conflict most with maintaining their ethnic identity. Besides encouraging their children to work hard, these parents also say they do things specifically and deliberately to help their children strike out on their own. They want their children to be independent, to find themselves, and to make maximum use of their talents. "We expose them to everything we can afford," says one parent. Another says she tries to reinforce the "belief that they are unique and have a contribution to make." Others mention encouraging their children to "expand their horizons," exposing them to "different people and ideas," telling them they are "special," and teaching them that the "U.S. is a country of opportunity." These are the kinds of values that encourage young people to seek new horizons and think for themselves, even if that means moving away, choosing a career different from that of anyone in their family, and marrying someone from a different ethnic group or religion. "It's good for children to be well-rounded," the mother from Hong Kong says. She wants her children to study European history as well as Chinese history. Although she wishes her children would learn to speak Chinese, she quit sending them to an after-school language program almost as soon as they started; it conflicted with Scouts.

How is it possible for someone who values ethnic tradition so deeply to give it up so readily? Scouts takes precedence over learning Chinese through a process of mental accommodation that probably even the person herself could not recount. It does involve a serious trade-off, which is why motion pictures and novels about immigrants so often emphasize the struggle to preserve an ethnic heritage in the face of competing alternatives. At a deeper level, though, choosing Scouts over Chinese lessons is easier to understand. This is because ethnicity itself has for many Americans become an expression of something they *liked* while growing up—or came later to realize nostalgically that they wished they had liked. Preserving one's ethnic heritage thus becomes a matter of *enjoying* beans and rice and tortillas, just as one might have a taste for French wine or German cars. A person can enjoy these small pleasures and do very little else reflecting his or her ethnicity. Ethnicity is not an all-or-nothing proposition. If learning Chinese is too demanding, going to a Chinese restaurant can more easily be reconciled with Scouts.

In the past, parents who wished to uphold distinctively ethnic values were always helped by having friends and family who shared these values and traditions. Mama might be easily swayed, but Grandma would staunchly defend the old ways. Mama could thus call in reinforcements from the older generation when she needed them. That image was never quite accurate, for Grandma was not always present. It did reflect the realities of life in ethnic enclaves, though. Nowadays, those coethnic neighbors and extended families are sometimes present but often missing. For instance, a majority of those interviewed (63 percent) said they had some neighbors of the same ethnic background, but only a third (35 percent) said they ever see neighbors of the same ethnic background socially. It is not hard to imagine why this might be the case. The long work hours that most of these people put in mean they have little time to socialize with anybody in their neighborhood. Their career trajectories have also required them to move around, and in many cases they have settled in upscale neighborhoods, rather than remaining in ethnic enclaves.

As for extended families, relationships with parents and siblings are important, and these relationships can be a significant avenue through which distinctive ethnic values and traditions are preserved. Remittances are one of the ways that immigrants stay in contact with their families of origin. Among financially successful immigrants, it is not uncommon for remittances of some kind to be provided to parents or other relatives. In fact, 63 percent of those in the New Elites Project said they had provided financial help to their parents at one time or another. And remittances of this kind appear to be more common among the groups whose parents are least likely to have been financially successful themselves; for instance, 86 percent of the Hispanics said they helped their parents financially, compared with only 48 percent of the Asian American Christians and 59 percent of the Hindus.[20] In most cases, these remittances are not like the arrangements social scientists have studied in which an immigrant working in the United States regularly sends money back to his family in, say, Mexico or El Salvador.[21] The arrangements are more sporadic. "There was a government lien on my parents' house, and my brothers and I hired an attorney to clear that up," recalls a man whose parents immigrated from Mexico. "I helped them out by working when I was in school so they didn't have to buy my clothing," says a woman raised in Mexico, "but I don't help them now." These arrangements demonstrate family loyalty and provide a basis for maintaining ethnic values. It would be an overstatement, though, to say that upwardly mobile first- and second-generation immigrants are tied *closely* to their parents in this way.

Just as with previous immigrants, the current generation that came to America is easily distinguished, by its values and lifestyles, from their counterparts who stayed in their country of origin, and second-generation

Americans' self-image often differs from that of the first-generation group. These differences are evident in the comparisons people draw between themselves and their parents. "I'm much more affluent." "I have money; they didn't." "I have a more comfortable life." "Just a lot more disposable income." "I attend movies and go out for dinner." Having attained financial success, these first- and second-generation immigrants emphasize the opportunities and social class differences that separate them from their parents. They may not boast about how much money they have, but they aren't shy about acknowledging it, either. With financial success also comes greater freedom to be themselves and to pursue what they, as individuals, want, rather than having to follow certain customs and being restrained in their pursuits. "I am very creative and free from society," says one. "I do a lot more personal enrichment things," says another. Other comments also suggest having greater freedom, flexibility, and room for individual decisions. "I have a very flexible lifestyle." "I live the way I want." "We have more freedom." "I have choices in my life."

Having more money, more choices, and a more comfortable lifestyle doesn't mean that people disagree with their parents about everything. Indeed, many of these people say they are not different at all from their parents when it comes to basic values, or they deny having any fundamental disagreements about politics, religion, or other topics on which people often have conflicting opinions. But being more successful and having different experiences does take its toll on family relationships. "My parents and I disagree on just about everything," says one woman. "I'm more flexible in my thinking," says a man who describes his father as being set in his ways. Another says his parents are "old-timers" and thus not very rational in their approach to life. Others acknowledge that there are subjects they just don't talk about with their parents because such discussion would only lead to arguments. The topics on which there seems to have been the most violent disagreement usually involve dating, romantic interests, and marriage. "Mostly who to get married to." "Boy/girl relationships." "Choices of mates." "Dating Caucasian girls." The next most common sources of dispute are conflicts with same-gender parents and clashes involving gender roles. "My mom always says I give away too much," says one woman. "Women's identity, women's role," says another. "Business disagreements with my father," a man says. Another says his father wanted him to be an engineer instead of a doctor. Yet another says his father is much more conservative in his views than he is.

Being of the same generation, immigrants and their siblings are less likely to experience conflict than immigrants and their parents. Yet relationships with siblings vary considerably, depending on whether one's siblings are also immigrants or have remained in their native country, and whether they are also financially successful. Helping siblings financially is much less common than helping parents, for one thing. Only a third (34 percent) of those interviewed say they help their siblings in this way, compared to the nearly two-thirds who have helped their parents.[22] It is also striking how rarely many of these financially successful immigrants visit their siblings. A quarter say they never see their siblings at all, and another 20 percent see any of them only once a year. Of course they may stay in contact by telephone or email. But there is little sense of tight-knit families gathering regularly to celebrate holidays, commemorate anniversaries and birthdays, retell the old stories, and preserve the ethnic customs.

The idea of symbolic ethnicity suggests that people may practice ethnic customs in their homes or by eating occasionally at ethnic restaurants. But what about workplaces? Ethnicity becomes more complicated in these *public* settings. On the one hand, it may be useful to be identified by an ethnic label because the employer has an interest in demonstrating that the organization is inclusive and mindful of diversity. Ethnicity can be useful in less diverse settings, too, because it signals to the organization's clientele that they will find kindred spirits there—people who speak their language, share their customs, and understand their tastes. On the other hand, being labeled as a member of an ethnic group may put one at risk of discrimination in the workplace. Or, because there are relatively few coethnics at the organization, it may simply be easier to downplay or completely hide one's ethnic identity, insofar as this is possible.

How these opposing forces play out can be seen in the fact that 64 percent of these interviewees say that people at work relate to them as a member of their ethnic group, and a majority (53 percent) say that some of their coworkers are of the same ethnic group, compared with only 22 percent who say none or only a few of their coworkers are. Thus there is a kind of ethnic presence or visibility at work that cannot be hidden. Yet a majority (57 percent) also say they have been treated unfairly or discriminated against because of their ethnicity—meaning that some prefer to hide their ethnicity if they can.[23] The typical response to these opposing pressures is to acknowledge one's ethnic identity because it is evident anyway from one's physical appearance, but to emphasize it on some occasions and deny its importance on others. This is simply a way of being flexible about one's identity. It is an aspect of how a person chooses to relate to others, dictated sometimes by circumstances alone, but at times also playing a strategic role in the presentation of oneself. "I have tried not to be pigeonholed as an Indian American," says a government official who grew up in India. "I'm not ashamed of it, but I want to be judged for the quality of work I do." He figures his coworkers surmise his ethnic heritage from how he looks, but it never really comes up in anything they say or do. Another man with a similar background provides a contrast. He is a physician, and about half of his patients are Indian American. He is happy to be identified as Indian American. Besides having an Indian name, he participates actively in an Indian American organization in his community, where he sometimes meets patients or prospective patients. At the same time, he creates distance between himself and this community by participating in other professional organizations and doing pro bono medical work in a low-income neighborhood populated by different ethnic groups.

By saying that ethnicity is sometimes *strategic*, I do not mean to suggest that people consciously manipulate their public persona for self-interested reasons (although that may sometimes be the case). I do mean that people exercise choice in how much or how little they decide to work with coethnics, participate in ethnic organizations, marry endogamously, and raise their children to respect ethnic traditions. Ethnicity is in this sense neither a characteristic that significantly restricts people's decisions nor an obligation to which they are deeply beholden. This has nothing to do with the fact that people from different ethnic backgrounds face different hurdles in attaining higher education or entering prestigious occupations. That much is clear. It is rather *how* ethnicity is worn, managed, and presented within these particular circumstances that is at issue. Ethnic identities typically evoke ambivalence as people describe how they think about these identities. Ethnicity provides roots, but most Americans seem comfortable with keeping those roots shallow. We want portable identities that we can carry with us. Ethnicity is like the family photo album—a collection we take out once in a while to show our children, but not one that takes much time away from the hustle and bustle of daily life.

Comments about being discriminated against and being treated unfairly are probably the most revealing in illuminating how ethnicity
actually constrains behavior—and why these constraints are not perceived as more serious by those experiencing such treatment. The typical
incidents people describe when asked about unfair treatment are associated in their minds with ignorance and insensitivity, not with outright
hostility. They involve stereotypes, such as associating bad food, laziness,
or cunning with a particular ethnic background, or other false assumptions, such as the notion that people from a given country lack certain
skills or interests. These are painful, and there can be no question from
the vividness with which they are remembered and described that they
cut deeply. "We could not speak Spanish in school," says a Latina who
grew up in New Mexico. "There would be things said about Hispanics,
inappropriate things about lazy and uneducated. Being passed over because of the number of vowels in one's last name." Yet these incidents
are usually described in ways that also suggest reconciliation or the ability to transcend them. "I think to a great extent when people feel they're
being treated unfairly," says a Cuban American in Miami, "that it really
is something they drive." He thinks people respect the individual more
than anything else. "If you have a good personality, if you're charismatic, if you're able to not have a chip on your shoulder and present
yourself as an intelligent individual, then people will respect that." Being
strong, he feels, has given him the ability to rise above prejudice. Others
take credit, too, for keeping the ill effects of discrimination at bay. A
Muslim who works for a large electronics firm, for instance, says he just
nips any stereotyping in the bud by confronting people and correcting
whatever they have said. Ironically, the unfair treatment that people
have experienced is sometimes the result of others' going out of their
way to respect ethnic differences. For instance, an Asian American man
says he got a job as a clerk one time early in his career because (he
thinks) the manager thought he would be good with numbers. An Asian
American musician makes a similar point about how she is treated by
the press. "I don't know if it's unfair, but, yes, in a way different." The
press associates being Asian American with being a good musician, she
says, so reviews often mention her ethnicity. Because they have attained
success in their careers, few of the people we spoke to expressed such
bitterness as might be felt by people whose aspirations had been
thwarted. But those who had not been as successful as they had hoped

seldom blamed discrimination, either. "Sometimes the idea comes to me that I have been discriminated against," says a Muslim who came to the United States from India in 1968. "But, honestly, I don't think I was treated unfairly. If I was, I don't think I would have made so much progress." He describes how he was able to attend a Jewish college, even though he was Muslim, and how he has accomplished a lot in his profession, despite not having gone to an elite university. Other Muslims are less sanguine, especially about the climate of opinion in the United States since September 2001. They speak of being called terrorists and of having, as one says, "an uneasy feeling that we are now the enemy." That does not sit well. It makes them worry about how their children will fare at school and whether some crazy person might attack them on the street. Their response, though, is to go on as before. Having an ethnic identity is neither something to hide nor something to wear on one's sleeve. It is just a piece of who one is.

As these examples suggest, ethnic identities among the most recent wave of upwardly mobile American immigrants are meaningful and yet highly negotiable. Passing along very much of an ethnic heritage to one's children proves extremely difficult. Commitments to extended family members are in many cases sporadic. An employer may benefit from hiring someone as a "minority," but being treated as one is undesirable. There are, in fact, strong norms against taking ascriptive characteristics into account in workplace decisions. We want success to be based on achievement, rather than inherited traits. The drive for success, moreover, typically requires ethnic identities to be compromised. Ethnic businesses are often small, and many depend on low-wage labor. The longer immigrants are in the United States and the more training they acquire, therefore, the less likely they are to work with coethnics or depend on ethnic networks to locate jobs.[24] For those who attain higher education, the pressures to abandon ethnic commitments are particularly notable. A person who attends college close to home gives up the advantages gained by someone who "goes away" to an elite university. Being unwilling to give up ethnic holidays or relocate to a new community is likely to restrict career opportunities as well. In place of ethnic identities that truly link people to ethnic networks, neighborhoods, and organizations, then, an ethnicity of symbolism develops that can more easily be accommodated by the marketplace. Ethnic foods and bumper stickers are marketable commodities easily purchased by people who want some ethnic ties, however weak. Ethnic identities in the political arena take on similar characteristics. The white Anglo candidate who speaks a little Spanish is more marketable than the Hispanic candidate who is too easily associated with a "special interest." An entertainer (such as Arnold Schwarzenegger) who can remind voters at the right moments that he or she comes from "immigrant stock" is more likely to be elected than someone who fights for immigrant rights. Despite the efforts that have been made in recent decades to transform America into a more genuinely pluralistic society, therefore, immigrants still feel pressure to assimilate, to fit into a single mold, and to express ethnic variations in largely symbolic ways.

Military strategists point out that commanders sometimes engage the enemy in new battles through the lens of what went wrong in the previous war. One interpretation of the battle plan the United States used in its war against Iraq, for instance, is that it emphasized the overwhelming use of force ("shock and awe") because the military blamed its failure in Vietnam on not deploying enough force. That same interpretation attributes the United States' apparent failure in planning an effective postwar strategy in Iraq to not having had the occasion to need one in Vietnam. Whatever the merits or demerits of these examples, the point is that responses to events are very likely conditioned by responses to previous events.[25] Just so, it is not entirely a coincidence that ethnic diversity is following some of the same patterns that it did in the past. Our nation's history is a history of immigrants and their struggles to thrive in a new land. For that reason alone, we find it easy to consider the recent wave of immigration as just that—the latest in a long series of waves, each fairly similar to all the others. A more specific reason for viewing ethnicity through the lens of the past is that many of the public intellectuals who have written about ethnicity were themselves immigrants or descendants of immigrants and were interested in the topic for this reason. The list of such figures is long and distinguished, including such names as Daniel Patrick Moynihan, Nathan Glazer, Oscar Handlin, Robert Gordon, Michael Novak, Seymour Martin Lipset, and Andrew Greeley. Their contributions have been insightful and have illuminated many of the ways in which recent immigrants face dilemmas similar to those faced by immigrants in the past.

The difficulty arises when attention to the similarities clouds attention to the differences. For instance, the new ethnic communities of the early twentieth century were established against the backdrop of an overwhelmingly white Protestant culture that was not only fairly homogeneous in origin but also wedded to a self-congratulatory history that saw itself as the culmination of an inevitable march of progress toward enlightenment. The prejudice and discrimination against new ethnic groups that resulted in this context were considerable.[26] Assimilation was the solvent that overcame such prejudice and discrimination. For the majority culture, there was less reason for prejudice if it could be shown that new immigrants were becoming Americans "just like us." And for their part, new immigrants learned that blending in was the best way to behave, and that their friends were people who encouraged them to assimilate in this manner. The recent wave of immigration has by no means escaped prejudice and discrimination. It has, however, occurred at a time when overt prejudice and discrimination are less likely to be tolerated by the courts or in simple norms of etiquette and decorum. Blending in to the point of eradicating all but symbolic traces of ethnicity makes less sense under such circumstances than it does when bigotry is rampant. Lessons of the past also become less than helpful when they are used to justify current policies simply by way of analogy. For instance, it may have been the case that the New York City public schools provided no instruction in Jewish history and culture at a time when one-third of the pupils in these schools were Jewish; it may also be true that this neglect stemmed *partly* from the concerns of Jewish parents themselves about negative reactions from Gentiles or about which particular historical and cultural aspects would be emphasized. But that experience alone should not be used as an argument against including Spanish-language instruction or lessons about Asian American history in classrooms now. Against the backdrop of discrimination, it is easy, as assimilationists do, to applaud statistics demonstrating increases in interethnic marriage and geographic dispersion of ethnic populations. It is harder to remember that those statistics fail to reflect social disruptions that may be less beneficial for families and communities than they are for economic advancement.

## THE COSTS OF HALFHEARTEDNESS

Symbolic ethnicity is arguably not such a bad thing. If it didn't work so well, millions of Americans would probably either become more serious about maintaining their ethnic commitments or abandon them altogether. Halfhearted commitments mark many aspects of our daily lives (a little quality time with the children, putting in one's two cents at work). They are ways of hedging our bets. When we need to move on, we can. Stakes are easier to pull up than roots. Yet there are costs associated with our shallow commitments.

The strong pressures encouraging people to assimilate in our society put those who choose not to—or who are unable to—at a decided disadvantage. African Americans provide the clearest example. Racial barriers and de facto residential segregation make it harder for them to achieve economic parity. The black middle class achieves financial success by transcending these barriers. Those who are left behind in segregated neighborhoods may have strong identities but lack access to jobs and social services.[27] The same is true among other ethnic groups. When symbolic ethnicity is so highly valued, it becomes easier to assume that people who choose deeper ethnic or racial bonds are inferior. The way to "help them" is to draw their most talented young people away from their families and neighborhoods. Give them scholarships. Encourage them to attend colleges hundreds of miles away. Encourage them, once they are there, to mix with students from other backgrounds. Inspire them with stories of jobs in different cities and other states. The young person who refuses to play the game is only hurting his or her own chances.

If a person engages strategically with symbolic ethnicity, though, there are costs as well. This is the person who is accused of playing the "race card." The cost incurred comes in the form of cynicism. Symbolic ethnicity is so easily manipulated that it plays easily into the hands of critics who regard it cynically as simply a way of attaining an unfair advantage. The criticism sticks because it points to the better assimilated members of an ethnic group and says their ethnic loyalties are shallow after all. The criticism takes a step further when it becomes a policy recommendation. Have a racially and ethnically blind policy for education and hiring. Let everyone assimilate. Give no special consideration to those who retain deep ethnic loyalties.

Another cost is that genuine learning from participating in different cultures is lost. We give lip service to diversity, but when it comes down to it, cultural differences amount to cigar-store Indians and made-in-China menorahs. Symbolic ethnicity is the kind of token measure that accepts ethnic diversity as long as people all act the same most of the time. "I wish we could get to a time when we think, 'Hey, spice is good,' " says a woman who grew up in Latin America. She envisions a future United States where people are not only free from discrimination because of how they look, but also genuinely valued because they are different. "That's why we put in salt and pepper. Spices are good. Differences are good." Ironically, we are of course a salt-and-pepper society—a culture in which the contrasts between white and black are inescapable. Yet it is the broader mix of aromas and colors that gets lost in this emphasis on white and black. "All of my life I have listened to the black and white conversation, like listening to a quarreling couple through a thin motel wall," complains essayist Richard Rodriguez. What he calls the "browning of America" gets lost in that conversation.[28] So does yellow, as Frank Wu argues in a book by that title.[29] The problem is partly that large segments of white America still prefer to think in assimilationist terms, hoping against hope that a color-blind society can be created, in which all hues seem white. The problem is also that symbolic ethnicity reinforces cultural stereotypes without resulting in the sustained interethnic dialogue that pluralism requires.

Immigrants who have attained educational and occupational success in the United States see another problem. Their families suffer. Children suffer from a lack of parental involvement. Parents are too busy with their careers to spend time with their families. It took enormous commitment to make it to the top in their professions, and now they wonder whether the cost was worth it. "Both parents have to work and, quite frankly," says a Cuban American man, "by the time they get back from work at six o'clock, they're just too pooped to care." He says parents need to help children develop a strong sense of personal identity. When children are not part of a family that maintains its ethnic heritage, they seek other groups as replacements. "They go out with their buddies. They get into a group, and that group becomes their identity." Like generations of upwardly mobile immigrants in the past, these parents worry especially that their children are being spoiled by having a comfortable life. Assimilation produces conformity to mass culture. They look at their children and wonder whether the next generation will know how to work hard for a living or will simply take the comforts of middle-class life for granted. Their children have many more possessions than their parents did at the same age. "My kids, they have so many toys," says a mother of Peruvian ancestry. "If you only have one toy, you value it.

Here, it's so easy to have so much that you don't appreciate what you have." Still, the children seem always to want more. "There is this consumer focus in this country," says a woman of Mexican background. "I don't see that when we visit in Latin America." She says "wanting things in excess" is the biggest problem children face growing up in the United States. It is hard for children to have other values when this is what they see among adults. "Everybody wants the big cars and the big houses," says a man who grew up in Palestine. "Materialism has taken over. It will only lead to greed and dissatisfaction."

These parents are too smart to believe that stronger ethnic ties would necessarily solve these problems. They know that children need certain material possessions to fit in at school and that the mass media constitute too powerful a force for anybody to fight. Yet there is a lingering regret that life is not better. "I wish we were back home in Turkey," says a man who grew up there. He remembers the neighborhoods where children played. He regrets his children's watching so much television here. It is easy to misunderstand such expressions of regret. They sound like nostalgia, a longing to return to the simpler life of one's parents or grandparents, which of course is part of many first-generation immigrants' outlook. That interpretation is on the whole inaccurate, though. What these parents want is forward-looking. It is a vision of an America that truly lives up to an ideal of providing economic opportunities without destroying families and communities in the process. "I just want a quality life with my family," says a woman from India. "I can live in a smaller house. I don't need to have the best of everything. Why go out and earn more and more money if it kills my family?" She looks around her and sees the erosion of family and religion and the moral values that are associated with both. In their place, she sees young men in dirty jeans and college-age women "showing half their buttocks." It is not a pretty sight.

### TOWARD BETTER PRACTICES

The response from assimilationists to concerns like these is that immigrants and their children are free to choose. If they want to maintain ethnic ties, they can start their own voluntary associations. If they dislike what they see at the shopping mall, they can stay home. It is a free country after all; nobody is stopping them. Nathan Glazer, for example, suggests that Latino and Asian American parents could start parochial schools as Irish and Polish Catholics did in the nineteenth and twentieth centuries. Or weekend classes for instruction in ethnic and religious customs the way Jewish parents did. That would be a better solution, he suggests, than trying to incorporate greater respect for ethnic diversity into the public school system.[30] Glazer also argues that, if left to choose, the children of immigrants would probably opt out of their ethnic traditions because "American culture"—by which he apparently means the culture of consumerism ("How can one fight rock and jeans?")—is simply more attractive. Rock music and blue jeans, by this reckoning, are morally and aesthetically neutral compared with anything that might be more authentically ethnic as long as they are freely chosen. One does not have to consider the power of advertising, for instance, or any of the other social and cultural factors shaping such choices. All that matters is the individual.[31]

But this way of thinking emphasizes the positive value of freedom at the expense of considering any other values. It begs the question, freedom to do what? Freedom becomes an end in itself, rather than a means toward achieving greater ends, such as human flourishing, alleviation of suffering and injustice, or better lives for the next generation. People who have not been so thoroughly schooled in the idea that freedom is an end in itself can see more clearly the negative consequences that unrestrained freedom can have. "The great thing about this country is that it offers freedom," says a man who came here from India. "However, I think this country offers so much freedom that you find yourself not having any structure within which to investigate yourself." This is the classic insight that a clear sense of personal identity can be attained only through interaction with others. And not only that. Interaction that is structured enough to provide a stable set of reference points. The reflected self-image that comes back from those reference points is thus stable as well. It is still possible to question the structures in which one lives and to gain individuality through the process of questioning. Individuality of this kind is different from trying to find oneself by absorbing some pieces of identity through casual exposure to a great many different subcultures and groups. It is anchored within a tradition that does impose obligations and is thus limiting, but at the same time teaches one how to honor obligations and how to accept the limitations of which life is inevitably composed. In the absence of such structure, this man says, "you are very free and very lost. You are like water. You can go anywhere, do anything, and just spend your life doing that." The result is that "you spend a great number of years trying to figure out who the hell you are." And by that time you realize you have already lived most of your life.

Policy discussions seldom take very seriously the complaint that people with too much freedom on their hands may spend half their lives finding themselves. Policy making has focused more on the potential problems arising from ethnic loyalties. These problems include conflict between ethnic groups, people's self-interestedly helping members of their own group while ignoring the needs of other groups, mistrust of outsiders, and a lack of cohesion spanning the entire society. A good example of how troublesome these problems can be comes from the political scientist Robert D. Putnam's *Making Democracy Work,* a wide-ranging empirical study of democratic processes in Italy.[32] Putnam found that extended family networks were especially strong in southern Italy. These kinship bonds were in many ways beneficial, for instance, in preserving ethnic customs. However, they did not enhance efforts to promote effective democratic governance in the region. The voluntary associations that drew together more diverse groups in northern Italy were more suited to that purpose. They promoted trust within the wider society and of government officials, reduced cronyism, and encouraged people to participate in democratic elections. The analogous problem in the United States might be gang warfare between groups in tight-knit ethnic neighborhoods. Each gang may be intensely loyal to its ethnic traditions but incapable of working toward the common good.

The public policy implication of such examples is that ethnic loyalties should be discouraged rather than reinforced. The problem with drawing that conclusion, though, is that it fails to take into account the broader social and political structure in which ethnic groups are embedded. Putnam's observations of Italy focused on a particular time in the country's history when an experiment in decentralized democratic government was taking place. The political context in the United States is quite different. Decentralized democratic government has been practiced in the United States for more than two centuries, and there is a strong system of federal laws and institutions preventing tribalism from spinning out of control. Gang warfare in ethnic neighborhoods is no better a source from which to generalize. It exists in a vacuum of economic opportunity and often in the context of weak governing structures for democratic representation and law enforcement. Most of the research on ethnic conflict has focused on its potential for inhibiting democratization processes in developing countries, rather than on its relation to ethnic loyalties in democratic settings. This research nevertheless points to the potential for violent conflict between ethnic groups when ethnic identities are accompanied by extreme economic disparities rooted in discriminatory policies.

Better practices would involve paying more attention to ethnic loyalties, not less, and doing so by focusing on the need for equal provision of services to ethnic neighborhoods. People should not have to choose between living near their extended families and living in safe neighborhoods. They should not have to adopt an itinerant lifestyle to make it in corporate America, especially when companies themselves are decentralizing and conducting more business electronically. Public housing policies should take account of the fact that many people prefer to live in communities with shared values and traditions, rather than being scattered wherever low-income tracts can be built. School policies especially need to consider whether breaking up neighborhoods and encouraging symbolic ethnicity are the best ways to mold America's next generation of citizens and workers. "When immigrant children lose their expressive culture, social cohesion is weakened, parental authority is undermined, and interpersonal relations suffer," writes one observer.[33] No matter how good they may be at communicating instrumental skills, educational programs that strip children of their cultural heritage result in personal loss and social disruption. Magnet schools that draw children out of their neighborhoods need to be rethought. Grant programs to schools in low-income neighborhoods probably need to be expanded. Lessons about the dangers of prejudice and discrimination still need to be taught, but these lessons should be augmented by opportunities to learn more about the distinctive values of one's own ethnic tradition.

How practical might it be for school systems to adopt policies more favorable to the strengthening of ethnic communities? Most of the discussion about ethnicity and schooling has focused on questions about bilingual education and school vouchers. Bilingual education makes sense in some school districts and is entirely impractical in others. Where there is a large Spanish-speaking population in the district, it is hard to see why bilingual education would not be beneficial, both for children whose native language is Spanish and for children whose native language is English. In other districts, where nearly all pupils speak English or where many other languages are represented, bilingual education is harder to defend. School vouchers raise a host of questions that go well beyond those of ethnic pluralism.[34] One objection to school vouchers, though, is directly relevant: school vouchers lead to the balkanization of communities along ethnic lines and, in the extreme, result in the kinds of ethnic violence that have raged in Eastern Europe and North Ireland. That is a specter worth keeping in mind, to be sure. But it is unlikely. The ethnic violence to which critics point in other countries is rooted in histories of political and economic subjugation and has been perpetuated by regimes much less committed to democratic pluralism than the United States. We also need to understand that pro-ethnic school policies are not limited to bilingualism and school vouchers. The essential question is *how* ethnicity is portrayed in textbooks and how it is taught in the classroom. The rainbow approach depicts children of different racial and ethnic backgrounds (usually one representative of each) happily studying together. No matter what the subject matter (Columbus's voyage or slavery), the rainbow students smilingly learn the same lesson and agree on a single interpretation. A truly multicultural approach would go further than simply encouraging cooperation and agreement. It would also evoke discussions of the different interpretations one might have of common events because of one's racial or ethnic background. Even more, a multicultural approach would encourage students to take pride in their particular heritage and to learn more about it.

One of the major hurdles that educators face in the United States is the mass media. Children watch television instead of doing their homework. They are bombarded with thousands of commercials for junk food and toys instead of learning how to think on their own. The "messy media blast," in the words of an interviewee who had grown up in Egypt, exposes children to a constant diet of violence and sex. It is no wonder that teachers more often regard television as their enemy than as their friend. Yet this is a relationship that could be reversed. The media have found ways to deter pornography from finding its way into the hands of children. Tobacco companies have been forced to stop advertising cigarettes to teenagers. Efforts could be made to curb other kinds of socially destructive media. "There is a much better story to tell" than the one about violence and filth, says the man from Egypt. He recognizes the power of narratives rooted in ethnic traditions. Stories about violence and filth are not easily replaced by sterile philosophical arguments. At least not if the human desire for stories is as deep as many educators say it is. Much of what ethnic identity is about, even symbolic ethnicity, is narrative. The ethnic heritage that people express through Chinese or Mexican cooking is also preserved and communicated through stories. Family stories link one's personal history with the history of a people—their struggles to overcome injustice, to survive. These are the stories that convey messages of hope, not the sordid tales that television producers supply.

The complaint that so many first- and second-generation immigrants express about the deterioration of families and family time points to a need for serious rethinking of social policies affecting the family. Many of the pressures that keep parents at work too long to have energy left for parenting are not their own fault. They are pressures built into the norms of corporations and professions. The high divorce rate in the United States is another phenomenon to which many immigrants draw attention. "I see too many separations and too many divorces," says a man of Indian descent whose parents were divorced. "I've gone through that and it's devastating to the child." It is unclear whether divorce rates are any lower when people marry within their own ethnic group. Ethnic groups themselves vary in how much or how little they encourage parents to stay married.[35] But this man has a point worth considering when he suggests that extended families often become more important than ever for the children of divorced parents. "See that there is a family complex so the child has an uncle or a grandmother or cousins," he says. The same point can also be made with respect to intact interethnic families. With more than half of second-generation Latinos and Asian Americans marrying across ethnic lines, every effort should be made to encourage strong ties among extended families.[36] Programs concerned with strengthening ethnic communities would need to begin by resisting efforts to roll back family reunification policies on grounds that they bring in less talented immigrants. These programs would also resist guest worker policies that permit only breadwinners to immigrate, instead of providing schooling and services for whole families. It may be attractive to corporations and taxpayers to benefit from low-wage immigrants without having to cover the costs of services for their families. But family reunification policies have been one of the main ways in which a sense of ethnic identity has been maintained.

Because ethnic identity is fundamentally about culture, it falls, in the final analysis, to cultural institutions to foster efforts to preserve meaningful forms of ethnic identification. Educators, leaders of universities, and heads of neighborhood associations can do more to promote frank discussions of ethnic loyalties. Besides discussions, ethnic studies programs and ethnic student associations are needed in high schools and colleges and at community centers. Religious leaders, too, can play an important role in strengthening ethnic identity through congregational programs. Insofar as the workplace is an important source of identity for many Americans, it also needs to be included in considerations of ethnic diversity. Instead of priding themselves on having token representation of ethnic diversity, employers might want to consider the benefits of hiring coethnics in sufficient numbers to form a critical cultural mass. They might find it in their interest to encourage ethnic interaction as much as they do after-work softball games. The point of such efforts should not be to lock people into ascriptive identities from which they cannot escape. Such efforts should rather focus on the normative judgments built into the idea of being locked in and needing to escape. A society in which pluralism is genuinely valued recognizes that diversity means more than ethnic symbolism. It understands that ethnicity involves social ties and moral obligations—the kind that strengthen and sustain even the most ambitious individuals.

## CHAPTER 7

# SAVING OURSELVES FROM MATERIALISM

One of the more curious developments during the last third of the twentieth century was the coupling of America's fascination with material possessions with our perceptions of new immigrants. This was an ironic connection: the argument was not that new Americans sought material pleasures, but that immigrants' values could restore some sanity to our national psyche. And it was not the most straightforward connection that might have been made, for the period could just as well have been (and often was) described solely in terms of economics. It was one in which hard-nosed critics and even some defenders of the American economy worried that our pursuit of material gratification had gotten the better of us. The 1970s was dubbed a time of narcissism; the 1980s, a decade of greed; and the 1990s, a new Gilded Age, resembling that of the previous fin de siècle in ostentation and excess. The period included the notorious savings and loan scandals of the 1980s and the later fraud-ridden debacles of Enron and WorldCom. It seemed the culmination of what the poet Lawrence Ferlinghetti had earlier described as an America of "bland billboards / illustrating imbecile illusions of happiness / [for] maimed citizens / in painted cars."[1] Only now the imbecile illusions came from cable television infomercials, Internet ad-ware, and electronic spam. Sport-utility vehicles, laptop computers, digital cameras, electronic personal organizers, and cellular telephones all became necessities. Their use became so pervasive, the writer Howard Rheingold observed, that it was hardly surprising to hear about "a Plain order [Amish] businessman who called his stockbroker from his company car phone, pushing three taboos at once past their boundaries."[2] At the same time, the dramatic growth in immigration that took place after

1965 was, among other things, accompanied by arguments that new immigrants would somehow save us from our greedy ways.

## OUTSIDERS AS REDEEMERS

The idea that new immigrants might be the remedy for American materialism was not often in the foreground of public discussion, but it was seldom far in the background, either. The triumph of meanness, as the writer Nicolaus Mills called it, brought out the worst in American culture by combining materialism with bigotry toward immigrants; yet this same cultural shift had a better side, which drew together more critical views of materialism with more favorable attitudes toward newcomers.[3] In this interpretation, new immigrants may have come in search of the American dream, but they were relatively less sullied by the quest for possessions than were the native-born. Immigrants worked harder for what they earned, spent less on luxuries, were less easily swayed by mass marketing, led simpler lives, and cared more for their families. Some of them put European Americans to shame by valuing the sacred above material goods, as a reporter for the *Grand Rapids Press* noted about a Muslim vocal group that put "the Prophet before profit."[4] Most—whether Hispanic, Asian American, or Muslim—were viewed as hardworking breadwinners, motivated more by the need to make ends meet than by aspirations for lavish lifestyles.[5] "I know a lot of Hispanics who are even better people than some of my own family," a ninth-grader wrote to her local newspaper in Georgia. "The reason they get jobs over here is because they are willing to work hard and, not to mention, for less."[6] Advertisers naturally treated new immigrants as new consumers but also cautioned that different appeals would be required. Asian Americans and Hispanics were described as value conscious, traditional, family oriented, and less individualistic than other Americans. "They feel the need to become more involved in the life of their community or neighborhood," counseled one marketing firm. "Therefore, their community events offer excellent opportunities for advertisers."[7] Observers also noted that immigrants would be absorbed into mainstream culture and would thus become materialistic themselves, but in the meantime an open-door policy would help keep American values properly aligned. Comparing immigrants in Miami in the 1990s with those who came in the 1960s, *New*

*York Times* reporter Mireya Navarro emphasized, "The newer immigrants see themselves as less materialistic and money hungry."[8]

The national self-scrutiny that emerged after September 11, 2001, seemed especially sensitive to the accusation that the rest of the world disliked Americans for being too focused on money and possessions. Terrorist attacks, a man from Portland wrote to an on-line chat room, were a way of saying, "you bloody yanks are greedy selfish imbeciles." Patriotism meant denying these images while continuing to go shopping to keep the economy from faltering. "Too many have the wrong idea of Americans as shallow, materialistic consumers who care only about getting rich and getting ahead," President Bush said to a crowd in Atlanta a few weeks after the attacks. "This isn't the America I know."[9] Yet it *was* the America most Americans knew, or at least thought they knew. In one national survey, 82 percent said Americans were "materialistic," and 77 percent said Americans were "self-indulgent."[10]

What Americans meant by *materialism* was better determined from interviews and news commentary than in surveys.[11] Materialism was not the philosophical outlook that scholars might have identified, if asked, but the rather more general view that Americans were somehow caught up in a cycle of getting and spending. The object of this getting and spending was consumer goods and consumer services. And the affect associated with materialism, much more even than with consumerism or consumption, was decidedly pejorative. Qualifiers such as "crass" and "shallow" were common, while words like "vulgar" and "philistine" sometimes surfaced as well. To be materialistic meant that a person was flat, uninteresting, uncultivated, ungenerous, and uncaring. Such a person lived in a kind of cultural wasteland, overpopulated by cheap (or not so cheap) gadgets and purchases that revealed unrefined tastes. To be a materialist might mean having money, living well, and enjoying the latest in consumer goods, but it also implied that one was not a deep thinker, a man or woman of principle, or, for that matter, a very interesting person to be around. Materialists were too much influenced by advertising and the marketplace to have firm convictions or even to be authentic as individuals. At the least, materialists were boring; at the worst, they were immoral, absorbed only with their own gratification, and thus a burden on the world. Saying that Americans were materialistic, whether or not one believed it, was a way of casting aspersions on the national character. It implied that we were, indeed, greedy and selfish.

Just *how* new immigrants would redeem the nation from materialism was a topic on which there was a wide range of views. "Students who enroll in courses in which they study diverse people and their culture," wrote an administrator at Southern Illinois University, would not only "achieve a higher level of satisfaction with college" but also "tend to be less materialistic and more supportive of social change."[12] An observer of Latino immigrants concluded that they were beginning to transform American values by questioning the materialistic messages of television.[13] An expert on Muslim Americans thought their numbers would increase because of Islam's "simplicity."[14] "Liberal society's much-vaunted individualism and materialism are eroding the moral foundations of the West from inside," another scholar wrote. "Muslim piety and practice can help open our eyes to God's real presence among us."[15] Buddhist immigrants were especially interesting because they seemed to lead simple, introspective lives that other Americans could emulate, either by taking up Buddhist-inspired spiritual practices or by learning from the example of Buddhist coworkers and neighbors. "If the focus of the 20th century has been on outer space, the focus of the 21st century may well be on inner space," pollster George Gallup predicted in response to a reporter's question about the potential impact of Buddhism.[16] As far as we know, relatively few Americans actually became Buddhists, yet in a national survey conducted in 2003, fully a quarter (26 percent) of Americans said they found the Buddhist religion "appealing."[17]

The argument that new immigrants can—and should—help move America past the worst aspects of its materialism is part of the broader understanding of America that has come into prominence in the past few decades. This understanding emphasizes that the United States is now a multicultural society and must become even more respectful of its cultural diversity if it is to remain a great power in the world. The role of immigrants in this understanding contrasts sharply with the pattern of assimilation that we recognize in retrospect as the model to which previous waves of immigrants were subjected. In the recent criticisms of that model, immigrants who succeeded economically did so by making a clean break with the past, giving up their distinctive ethnic traditions, and following a unilinear process of assimilation.[18] There was a dominant white Anglo-Saxon Protestant culture to which they were expected to conform. And as they lost touch with their roots, they were thus vulnerable to absorbing the crude materialistic values of the consumer society. The newer understanding suggests that this is an experience that should not be repeated. If multiple cultural traditions are given due respect, then the consumer culture can be held at bay. Ethnic traditions will be preserved, and, paradoxically, the United States will also be in a better position to interact economically and politically with the diverse cultures of the world. "Today there are clear and unequivocal advantages to being able to operate in multiple cultural codes," writes psychologist Marcelo Suarez-Orozco. "There are social, economic, cognitive, and aesthetic advantages to being able to move across cultural spaces." Immigrants and the children of immigrants who can negotiate multiple cultural codes, he argues, will play an essential role in the "remaking" of America within the new global economy.[19]

The idea of immigration as an antidote to materialism is important not so much because a few Americans may have actually adopted different lifestyles, but because it reveals the deep ambivalence within our culture toward the material life itself. This ambivalence has been a recurring theme throughout our history. Indeed, the idea that new immigrants with frugal lifestyles and good values might set America back on track has been just one of many sources to which we have looked for salvation from commerce, spending, and greed. One of the oldest is what historians term the agrarian ideal.[20] Jefferson famously articulated this ideal in a letter to James Madison in 1787 when he wrote that "corruption of morals"—among which he included "the designs of ambition"—is a phenomenon "of which no age nor nation has furnished an example" among the "mass of cultivators." If only America could keep its population employed on the land, Jefferson believed, it would be possible for the "manners and spirit" of the people to preserve a vigorous republic.[21] This is an idea that continues to resonate in the recent "homesteading" movement, about which the historian Rebecca Kneale Gould has written so perceptively, or in the popular writing of Wendell Berry and Kathleen Norris.[22] "America's urban majority, native born or not, might be seen as immigrants to a world of asphalt and cement," Norris writes, "and what they need more than anything is access to the old ways of being. Access to the spirits of land and of place."[23]

Not so different from the agrarian ideal has been the hope that music and art would redeem us. In a 1780 letter to his wife, Abigail, John Adams wrote, "I must study politics and war that my sons may have the liberty to study mathematics and philosophy, geography, natural history, naval architecture, navigation, commerce and agriculture, in order to give their children a right to study painting, poetry, music, architecture, statuary, tapestry and porcelain."[24] The arts were like a millennial dream for Adams, a vision of the Promised Land that he, like Moses, could only view from afar with an expectation of its being realized by generations to come. For subsequent generations, the trade-off between beaux arts and the more mundane worlds of getting and spending has been often imagined and sometimes achieved. Emerson, though hardly a critic of American commerce, wrote of the necessary tension between the quest for beauty—"alive, moving, reproductive"—and the "economical use," the "mercenary impulses," giving the mills, railways, and machinery of his day their "selfish and even cruel aspect."[25] More recently, the poet Greg Glazner is one of many artists and writers who skillfully remind us of the difference between beauty and the distractions of our material possessions. "Here are some diversions," he writes, "buying wealth on credit, boxing, the visionary buzz of brain-damaging substances, alligator shoes, weekend Buddhism, fission, television brain-lock."[26] There is at present some evidence, too, from the American public at large that people who have been more interested in and exposed to the arts are more likely to view materialism as a problem than those with less interest and exposure. For instance, in a national survey conducted in 1999, 69 percent of the public thought "materialism" had become a "serious" or "extremely serious" problem in our society. Among people with the least exposure to the arts, this proportion was 50 percent, while among those with the most exposure, it was 77 percent.[27]

Then, from time to time, we have pinned our hopes for redemption on the ideal woman, or perhaps better, the feminine ideal, the one historians tell us was first expressed in early nineteenth-century discussions of the bourgeois domestic sphere.[28] Private, feminine space was a protected zone, free of the marketplace and therefore of striving; although it was to be comfortable—and therefore outfitted with devices that only money could buy—it was supposed to shield children from the outside world, teaching them simple virtues, while also providing the breadwinner a retreat in which to escape from the potentially corrupting influences of commerce. The ideal woman, above all, created a domestic space in which good manners prevailed. Good manners were very nearly the opposite of paying attention to one's material possessions, especially of flaunting them in the unseemly style that Thorstein Veblen would later refer to as conspicuous consumption.[29] Good manners, Catharine E. Beecher wrote in 1842, were "the expressions of benevolence in personal intercourse by which we endeavor to promote the comfort and enjoyment of others, and to avoid all that gives needless uneasiness." The woman of the house, Beecher wrote, should create an atmosphere emulating the "divine precept" of doing to others as we would have them do to us. There should be "kindly feelings," sympathy, and courtesy.[30] That image of the home as a protected space in which values other than materialism are emphasized has certainly prevailed.

Intermittently, white middle-class Americans have also sought cultural redemption from African Americans. The argument, in bald outline, has been that slavery and discrimination taught African Americans deeper, less materialistic values that white European Americans could do well to emulate. In retrospect, one of the most astonishing expressions of this argument was a 1957 essay that included the following passage:

> Knowing in the cells of his existence that life was war, nothing but war, the Negro (all exceptions admitted) could rarely afford the sophisticated inhibitions of civilization, and so he kept for his survival the art of the primitive, he lived in the enormous present, he subsisted for his Saturday-night kicks, relinquishing the pleasures of the mind for the more obligatory pleasures of the body, and in his music he gave voice to the character and quality of his existence, to his rage and the infinite variations of joy, lust, languor, growl, cramp, pinch, scream, and despair of his orgasm.[31]

These lines were written by the young Norman Mailer in his essay "The White Negro." Mailer argued that the United States—indeed, the West—had become so governed by economic striving and cultural conformity that the only existentialist hope lay in emulating the Negro, becoming, as it were, white Negroes. It was, he wrote, the "hipster" who most clearly did this. "The hipster . . . is rarely an artist, almost never a writer. He may earn his living as a petty criminal, a hobo, a carnival roustabout or a free-lance moving man in Greenwich Village. . . . The hipster [has] absorbed the existentialist synapses of the Negro, and for practical purposes could be considered a white Negro."[32] A half century later, Mailer's remarks seem naive, even crude. And yet African Americans continue to provide white European Americans with a cultural "other"—whether in misreadings of the anthropologist Carol Stack's

*All Our Kin* that erroneously take her study as evidence that extended kinship networks in African American neighborhoods provide a model for living without material goods, or in a recent report on Houston which suggests that African Americans there have learned through hardship to be "more generous and compassionate" and to "make the most of bad situations"—an other from which cultural redemption may be gained.[33]

The common feature of these arguments about the redeeming qualities of immigrants, artists, homemakers, and African Americans is that they all look for cultural solutions from outsiders. To their credit, they view outsiders largely in positive terms, rather than as extraneous material that must be expunged from the body politic. Yet they are the kind of cultural constructions that are typified by the stranger, the Lone Ranger figure, who rides into town to save the townspeople from their own mistakes and ineptitude. "Because he is not bound by roots to the particular constituents and partisan dispositions of the group," the sociologist Georg Simmel wrote, the stranger "confronts all of these with a distinctly 'objective' attitude, an attitude that does not signify mere detachment and nonparticipation, but is a distinct structure composed of remoteness and nearness, indifference and involvement."[34] The outsiders who may save us from materialism are thus people who can understand it better because of having some critical distance from mainstream culture, and who are yet sufficiently assimilated to it, even victimized by it, to appreciate its power.

Whether any of these salvific notions has a connection with reality is largely beside the point. It would be difficult to determine whether immigrants are any less materialistic than native-born Americans; from what little can be learned from public opinion surveys, they probably are not or at least are no more concerned about materialism than other Americans. In one survey, for instance, first-generation Americans were only slightly more likely than other Americans to say materialism was a serious national problem, second-generation Americans showed no differences, Latinos were indistinguishable from white Anglos on the question, and Asian Americans were actually less likely than other respondents to think materialism was a problem.[35] For each image, there is also a corresponding counterimage. African Americans with meager incomes are stereotyped as living above their means to make a statement of well-being to friends and neighbors—what is colloquially known as being "hood rich."[36] Women are stereotyped as compulsive shoppers just as often as they are portrayed as thrifty homemakers. And people who intentionally opt for simple living are accused of spending more money on their lifestyle (purchasing organic foods, hiking equipment, and magazines about simple living) than they would if they lived like everyone else.

## DEEP AMBIVALENCE

With these many ways of searching for alternatives, we need to ask what it is that concerns us so about the materialism of middle-class America. For we do seem to have a troubled relationship with our possessions. We expend a great deal of energy in pursuit of them, and yet we are far from persuaded that these pursuits are worthy of us. One has only to look at opinion polls to see evidence of this deep ambivalence. In one national survey, 78 percent said "selfishness" was a serious problem in our society.[37] Another poll, this one among parents of teenagers, found—perhaps not surprisingly—that more than three-quarters were concerned as parents about the extent of materialism in the society.[38] In yet another survey, this of people with jobs, three people in four said materialism is a serious or extremely serious problem in America, and the same proportion said this about "too much emphasis on money." How much these concerns might matter, though, was debatable, given other responses in the same survey. When asked about their important values in life, 80 percent included "having a high-paying job"; 78 percent, "having a beautiful home, a new car, and other nice things"; 75 percent, "wearing nice clothes"; and 72 percent, "being able to travel for pleasure and see interesting things."[39] In short, we seem to place high value on material goods at the same time that we worry about being overly materialistic.

Ambivalence of this sort raises the possibility that we are, in fact, overly materialistic. *More* than a possibility, some would say; *of course* we are overly materialistic: just look at the cars we drive, the gadgets in our homes, how often we eat out, and so on. But responding this hastily is not helpful. It begs the question of how we might know that the material goods and pleasures—which any right-minded American would admit enjoying—are actually taking too much of our time and attention. Responding so hastily also cuts off discussion of what we mean by materialism, or its absence, and thus prevents us from being more reflective about the place of material goods in our society and in our lives. We need to start by examining several of the more obvious ways of thinking about materialism, if only to recognize their limitations.

One approach to considering how materialistic we are is to look at how much the average household spends each year on goods or services that are, in some way, unnecessary. For instance, we might find it interesting that recent U.S. Labor Department figures show the average household to have spent $2,235 a year eating out, $1,953 on entertainment, $349 on alcoholic beverages, and $308 on tobacco products.[40] A recent book called *Affluenza* takes this approach a step further, observing that we spend more annually on shoes, jewelry, and watches than we do on higher education, and that we have twice as many shopping malls nationally as high schools.[41] If those figures set the stage for arguing that we are indeed a materialistic society that could live with fewer malls or consumer goods, they are probably effective. Yet, in themselves, they may just as well be cause for celebration. Shopping malls are harmless enough as entertainment, provide employment, and help stimulate the economy. One has only to remember President Bush's urging the nation after 9/11 to go shopping, or to consider the argument of a recent book—one with many predecessors—explaining that even God loves American capitalism.[42]

A second approach involves comparisons between the United States and other countries. Such comparisons focus on material goods themselves or on our attitudes toward them and toward ourselves. Good evidence on what we actually do with our money, compared to people in other societies, is surprisingly hard to come by, especially in view of the vast attention our government pays to economic indicators. A few comparisons, though, can illustrate the difficulties we face in trying to assess our nation's attachment to material goods simply from the extent of our possessions. For instance, think again about Howard Rheingold's interest in cell phones as a barometer of material life. According to one report, there were slightly more than 69 million cell phones in the United States. That was one cell phone for every four people—men, women, and children—in America. But was that actually a high proportion? It was higher than in France, where cell phones were only a fifth as numerous as people, but it was lower than in England or Germany, where there were about three-quarters as many cell phones as people. Other consumer items suggest equally complicated conclusions. The number of regular telephones, taking account of differences in population, is only slightly larger in the United States than in England, France, and Germany. The number of radios (averaging about two per person) and televisions (averaging more than one per household) are both substantially higher in the United States than in the other three countries, as is the amount of electricity consumed per capita. Yet the percentages who use the Internet are the same in England as in the United States, although higher than in France and Germany.[43] The differences are more striking again if the ratio of savings to disposable income is taken as a measure of whether people are living at the edge of their means, or exercising more restraint. In the United States, savings rates have consistently been lower over the past two decades than in France and Germany, and since 1995 lower than in England.[44] If we move beyond comparisons with other advanced industrial countries, then of course the picture looks quite different. One especially telling statistic is that carbon dioxide emissions from consumption of fossil fuels in the United States alone accounts for 24 percent of all such emissions in the world.[45] Broader comparisons are sometimes expressed more eloquently, too, in narrative summaries than in statistics. The U.S. Central Intelligence Agency has not always been known for its accuracy, but in its characterization of the U.S. economy, it seemed squarely on target. "In this market-oriented economy," the CIA's *Factbook* observed, "private individuals and business firms make most of the decisions. . . . U.S. business firms enjoy considerably greater flexibility than their counterparts in Western Europe and Japan in decisions to expand capital plant, lay off surplus workers, and develop new products."[46]

If we assume for the moment that the United States is at least as materialistic in reality as other countries, if not more so, then how do we understand surveys that seem to suggest widespread concern about materialism? Is it that we are materialistic and wish we weren't, or is it possible that people in other countries are even more concerned about materialism than we are? During the 1980s and 1990s, surveys were conducted in seventy countries among more than 160,000 people, and one of the questions included in these surveys asked whether "less emphasis on money and material possessions" would be a good development or a bad development. In the United States, 70 percent said this would be a good development, and only 11 percent thought it would be bad. Among all the countries, the 70 percent in the United States was one of the higher proportions favoring less emphasis on material possessions.

And the countries that resembled the United States were also (like the United States) relatively affluent. The pattern was what one of the architects of the survey termed "post-materialism": in other words, having enough possessions to think that having fewer might be a good idea.[47] Yet the surveys left unanswered the question of *why* people with possessions might want fewer, or, if people really thought materialism was such a bad idea, what they might see as the pathway out of it.

From comparative studies, it would also be interesting to know whether people in other countries think Americans are too materialistic. Unfortunately, such questions have not been asked. In one study, though, people in a number of countries were asked whether they thought "consumerism and commercialism" represented a threat to their own culture. This question is interesting in view of anecdotal impressions that people in other countries hold the United States responsible for exporting commercialism.[48] High percentages in nearly every country agreed with the statement. The percentages ranged from 72 in Bolivia, to 65 in Tanzania and 64 in Mexico, to 56 in Guatemala and 53 in India (in this study, Americans themselves were about evenly split on the question of whether commercialism was a cultural threat).[49] International comparisons, therefore, point to a global perception of America as a materialistic society but remain ambiguous with respect to some aspects of the important questions. Some affluent countries spend more on consumer goods than we do, some less; and some are more worried about the ill effects of materialism than we are, but we are more worried than people are in many other countries.

The other way to think critically about American materialism is through comparisons with the past. These are the comparisons implicit in remarks about people's having it easier now than their parents or grandparents did. And if we look back to, say, the Great Depression or even the average American during the Gilded Age, it is easy to find evidence of greater material comfort now than then. For instance, a study by one economist found that expenditures on recreational activities in the United States increased from 1.9 percent of the average family budget in 1890 to 3.2 percent in 1919, staying at roughly the same level until the end of the Depression, and then rose to 5.5 percent by 1991.[50] Recreational activities are not the same as material goods, but the upward trend suggests that Americans have gained more discretionary income to spend on, among other things, consumer goods. An associated

trend has been the growth in recent decades in mass marketing and especially in television advertising. Since more and more people are exposed
to television, researchers have assumed that any effects associated with
television advertising might indicate that things were changing for the
worse. It has been estimated, for instance, that the number of commercials the average child sees annually has doubled since the early 1970s
from 20,000 to 40,000. One reason for this increase is that television
programming devotes more time to commercials—as much as one minute for every minute of program content on many channels. Another
reason is that a quarter of all preschoolers, one-half of all older children,
and two-thirds of all teenagers now have televisions in their bedrooms.[51]
Moreover, a quarter of the nation's schools now subscribe to an in-school
television channel that pipes two minutes of commercials to classrooms
for every ten minutes of content. Research conducted among young children shows that they lack the cognitive development to think critically
about television advertising and that there is a direct relationship between children's exposure to such advertising and their desire for material goods.[52] The burgeoning role of television advertising, together with
increases in disposable income, is probably responsible for the rising
material aspirations of American adults as well. In his book *Living It Up:
Our Love Affair with Luxury,* the writer James B. Twitchell reports, for
instance, that the proportion of Americans who identified owning a vaca-
tion home as part of "the good life" grew from 19 percent in 1975 to 35
percent in 1991; and during this period, the proportion who associated
having a swimming pool with the good life grew from 14 to 29 percent,
while the number holding this view about owning a second color television rose from 10 to 28 percent.[53]

Comparisons with the past, even those involving a relatively short time
span, partly explain why Americans both desire material possessions and
consider this attraction problematic. Our desire has simply grown faster
than our capacity to pay, thus leaving us frustrated and wishing we were
not as materialistic as we are. One survey of U.S. households found that
the level of income needed to fulfill one's dreams doubled between 1986
and 1994 and by the latter date amounted to more than twice the median
household income.[54] There is, however, a longer history of concern about
materialism—evident in John Adams and Catharine Beecher and many
others—that runs deeper than whatever frustration may be associated
with this recent rise in consumer expectations.[55]

A longer-term historical perspective helps to make sense of the view I mentioned earlier that immigrants can somehow save us from too much materialism. There has been a tendency among the descendants of previous waves of immigrants to romanticize the lifestyles and values of their forebears. The religion scholar Will Herberg noted this tendency in the 1950s in citing the historian Marcus Hansen's "law" that what the son forgets, the grandson remembers.[56] Having successfully assimilated, the third generation now found itself without roots—and not only that, but longing for the simpler life, the authenticity, and the wisdom that surely belonged to the generation who immigrated. The historian Beth Wenger notes that by the 1920s Jews in New York City were already feeling nostalgic about the Lower East Side, a neighborhood once "teeming with life and feverish activity, rich in movements and 'isms,' and marked by squalor, poverty, and sordidness, by energy, ambition, and idealism."[57] The historian Jenna Weissman Joselit has noted the same tendency, one fraught with tension in Jewish families of the 1930s who filled their homes with the material "wonders of America" but also sought to remember the old ways of their parents and grandparents.[58] Among American Catholics, idealization of the past and the resultant sense of loss were also evident. Robert Anthony Orsi's study of Italian Harlem between the 1890s and 1940s shows affluent second- and third-generation immigrants returning home from the suburbs to the old neighborhood for the annual *festa* and the authentic domestic values of their mothers and grandmothers.[59] From what we know about the generation who came to America, most of the immigrants themselves were happy enough to see their children and grandchildren adopt the materialistic aspirations of the new country. There was nevertheless regret as well. Part of what they had left behind was a simpler life in which money and possessions did not matter as much. Vito Cacciola was one of many first-generation Americans interviewed in the late 1930s for the Federal Writers' Project. A humble man from Sicily who earned his living repairing shoes, and who spent much of his spare time in his garden and listening to music on the radio, he mused in broken English about people's not singing as much in America as they did in Sicily:

> Maybe its de American custom what spoils de music. . . . De Italians maka more labor in Sicily, but they does not hurry and worry so much. They work in de sunshine with nature. They does not get so

mucha greed and ambition. . . . It is de truth. Nobody singa who must make de payment on automobile and washing machine. Peoples what paya all de time through de nose, maka disharmony when they opens de mouth.[60]

It is perhaps the perceived contrast between a more materialistic present and a more authentic immigrant past that explains our proclivity to connect criticism of materialism with the immigrant experience. Calling for American Catholics to focus more on the poor and less on themselves, the liberation theologian Gustavo Gutierrez notes that the first-generation immigrants built schools and hospitals to help the poor, but then Catholics "moved up the social ladder [and] began to adapt more and more to the prevailing culture of consumerism."[61] His reference to the immigrant experience implies that American Catholics might yet redeem themselves by remembering it.[62] Or we all might do so by remembering that immigration was the taproot of cultural criticism, as former student activists Tom Hayden and Dick Flacks did in an essay in which the social critic C. Wright Mills—a plain home-bred American if ever there was one (a third-generation citizen reared in Texas)—was remembered as a descendant of Irish immigrants.[63] Understandably, there has been a similar yearning for the past in recent discussions of the critical literature written by the generation of Jewish immigrants that included Irving Howe, Isaiah Berlin, Theodor Adorno, and Saul Bellow. "The American Jewish sensibility once was characterized by a skepticism about current conditions," the literary critic Lee Siegel writes. "It . . . was devoid of the cold calculation that wears sentimentality like a fig leaf. It seemed to come from nowhere. American Jewish literary expression had a special kind of ethical beauty; an inconsolable joy; a pregnant mirth drawn out of life's sadness."[64]

## THE NORMATIVE QUESTION

As helpful as comparative and historical approaches may be, I want to suggest that both beg the question that prompts them in the first place. That question is a normative one and, as such, is harder for those who call themselves social scientists to confront directly than to attempt to address through the stealth maneuvers of cross-national and historical comparisons. Yet it is odd that social scientists are reluctant to grapple with *this* normative question when almost everything else they study—inequality, race, gender, public policy—has such clearly discernible normative underpinnings. There has to be some normative standard against which we compare our interest in possessions in order to know whether this interest is somehow askew.

How clearly this normative aspect is present in broader discussions of American culture is evident if we shift momentarily from social science to a different venue. Sermonizing may not have the place it did when Jonathan Edwards or Cotton Mather was the most distinguished figure in his community, but consider what one preacher said recently on the subject at hand:

> Time's up! It is time not to feel bad about being materialistic, but to be less materialistic. We're bombarded all the time with messages out to persuade us that having this or that thing will make us happy, that having stuff is the key to happiness. That's a lie. You know that and I know that. It's time for us to stop living as though that lie were the truth. If you're not happy now, then the new car, the new house, the new sweater, the new CD, the new golf clubs, the new computer will not make you happy. "Retail therapy" is a lie.[65]

This pastor's normative position is unmistakable. He may even have a receptive audience in speaking against materialism from the perspective of religious teachings. Judging from surveys, many Americans perceive a particular trade-off between materialism and religious values. For instance, in one survey, 57 percent of the U.S. public said materialism is a threat to religious faith.[66] In another survey, respondents were asked what would happen if Americans "were to become deeply religious," and 69 percent thought "greed and materialism" would likely decrease.[67] Underlying these sentiments seems to be some general awareness that religious teachings include warnings about excessive emphasis on money. For instance, in another survey, 71 percent agreed that "being greedy is a sin against God."[68] There is, however, a difficulty. Normative criticism, whether in religious or in secular language, ultimately fails if it is not substantively grounded. The principles on which normative criticism rests must be clearly articulated. We do have such principles in our culture, but, as with many other topics on which there is ambivalence, we have found it difficult to think clearly about these principles and thus to identify the normative standard from which our sense of unease about material possessions derives.

This normative standard is not one about which there is universal agreement; it is, nevertheless, widely present within American culture. To identify it, we need to begin by acknowledging how deeply American culture has been influenced, both in its formative period and throughout much of its history, by its religious heritage. "The authentic American Religion," the literary critic Harold Bloom wrote, "rarely proclaims its full knowledge, or its knowledge of the Fullness. And since the American Religion was syncretic, from the start, it can establish itself within nearly any available outward form."[69] Being so adaptable, Bloom reminds us, American religion became not only popular but also introspective, inhabiting private hearts even more than public pulpits. We cannot understand American religion, though, without recognizing the distinctively powerful impetus of biblical tradition, and especially of Protestant Christianity, in the founding sentiments of our nation.

The two principles about material possessions that emerge most clearly from the biblical tradition are those about injustice and idolatry. There is no clearer statement of the principle of justice than in Micah 6:8: "Do justice, love mercy, and walk humbly before your God." Its connection with questions about possessions is equally straightforward: possessions are sinful if they or the means by which they are attained involve oppressing or otherwise harming the poor, the disadvantaged, or the needy. Teachings about idolatry, which find expression in the second commandment, come into vivid relief in Jesus' story about the rich man who built bigger barns only to have his soul required of him the same night, and in Jesus' observation about how difficult it was for a rich person to enter the kingdom of heaven.[70] There is ample reason to think that these were not condemnations of wealth as such but warnings about wealth's taking the place of that which is truly and ultimately holy.

These principles came early to be the basis from which religious and secular leaders alike articulated normative ideas about the proper place of material possessions in American life. Having invoked Catharine Beecher earlier, I want to draw from her widely influential work for an additional illustration. After counseling women of her day at such length about the many domestic duties to which they should attend, Beecher wrote:

[I]t is sometimes the case that a woman will count among the *necessaries* of life all the various modes of adorning the person or house practiced in the circle in which she moves; and after enumerating the many *duties* which demand attention, counting these as a part, she will come to the conclusion that she has no time, and but little money, to devote to personal improvement or to benevolent enterprises. This surely is not in agreement with the requirements of the Saviour, who calls on us to seek for others as well as ourselves, *first of all*, 'the kingdom of God and his righteousness.'[71]

Beecher touches here on the need to be charitable, about which she subsequently writes more, but her statement pertains mostly to keeping the "necessaries of life" properly subdued to the "kingdom of God."

In Beecher's contemporary, Abraham Lincoln, there is recurrent recourse to the principle of justice. Lincoln's opposition to slavery is, more than anything else, grounded in the conviction that it is an unjust means of attaining material goods. "It may seem strange that any men should dare to ask a just God's assistance in wringing their bread from the sweat of other men's faces," Lincoln declared in his second inaugural address. "But let us judge not, that we be not judged," he added with unmistakable irony. The next lines mince no words in applying the principle of justice to slavery. "Woe unto the world because of offenses; for it must needs be that offenses come, but woe to that man by whom the offense cometh," Lincoln quotes. Then, referring to the "terrible war" in which the nation has so long been engaged, he proclaims, "If God wills that it continue until all the wealth piled by the bondsman's two hundred and fifty years of unrequited toil shall be sunk, and until every drop of blood drawn with the lash shall be paid by another drawn with the sword, as was said three thousand years ago, so still it must be said 'the judgments of the Lord are true and righteous altogether.' "[72] Lincoln was not a churchgoer and did not consider himself a Christian, as historian Mark A. Noll has recently reminded us, but the biblical language, and even its cadence, were indelibly imprinted in Lincoln's thinking about justice.[73]

For those educated in the twentieth and twenty-first centuries, it is perhaps more common to seek principles for judging the propriety or impropriety of economic behavior in secular sources than in biblical traditions. Those schooled in social theory need look no further than the writings of Karl Marx and Max Weber. Especially in his earlier work,

Marx brought to the fore, as no writer before him had, the harsh realities through which the fortunes of the "haves" are linked with the immiseration, as he called it, of the "have-nots." We need to remember that Marx was profoundly concerned with the problem of alienation in modern societies—alienation from our work, from those around us, and from ourselves.[74] Fundamentally, he believed, alienation resulted from injustice, which, in market economies, was exacerbated by the desire for profit, by the accumulation of wealth among the few, and by the tacit and overt exploitation of the many. Marx's ideas for many reasons proved unattractive in the United States, and yet for a time variant expressions of concern about social class and economic injustice were evident in such widely diverse contexts as agrarian populism, syndicalism, utopian socialism, and so-called Marxian-Christian social movements. Weber, too, was profoundly interested in the normative implications of economic behavior, devoting much of his prodigious energy to writing about the complexes of meaning through which economic behavior was motivated and made to seem obligatory. Toward the end of his famous treatise on the Protestant ethic and the spirit of capitalism Weber wrote, "Material goods have gained an increasing and finally an inexorable power over the lives of men as at no previous period in history."[75] This statement comes just after Weber's much-quoted observation about modern economic life's becoming an iron cage, and it is in this light that the statement must be interpreted. The Puritans, Weber argued, regarded their work as a calling and thus viewed it as a means to an end, or what he elsewhere termed *wertrational* (value-rational) action, whereas in his own era, work was an end in itself, or *zweckrational* (means-rational) action, in which the availability of means was all that mattered.[76] Weber thought this substitution of material acquisition for higher-order values had reached its pinnacle in America. "In the field of its highest development," he wrote, "in the United States, the pursuit of wealth, stripped of its religious and ethical meaning, tends to become associated with purely mundane passions, which often actually give it the character of sport."[77]

Weber's reference to material pursuits' taking on "the character of sport" reminds us that normative judgment is far different from the lighthearted tongue-in-cheek commentary that usually passes for cultural criticism of American materialism. Such commentary expresses its disdain for materialists on aesthetic grounds, pointing out that they spend money on imitation art instead of the real thing, or that they make boring conversationalists at parties. Humorous depictions of materialists can create a new perspective that opens the door for normative criticism, but it often falls short of the mark by attempting to please the very consumers it criticizes. When the problem with materialism is only one of bad taste, marketing specialists are all too ready to counter that bad taste is still simply a matter of personal preference, or to respond with new consumer products marketed at higher prices because they represent more refined tastes. Packaging being what it is, new slogans with different adjectives may fill the bill. Old words signaling good taste, such as "respectable, decorous, opulent, luxurious, elegant, splendid, dignified, magnificent, and extravagant," journalist David Brooks writes, have been replaced by new words, such as "authentic, natural, warm, rustic, simple, honest, organic, comfortable, craftsmanlike, unique, sensible, sincere."[78] The new elite, he observes, continues shopping, but avoids feeling materialistic by using the new vocabulary. Rendering moralistic judgments about such matters seems, well, moralistic and old-fashioned.

But unless we dismiss them as simply the manners of a bygone era, injustice and idolatry are two criteria against which to evaluate the social role of material goods and the pursuit of these goods. At whatever the level of abundance or lack thereof, possessions acquired in ways that produce injustice or that become ends in themselves are normatively problematic. These are moral concerns, insofar as they pertain to the lives of individuals, and ethical concerns, insofar as they pose problems for our relations with one another. Indeed, considerations about injustice and idolatry also bring us back, as so many contemporary social issues do, to basic questions about the vitality of democracy. If the pursuit of material goods is not accompanied by a strong collective commitment to justice, an oligarchic concentration of power of the kind that worried Tocqueville is the likely result. And once the quest for possessions becomes an end in itself, democracy is endangered because the culture has no higher values by which to set its priorities than conformity to the same standards of acquisition. "If this process of leveling down . . . is allowed to continue," the Norwegian immigrant Ole Edvart Rolvaag wrote in the 1920s, "America is doomed to become the most impoverished land spiritually on the face of the earth; out of our highly praised melting pot will come a dull . . . smug complacency, barren of all creative thought. . . . Soon we will have reached the perfect democracy of barrenness. . . . Dead will be the hidden life of the heart which is nourished by tradition, the idioms of language, and our attitude to life. It is out of these elements that character grows."[79]

The "culture of consumption," as the historian T. J. Jackson Lears called it, has proven more capable, though, of sustaining ethnic diversity than Rolvaag imagined it could.[80] Although there is a sense in which American culture has become a "democracy of barrenness" (as chain stores and fast food franchises so clearly illustrate), the American consumer can also spend a small fortune attending ethnic festivals, eating at ethnic restaurants, purchasing ethnic music and art, traveling to his or her country of origin, or decorating the home with more distinctive, traditional, and therefore presumably "more authentic" furnishings. Consumer markets are, in fact, quite good at fulfilling, if not also cultivating, diverse tastes. It is rather when the logic of the marketplace becomes the dominant feature of our culture that we must worry.

Marketplace thinking, much like air and water, is such a part of our existence that it is hard to fully appreciate our dependence on it. One reason for this is that we in the United States have been the beneficiaries of an expanding global economy in which inexpensive consumer goods are produced abroad. This, along with technological development, has meant that basic necessities, such as food and clothing, constitute a smaller share of the average family budget than was true in the past, and thus seem easier to attain. In 1890 food and apparel alone accounted for 61 percent of the typical family budget, whereas by 1991 this proportion had fallen to 26 percent.[81] Although some of this decline resulted from higher standards of living in general and from smaller households, specific items also cost less. For instance, in 1890 a five-pound bag of sugar cost 34 cents; in 1970, it cost 65 cents, or about twice as much, whereas average family incomes over the same period had risen by a multiple of four. In 1920 a dozen oranges sold for 63 cents; in 1970 the price, at 86 cents, was only slightly higher. In 1912 a pair of men's trousers cost $2.95: if the price had kept pace with average incomes, they would have cost almost $600 in 2003 instead of a tenth or twentieth of that amount.

In the earlier period, the high cost of consumer goods relative to the low earnings of working Americans was enough to provoke periodic efforts at grassroots mobilization to resist what was viewed as economic injustice. One of these now largely forgotten efforts was the Farmers Alliance, a collective bargaining movement that began in several scattered locations in the 1870s and became a national organization in 1890, enlisting as many as a third of the farm population in some states. A meeting in Lyons, Kansas, in 1888—a town of only 500 people at the time—drew representatives from 600 of the 1,200 local organizations with a combined membership of 70,000 throughout the state.[82] The movement attracted members persuaded that collective action was necessary to combat economic injustice. "They say the money trusts, corporations, and monopolies are sucking [their] life blood," a reporter in Kansas wrote for the *New York Times* in 1889. "The farmer must pay ruinous prices for everything he buys and get next to nothing for everything he sells; he sells corn at 17 cents per bushel and then buys it back in the form of meal at about $1.20 per bushel," and just so with sugar, wheat, and flour.[83] The Farmers Alliance lasted only a few years and achieved none of its immediate aims. Subsequent efforts, though, sometimes fared better. For instance, grassroots movements in the 1920s and 1930s were successful in banning corporate farming in Kansas for more than forty years and chain stores for nearly as long.[84]

The story of the Farmers Alliance illustrates another lesson that we risk ignoring at our peril: economic history is nearly always a struggle in which the powerful triumph over the weak. At about the same time that the Farmers Alliance was emerging, huge reservoirs of minerals, especially salt and oil, were discovered in the midwestern states. Within a few years, most of these resources were in the hands of giant trusts that bought up small businesses and drove into bankruptcy the ones that refused to sell. The trusts were eventually outlawed, of course, for powerful as they were, they were largely located within the territorial United States and thus subject to legislative action. It is much less clear how the workers today who toil at subsistence wages in Bangladesh or Peru, making clothing for American consumers, might achieve greater equity. This dimension of our relationship with possessions is easy to overlook and convenient to neglect.

One might wonder, though, within our own borders, why more attention is not paid to questions of injustice. Corporate mergers have concentrated greater power in the hands of a few, while the decline of labor unions and the self-disenfranchisement of the poor have weakened the political hand of those at the bottom. Economists point out that the richest Americans have grown even richer in the past few decades while families at the bottom are earning less. One study, for instance, showed that between 1983 and 1998 the average wealth of America's richest 1 percent grew by 42 percent, while that of the bottom 40 percent shrank by almost 77 percent.[85] The standard summary measure of income inequality in the United States is also higher than in other countries with similar economies and governments.[86] Discussions of materialism seldom pay much attention to these realities, however, except to note that everyone would like to be more like the rich. The same economists who provide this information argue that extreme inequality of this kind is simply the price of freedom—and that if entrepreneurs earned less, they would simply take their business to some other country where the profits would be better.

## SELF-SERVING REDEMPTIONISM

The idolatry of the consumer mentality is not easy to confront, either. We might seriously underestimate it, especially if the absence of idolatry is taken to mean worshiping God rather than mammon. The vast number of churches and synagogues, mosques, temples, and fellowship halls to which so many Americans flock would seem to indicate that we are a society in which obeisance to something other than the material life is routinely made. That conclusion is less convincing, though, when we consider the great extent to which American religion has become, in the sociologist Wade Clark Roof's apt phrase, a spiritual marketplace.[87] When marketplace thinking invades the sanctuary, the norms by which we make consumer purchases govern how we behave spiritually as well. What matters is not truth but gratification. Religious commitment ebbs and flows, Roof finds, as life events and personal needs dictate. The need to worship is driven not by a numinous sense of the holy, but by the feeling that this may be good for one's personal well-being. Whatever sense of cultural redemption may remain in this kind of religion, it is best characterized as what the theologian Murray Joseph Haar calls "self-serving redemptionism." In Haar's view, historic teachings about divine authority, salvation, and forgiveness are now adhered to, if they have meaning at all, "because I find that it benefits 'me.'"[88]

When they work well, religious congregations function as communities of obligation, not as spaces for individual gratification. Communities of obligation pose expectations to which individuals voluntarily submit, and which over time become such a part of individuals' identities that they are, in a sense, binding. In her book *The Overspent American: Why We Want What We Don't Need*, the sociologist Juliet Schor argues that Americans have succumbed to overspending because they no longer have strong reference groups that help keep their material desires within bounds.[89] The typical reference point, she argues, used to be the Joneses down the block who probably earned about as much as we did, whereas now the Joneses live in Aspen or Beverly Hills. Congregations were once a reference group of that kind, too. They were composed of Norwegian farmers in Minnesota, Welsh miners in Pennsylvania, or Baptist sharecroppers in Mississippi. The typical congregation almost always included a few members who were better off financially than the others. But knowing each other and worshiping together also meant knowing one's place in the economic hierarchy. In these tightly knit communities, people did not have to talk very much about their money or their purchases; everything was in easy reach of the local gossip network. All that has changed. If people are still reluctant to talk about their finances (and we know that is the case), then their financial decisions can truly be matters of the heart.[90] Instead of being guided by one's reference group, decisions about getting and spending can be shaped entirely by advertising. Congregations that seek to be reference groups for lifestyles and financial considerations must therefore work harder now to be effective. Some create a kind of counterculture in which simplicity and service are rewarded; others divide attendees into small homogeneous groups and encourage them to pray about their financial problems and hold one another accountable. The difficulty with all such reference groups—small groups, congregations, neighborhoods, or extended families—is that they are now much harder to maintain. People aspire to be like the Joneses in Beverly Hills not because their own neighborhoods have broken down (although they may have), but because television daily bombards us with images of those Joneses in order to mold us into consumers. Immigrant enclaves and the better values that might be inspired by these enclaves are weak in comparison.

It is nevertheless the dim awareness that material acquisition, or even personal happiness, is not the ultimate standard against which to evaluate life that remains as the cultural residue of admonitions against idolatry. The suspicion that artistic pursuits, the home, and the hardships endured by immigrants hold meaning that cannot be reduced to material goods stems from this awareness. Were that suspicion to be lost, the consumer industry would have prevailed and yet would have lost its soul in the process. The love-hate relationship we have with our possessions at least inspires the token unease with the marketplace that keeps advertisers busy trying to conquer.

As America has reinvented itself and in the process become more self-consciously diverse and inclusive, it has thus remained as deeply ambivalent about its materialism as ever. The hope that new immigrants will somehow redeem the nation from its fascination with possessions—by retaining stronger family ties or by working harder and living more simply—seems as unlikely to be realized as was the faith in homesteaders, artists, or hipsters. The ease and frequency with which Americans of all ethnic backgrounds, ages, and incomes are besieged with opportunities for material gratification makes it nearly impossible to reflect for long on considerations of injustice or idolatry. Ambivalence is always dangerously precarious, too. The saviors to whom we look for help in overcoming materialism at one moment are the saviors we crucify at another. Hipsters become deadbeats, family-minded poor people become welfare chiselers, and hardworking immigrants become aliens intent on stealing our jobs.

Confronting injustice and idolatry is also difficult because it runs counter to what the marketplace teaches about good economics. Buying cheap and selling dear is easier to do if the poor are not organized. Focusing too much on injustice could sow the seeds of organization and power. Socially responsible investing may be attractive as long as it is as profitable as socially irresponsible investing, but deeper reasons than profitability may be harder to find in a culture that attaches so much emphasis to the bottom line. If the hope is simply that immigrants, the poor, or some other marginalized group will supply alternative values, then those values can easily be turned into consumer preferences and new markets. Subordinating money to happiness is not such a bad deal for the American economy, either, as long as the pursuit of happiness still requires spending money. But if the avoidance of idolatry means dramatically reducing one's participation in the marketplace, that choice clearly becomes more difficult for most Americans to consider.

Materialism is at its worst when it crowds out thinking about the larger realities in which we live. It is not so much that shopping takes more of our time, although it does, as that the getting-and-spending cycle envelops us in an all-encompassing logic of material gratification.[91] Immersed in short-term calculations, we find it harder to think critically about ourselves. Possessed by the quest for possessions, we are less able to reckon with the global relationships that make these possessions possible. Our new empire, Lawrence Ferlinghetti writes, has become "vaster than any in ancient days" but is likely to be remembered only for "carrying its corporate monoculture around the world."[92] Materialism lulls our conscience into a collective slumber. "Awaken now at last," Ferlinghetti writes, "And tell us how to save us from ourselves."

## CHAPTER 8

# VENUES FOR REFLECTIVE DEMOCRACY

T he cultural assumptions around which a society is organized provide stability to that society. These assumptions influence how we
think about individual responsibility, our roles as citizens, and our nation's place in the world. Although there are differing views in the
United States about how much or how little we should emphasize our
individuality, we are a society that takes our rights and freedoms as individuals very seriously. These rights and freedoms form the basis for
assumptions about moral obligations to ourselves and to one another.
Just as it is common for us to insist on individual autonomy in making
decisions about our lives, so it is generally accepted that *individuals*
should make up their own minds about what they should or should not
do, and should be rewarded accordingly. The connection between these
individual moral obligations and our understanding of democracy is
strong. We understand democracy to be diminished when a few individuals exercise too much control of government or when the majority
holds such monolithic views that diversity is weakened and the rights of
minorities are endangered.

An even deeper bond between the individual and society exists in our
cultural mythology. An anthropomorphic view of the nation likens its
role among other nations to that of the individual. Conceptions of justice
follow. Insofar as individual sacrifices have been made on behalf of the
nation, whether by fallen military heroes or struggling immigrants, the
collective privileges that the nation enjoys are culturally justified. Understandings of inequality within the society follow a similar logic. Success and the extraordinary rewards that come to some successful people
are morally justified by the effort from which success presumably re-

sults. The self-made American is a cultural trope that symbolizes and reinforces the pervasive belief that success stems not from chance but from hard work.

The United States is characterized by other powerful assumptions about religion and ethnicity. Religion is not only deeply embedded in the organizational fabric of our communities. It is a source of national pride, especially in our apparent capacity to embrace religious freedom by encouraging religious diversity. So with ethnicity. It is a source of cultural diversity, providing a sense of roots and belonging, even if these roots are shallow and the belonging consists of fungible attachments. Another component of our national mythology shapes our collective thinking about America's love affair with materialism, simultaneously encouraging us to be a society of consumers and allowing us to deny that we are.

The stability that accrues from these and other deeply held assumptions is of great benefit to the functioning of our society. The stories in which these assumptions are instantiated connect the present with the past. The narratives are the magnets around which narrative communities form—networks of people who share the same stories, identify themselves with these stories, and through them gain the capacity to remember. It is in this sense that we speak of tradition.[1] The narratives are more than rational arguments or intellectual knowledge and, as such, require a different kind of understanding from that usually suggested in discussions of political philosophy. The deep narratives of a society serve less as arguments and more as the context in which arguments take place. They point to an ambience of lived experience. They tell of national origins, ethnic customs, extended families, religious practices, and individual struggles and accomplishments. They are an ongoing part of our lived experience to the point that we are often reluctant to objectify them under the rubric of tradition. They are more the tacit ways in which we approach the world. They seem natural. Yet they are frequently anything but natural, at least if that means inevitable or simply the accumulation of human experience. The ambience of daily life is also produced—increasingly by the mass media and, through them, by the interests of large corporations or powerful individuals. Images of luxury automobiles are as common as images of motherhood and apple pie.

Some of these assumptions inform our understanding of the nation in which we live, telling us that America is a good place and worthy of our loyalty and admiration. These are sometimes called nationalistic assumptions, because they draw boundaries between our own nation and others. It is common for the narratives of our nation and ourselves to include references to religion ("God bless America"); for this reason, the term "civil religion" is sometimes used to describe them. The civil religion links the nation and its citizens to a divine purpose. Yet the deep assumptions on which social stability rests are at once more and less than terms such as nationalism and civil religion imply. The shared assumptions that give coherence to our society are about individuals and ethnic groups and communities, as well as about the nation itself. They are all-encompassing in that sense.

These shared assumptions are also less grandiose than often described. They are not philosophies of life or worldviews as much as they are fragments of experience. It is through the idioms of speech, the casual conversations we remember from childhood, the small rituals of daily life, and the stories we read or hear that we come to participate in the common aspects of our culture. These tacit understandings not only make it possible to communicate with others or to go through the day without having to think much about what we are doing. They also guide our institutions, giving moral meaning to events and providing community leaders with the public rhetoric required to elicit approval. Our best intentions are often rooted in these tacit understandings. We want our shared lives to approximate the ideals communicated in our stories.

However, the shared meanings around which a society is organized also limit its capacity to change and, for that matter, to realize its ideals. Sometimes these meanings hang heavily like the dead weight of the past. They are assumptions from a horse-drawn era that need to be superseded with new modes of transportation. Just as commonly, though, they are traditions and values that are worthy of preservation. If they are not to be a drag on our ability to achieve our aspirations, they need rejuvenation. They are assumptions that would work well again if they were better understood or applied in new ways to present conditions.

The trouble is that public discussion focuses so much on particular issues and policies that we fail to see what our underlying assumptions are. We struggle to move forward but fall short and wonder why. The problem is not that we have failed to commit sufficient resources. It is that we have gone forward without examining our assumptions. Thus we shoulder great and worthy tasks as a nation, such as welcoming new immigrants, ridding ourselves of racial and ethnic intolerance, rebuilding our communities, and renewing our commitment to democracy, only to find that we are not as welcoming or tolerant as we thought—that we are more individualistic, and even more dependent on the rich and powerful than we imagined.

To remedy cultural drag of this kind, we must be more deliberately reflective about our cultural assumptions. Reflection means looking beneath the surface, beyond the signifier to the signified, to the meanings that are implied as well as to those that are explicit. The story of a self-made billionaire may be inspiring, but why? It may be reassuring when a public official declares us to be waging a war for freedom and democracy or concludes an address by asking that God continue to bless America. Those, in fact, may be the more powerful messages, more so than information about a particular program or policy. Why are they powerful? When it seems obvious that success is the result of hard work, or that our communities would be stronger if people were less selfish, why do we think this way?

A reflective democracy is one in which individual citizens in their personal lives and in their life together devote effort to examining the cultural assumptions on which their behavior rests and is justified. A reflective democracy is more than just a republic of informed citizens. Being informed usually means knowing what is going on in the news or who one's public officials are and how they stand on various issues. Going a step further, informed citizens are people who do not engage in ill-considered judgments: they think long and hard about whether a particular dam should be built or a particular candidate should be elected. However, what I have in mind goes beyond these common usages of the term. Reflective democracy is more concerned with *why* we think certain actions are legitimate. It shifts attention, as some point out, to the society's goals and values, and is thus an antidote to the kind of thinking that focuses only on technology, costs and benefits, and efficiency. Reflective democracy focuses on the reasons public officials or private individuals give for their behavior—not, as is common in some circles, to determine only whether those reasons can withstand the test of rational logic, important as that is, but also to evoke the unstated reasons that guide behavior without our even realizing that this is the case.

Reflective democracy is something like the analysis of a great work of literature, probing it critically from different perspectives to understand

more clearly what is being said or not said, only here the work of literature is the text of our collective life. As with the analysis of literature,
reflection of this kind assumes that there is more to the story than meets
the eye. The story makes sense because it presents characters who are
recognizably good or evil, or because it plays on our fears or appeals to
our dreams. The plot consists of more than discrete episodes; it weaves
them together to form a meaningful whole. To engage in reflective democracy is thus to ponder. It involves thinking about the questions behind the headlines and putting oneself in venues where such thinking
benefits from the presence of others.

Some of what constitutes reflective democracy must be done alone.
We neglect this important aspect of democracy when we imagine, as
social scientists often do, that democracy is furthered only by getting
people out of their homes to work with others on political issues. Reflection is like doing one's homework in this respect. It consists of time away
from the hurried pace of public life—time to engage in introspection
about what truly matters in life and what the implications of those values
are for how one behaves as a citizen.[2] However, reflection is never effective if it is done only in isolation. We are social beings who take our cues
from others. We are influenced by what we learned as children from our
families, and by the casual remarks we overhear at work, and by the
images we see on television. This is why reflective democracy benefits
when we put ourselves intentionally in venues that prompt discussion
of our collective values.

Such venues are actually more abundant than we might realize. Although the price of living in a relatively affluent society is often having
too little time to do what we want, the benefit of affluence is that there
are opportunities to study, to think, and to deliberate with others. These
opportunities are especially encouraged in such venues as the town
meetings and other public forums we sometimes refer to as venues for
deliberative democracy. They occur in voluntary associations and in educational settings. And on the largest scale, they are provided by the mass
media and the entertainment industry. In each of these settings, however, there are challenges. Discussions are held and information is presented, but often without the kind of probing that truly facilitates reflective democracy. The challenge is to understand what goes on in these
settings so that this activity can effectively be nudged further in the
direction of reflective democracy.

Before we can consider the venues in which reflective democracy can take place, though, we need to consider two possible objections to the idea of reflective democracy itself. One objection is that too much examination of the taken-for-granted assumptions on which a society rests can be fundamentally destabilizing. In this view, it is not merely accidental that we do not often examine the deep meanings of social life; it is essential that we do not. Doing so would be disruptive of daily routines, just as obsessively pondering the norms governing driving down the highway might get in the way of actually being a good driver. The reason we take assumptions for granted is so that behavior can become habitual and thus effective in its very unreflectiveness. But this argument makes sense only if we assume that habits always produce the most desirable consequences—an assumption that we know is false. Habits outlive their usefulness. Habits are also shaped by the forces of power and wealth that influence and often corrupt the expression of good intentions. Certainly it is true that making our assumptions more explicit can lead to disturbing consequences (for instance, discovering how racist we are). Yet it is undoubtedly better in the long run for a society to face these disturbing consequences than simply to let them fester.

The other objection to the idea of reflective democracy is that it makes no sense to call for reflection unless there is some hope of discovering deeper narratives—deeper truths underlying the flawed narratives of the present—that can guide the social body into the future. The view of cultural narratives that I have developed in the preceding chapters neither assumes nor denies that such deeper narratives exist. My view on this question is that basic truths do exist, but that for a whole society they are unlikely to be found in some fundamental, underlying narrative, if only we dig deep enough. Narratives are inevitably personal, local, and context-specific, meaning that in a large, diverse society there will be multiple narratives. These narratives sometimes point to common truths, such as the value of fairness or the realities of joy and suffering, but this is not the same as saying that they give expression to these truths in commonly understood ways. A better view of what reflective democracy can do, I believe, is that it can generate clearer and more critical understandings of our deep narratives by bringing them into juxtaposition with other narratives. For instance, stories on which America's pride as a nation is built need to be examined in relation to stories of the nation's shortcomings. In the process, questions about good and evil are inevitably raised, as are possibilities for narratives about repentance and healing. Similarly, the narratives of self-made men and women that are so thoroughly engrained in our understandings of American success need to be retold with greater emphasis on the pain and dislocation experienced by the immigrants who have made us a strong nation.

This is the point at which my emphasis on falling short of our highest aspirations comes squarely again into the picture. We fall short, I have argued, because we pay insufficient attention to the cultural assumptions guiding our individual and collective efforts. We can now say more precisely what some of these assumptions are and how they limit our best efforts. The extent to which we value our individual freedom is one. How we legitimate our predominance as a world power is another. The proverbial rags-to-riches imagery that in new guises still undergirds our belief in the universal possibilities of individual success is yet another. So are our assumptions that ethnic and religious diversity have been working smoothly to provide equality and thoroughly grounded spiritual expressions for all, or the views we take for granted about how some "other"—whether racial groups or new immigrants—might somehow save us from the ill effects of materialism. It is not that these assumptions are false. It is rather that they are only part of the story. We do better when we examine the current balance between individuals and communities, not deciding in advance whether each is too strong or too weak, but considering more carefully the conditions under which we may need stronger selves or stronger community loyalties. By understanding the stories that new immigrants learn about America, we can bring into sharper relief the strengths and weaknesses of these stories. Our nation can justifiably take pride in its ability to absorb immigrants. Yet it must also reckon with instances of exclusion. Even more important, it must build into its collective narratives a clearer understanding of America's place in the world—not as a haven only, but also as a people capable of acknowledging its mistakes and working harder to do better. While the nation takes pride in the accomplishments of the few self-made men and women who gain exceptional wealth and power, it should also acknowledge the resources that went into these successes. In so doing, it can also increase the likelihood of a stronger commitment to ensuring that others have access to resources. The self-congratulatory stories about America's having achieved ethnic and religious diversity require similar reflection. These stories have often persuaded us that diversity is easy, and that it will prevail simply because it is in the best interest of all. Thinking this is a good way to avoid having to confront the hard work of actually living together in a diverse society. For a society that appears to be driven to its own destruction by such blatant reliance on advertising and consumption, the national mythos also needs to pay greater heed to such traditional values as simplicity and frugality. As long as our narratives imply that some romanticized group on the fringes of society holds the key to overcoming materialism, we are unlikely to do very much about overcoming it ourselves.

My purpose in mentioning these ways in which our deeply held cultural assumptions cause us to fall short is not to suggest that we can solve problems merely by recognizing that things are not always as good as they seem. Optimism, or at least hope, is itself a significant part of our culture that needs to be preserved. My point is rather to illustrate that reflective democracy requires individual and collective examination of when and how our narratives tell only part of the story. We can further that endeavor by being less willing to take the conventional wisdom implied in these narratives for granted. We can further it, in the first instance, simply by recognizing more clearly that we are shaped by our stories and not just by our economic or political circumstances. For reflective democracy to be truly democratic this awareness must also be infused into wider circles beyond those of clever advertisers and political operatives capable of manipulating the public consciousness for their clients or candidates. A degree of public mistrust, even cynicism, is a healthy aspect of any democracy. A renewed emphasis on the classical virtues of balance and harmony is also valuable, for these encourage reflection by raising questions about the other side of the coin. Narratives are typically built around understandings of balance and harmony, but these understandings are often one-sided. Thus when narratives of success are told, the failures implied may be there only for contrast, rather than for serious consideration. Such narratives are likely to require more sustained attention to less popular—but also long-standing—themes about the frailties of life and the need for support. The stories that make sense of life in terms of goodness and justice also require explanations of why life is meaningful when goodness and justice do not prevail. It is in these explanations that the direction to work harder at overcoming evil and injustice is likely to be found.

The most obvious place to encourage reflective democracy is in public forums. These occur in many locations and take different forms. The discussions that take place in the nation's capital on the floor of the House or Senate are one example. Increasingly, those discussions involve "hearings" before various congressional committees. In these cases, the deliberation occurs mainly among elected or appointed representatives of the public, rather than among the public itself. As a result, more attention has been directed in recent years to reviving earlier venues for deliberative democracy. The town hall or town meeting, for example, is generally a local event open to the public and long enough to include statements and rebuttals as well as questions and answers, but small enough to give the audience a sense of having actually participated. Most of the interaction at town meetings is between an official or panel of officials and rank-and-file members of the community. The typical "forum" takes a somewhat less participatory form. The participants are a panel who interact mostly among themselves, while the audience looks on, perhaps with the opportunity to ask questions at the end. A more participatory version of the town meeting or forum is the "roundtable" or working conference at which everyone is invited to speak and the number involved is sufficiently small to make this possible.

The assumption behind such meetings is that democracy will be furthered as participants question one another's statements. The questioning is supposedly a way to draw people out, forcing them to defend their positions and in so doing to state more explicitly their reasons for holding their particular opinions. Including divergent viewpoints in the discussion is conducive to such clarification because people are more likely to challenge those with whom they disagree than those with whom they agree. Both the participants and the audience leave the discussion with food for thought, as it were, having been exposed to various arguments, among which they must now make up their minds. A different assumption governs some public forums. This is the notion that the participants' actually reaching a consensus will further deliberative democracy. In Jürgen Habermas's treatment of rational communicative action, for instance, the rationality of the process involves iterative discussions that gradually result in agreement among the members involved.[3] The deliberations of a jury would be an example, although Habermas has in mind a process concerned with more complex social issues than the decision as to the guilt or innocence of a defendant.

Where town meetings and other such forums stop short of furthering reflective democracy is in focusing on an issue or set of issues, rather than discussing broader assumptions about morality, justice, values, or ethics. For instance, a public forum at which experts discuss whether gay marriage should be legal may provide an occasion for participants and the audience to discuss the implications of a particular legislative bill but skirt the deeper reasons why some people favor gay marriage and others oppose it. Public forums quite often focus on specific issues, such as a zoning law or school bond referendum, because there is in fact a pending piece of legislation to be considered. Because time is of the essence, a more wide-ranging discussion is out of order. Held, as they generally are, on an episodic basis and typically involving strangers, public forums are also limited because the familiarity and trust that would encourage discussion of deeper assumptions are missing.

The other limitation of public forums is that they involve relatively small numbers and have an arguably meager impact on the larger political process. A panel of experts may air their views in a public forum, and that may be a way of sharing information with an audience; but if those experts alone will decide the issue being considered, this is hardly a form of deliberative democracy in the ideal sense of that phrase. It is rather more like a seminar or a salon. Or, to take a different example, the kinds of town hall meetings that occur at the local level during primary election campaigns in states such as Iowa and New Hampshire bring people together by the dozens or hundreds and give them an opportunity to hear candidates speak and to ask questions. In creating this kind of forum, town hall meetings are an important part of the democratic process. *How much* of a role they play is debatable, though, especially when televised commercials are as important as they are, or when a candidate's fate is made or unmade by a sound byte–length remark, gaffe, or miscue. In those instances, greater opportunities for reflecting on such intangibles as style, personality, and perception are clearly needed.

The role of voluntary associations in strengthening American democracy has received considerable emphasis in recent years in view of evidence that participation in some of these associations has been declining. The interest in voluntary associations stems mostly from the view, expressed by Tocqueville among others, that these organizations do things for the good of the community and thus minimize the government's role in community affairs. Participation in voluntary associations appears to go hand in hand with voting, being interested in political issues, and doing volunteer work. All of this amounts to stronger social networks, which, in turn, help people get assistance when they need it, find jobs, make friends, secure emotional support, and feel integrated into their neighborhoods. The *cultural* role of voluntary associations has not received as much emphasis.

But voluntary associations are major producers of culture. Most of them put out newsletters and increasingly sponsor Web sites or host chat rooms on the Internet. Some of them focus specifically on civic topics or discuss books, while others bring in guest speakers or help organize town meetings. The information produced is usually a form of "narrowcasting" that gives it special value in comparison with the information people obtain from the mass media. For instance, newsletters tell how people can address needs in their local community, rather than simply describing those needs the way a television station might. Participation in many of these associations extends over longer periods, thus giving people a better opportunity to know and trust one another than they would have at a onetime public forum. Being well-acquainted means they can supply practical information informally, too, such as advice about raising children or referrals to doctors.

This cultural activity is limited, though, if it consists only of sharing information. Reflective democracy involves analyzing background assumptions as well as addressing practical questions. Associations often focus so much on specific issues that the background assumptions remain unexamined. In a study of voluntary service organizations in one metropolitan area, for example, the sociologist Paul Lichterman discovered that well-intentioned participants found it hard to think about social issues in terms other than those of problems facing specific individuals.[4] It was thus easier to provide charity to individuals than to work on larger community reforms. It took special effort to think about organization-to-organization relationships and to examine the individualistic assumptions that most participants shared. Associations also sometimes fail to encourage deeper reflections because, being voluntary, they attract a homogeneous clientele.

Religious organizations are especially important among the larger variety of associations to which people belong. They make up a large share of these associations, and they do a better job than many other groups do of drawing people into regular attendance at meetings. Religious organizations are ostensibly concerned with basic values, too, which means that they should be places for sustained reflection about these values. Where this happens best, it appears, is in Sunday school classes, Bible studies, prayer fellowships, and committee meetings. With proper guidance, participants can examine their assumptions about themselves or about social issues. Some groups, for example, have taken superficial discussions about gay and lesbian issues to a deeper level by examining assumptions about human nature, sexuality, marriage, child rearing, and spirituality. The shortcomings of religious organizations, like those of other associations, include their attracting a homogeneous clientele and focusing only on resolving personal problems.

If reflective democracy involves the kind of critical attention to cultural assumptions that one would expect in the analysis of a great work of literature, then it stands to reason that educational settings—especially higher education—would be one of the important venues in which reflective democracy is facilitated. Colleges and universities could serve as what Judith Rodin, the former president of the University of Pennsylvania, calls "communities of serious conversation" around the compelling issues of the day. Through such conversation in classrooms and lecture halls, universities could stimulate students to think more reflectively on their own about such issues as civil liberties, immigration, religious tolerance, and international relations.[5] That expectation, though, is often realized more in theory than in practice. The reality of American higher education is that it is frequently driven more by technical concerns than by an interest in critical philosophical and humanistic discussion. Students are oriented toward acquiring practical skills necessary to get started in a career or are motivated to learn only what is necessary to earn the desired grade, and even the better students sometimes have difficulty overcoming these campus norms. Administrative and funding considerations require that major attention be devoted to the natural sciences and engineering. Rapid change in these fields and the need for expensive labs and equipment mean that money and time must be spent to maintain them. No college or university is able legitimately to dispense entirely with the humanities. But humanities departments are often small and underfunded, relative to the number of students taking courses in them, and many of these courses involve basic language skills and writing.

The other serious limitation of educational settings as venues for reflective democracy is that very few adults spend any time in these settings
beyond the years they may spend as undergraduates or graduate students. Reflective democracy involves sustained thinking over the course
of a person's lifetime. The task is thus to instill these habits so that they
continue throughout life. That, however, is a tall order. The usual way of
thinking about critical reflection is that it occurs during the so-called
formative years when values are still fluid, but then needs less attention
once those values have been formed. With younger adults marrying later
and having families later, and with many people making major career
changes several times during adulthood, though, it becomes more important for people to have institutional settings beyond colleges and universities in which to discuss their changing values and aspirations.

Higher education is protected from the practical policy concerns that
may govern town meetings or voluntary associations. Yet it is difficult
to strike the right balance between ivory-tower isolation and engaged
policy intervention. On the one hand, humanistic studies for their own
sake are needed; for instance, to establish that the history of Civil War
battles is correct or that the latest translation of Aristotle is accurate.
On the other hand, foundation grants and government funding often
demand that scholarship in the humanities and social sciences have relevance to the immediate issues of today, rather than dealing with
longer-term questions. The appropriate balance differs from discipline
to discipline and from practitioner to practitioner. At minimum,
though, it requires that the critical distance from current events
achieved from a historical or philosophical perspective also inspire students to reflect on their own values.

By far the most powerful venue in which reflective democracy *could*
take place is the mass media. In standard treatments of democracy, the
media are viewed as comprising an institution that keeps the public informed and thus contributes to the preservation of democratic government by letting people know what their elected officials are doing. Information is key—which is why we think people who read newspapers are
better citizens, and why we worry that television may be giving only a
synopsis of the news rather than the full story. Generally we think, too,
that the news media play a more important political role than does the
entertainment industry; the latter is in business strictly to divert and
amuse but of course sometimes serves a critical function, such as

through a motion picture about apartheid or the life of Gandhi. If we consider the news media, their closest approach to cultural criticism is in the presentation of a major exposé, such as the coverage of the Watergate break-in and cover-up in the early 1970s, or the muckraking journalism of the early twentieth century. An exposé of this sort invites cultural reflection (how could something like this have happened?). Moreover, the news media sometimes follow up in those instances by presenting the thoughts and opinions of social commentators.

In fact, the commentator or columnist bears closest consideration as a facilitator of reflective democracy. Although it sometimes appears that there is more commentary than news, we must distinguish between two kinds of commentary—commentary that serves as filler on talk television and radio ("Well, sir, do you think so-and-so will be put in jail?") and commentary that seeks to interpret events by fitting them into a larger or longer-term framework. When the former is set aside, it can be seen that the latter is rare. Commentary of this sort is even more valuable because it specifically violates the canon of ostensibly objective reporting and deliberately brings the putative facts into juxtaposition with some normative framework. This is sometimes done through the lens of a public opinion poll, showing that an event does or does not square with public approval, or, more commonly, through the lens of what we might call a partisan position; that is, a pro-Democrat or pro-Republican perspective.

The more interesting kind of commentary seeks to cast the day's news in a larger perspective by extending the temporal horizon or widening the political context. For the former, news outlets increasingly rely on historians. The historian who can say, Yes, but you know, Herbert Hoover faced the same dilemma during his administration, is especially valued. That perspective reminds us that we can face adversity because the present travail is no different from the past, or shows us that there may yet be surprises in store. The political analyst is the commentator capable of giving a "political reading" to the day's events, explaining, for instance, that there was actually dissension among the president's advisers, or that this decision could pay big dividends during the next election.

What is harder to find is the same kind of cultural analysis—given, for example, by the person who can explain why a political speech was reassuring or how the recent welfare legislation fits well with our understandings of individual responsibility, or, even more valuably, by the historian or theologian who has examined the deep myths that guide our thinking about individuals, hard work, success, freedom, America, diversity, and money. The truth is that though such commentaries are rare, some exceptionally good ones have been articulated, and there is clearly the potential for more. Cultural analysis is especially helpful when it tackles not only the stated reasons for, say, a military campaign or major investment of public funds, but also the tales that are spun to defend these policies. Cultural analysis broadens the discussion by considering how media images are manipulated. It offers the opportunity to go beyond risk assessment and financial incentives. It takes a critical look at the stories we tell about America and about ourselves.

Cultural criticism is an art, one that is honed through specialized training—usually in the humanities, but sometimes in the social sciences and other disciplines. Unfortunately, it has become common in the social sciences and in some humanities disciplines, such as history, to view scholarship as a matter of little more than fact-finding and puzzle solving. Fact-finding amounts to collecting and processing information, such as conducting a survey or analyzing statistics from the census. Puzzle solving means providing an explanation for the facts observed, such as showing why racial segregation persists, or why more marriages dissolve now than in the past. In these endeavors, technical and so-called methodological concerns loom large: how do we conduct a reliable survey? which statistics give the best estimates of income inequality? Assumptions about what is right or wrong about society and about what is desirable can never be fully removed from such scholarship. These assumptions, for example, encourage scholars to study the ill effects of racial and gender discrimination or the social problems faced by families living in poverty. However, these normative concerns are more often left unstated than brought squarely into view. Reflective democracy means that more attention must be paid to these normative assumptions.

The human sciences were animated through most of their history by the belief that scholarly inquiry could unmask realities that had previously remained hidden. The role of inquiry was thus to do more than amass evidence. It was to show that beliefs and values were, unbeknownst to the common person, shaped by social conditions or deepseated personality dispositions. It suggested that democracies might not be as strong as imagined, that totalitarianism could reappear in unexpected places, that economic growth had unintended consequences, and

that social conflicts might too. Cultural criticism took on a similar interest in unmasking that which could not be seen with the naked eye. It
became, in Paul Ricoeur's memorable phrase, a "hermeneutics of suspicion" concerned with demythologizing taken-for-granted meanings.[6]
The role of cultural criticism was to show that there were power relations
hidden beneath the surface of social life. Cultural patterns persuaded us
that our worlds were inevitable, natural, even though they were our own
constructions. There were deep structures or patterns, myths, and false
views of reality. There were cultural cues that perpetuated masculine
domination or that maintained racial distinctions. The goal of cultural
criticism was thus not to produce a new orthodoxy, a "true" interpretation of culture, but to open the possibility of new meanings and thereby
to encourage reflection.

The major figures who developed what became known after World
War II as cultural criticism were committed to this belief that scholarly
inquiry could unmask hidden realities.[7] These writers were concerned
with both the substance and the forms that made particular cultural assumptions meaningful. They examined the kinds of "character" that
emerged in different family settings or showed how the demands of
the workplace created new understandings of the individual. Of special
interest were the questions of how nationalism worked, how authority
was reinforced, and what the relationships were between ideologies and
social classes. It is well to be reminded that many of these writers had
been influenced by the recent experience of totalitarianism or by first-
hand experience with the ravages of colonialism. Culture mattered, in
their view, not because it was the only source of domination, but because
it was one of them. Culture was powerful because people took it for
granted, rather than considering more critically their beliefs and values.
In the context of current evidence of an increasing concentration of
wealth in the hands of the few, and in relation to concerns about the
resurgence of elite dynasties in American politics, the need to be critical
of prevailing cultural assumptions becomes all the more important.

On a mountain road, probably in Switzerland, two young men hike
along, their gear in heavy backpacks, bundled against the chill
wind, exchanging conversation about their lives and their dreams. One

expresses his passion for art. He plans to major in ceramics. His goal is in ten years to have a small studio of his own. A car passes, slows, and stops. It is a luxury SUV. The well-dressed man and woman in the car offer the young men a ride. They accept. As they settle in the backseat, their eyes play over the rich leather, the sound system, the gauges, and the dials. Their pupils visibly widen. As the car eases forward, one young man says to the other, "You could always *minor* in ceramics." "Yeah," says his companion.

One can accept the story at face value or one can think more reflectively and challenge it. Accepting it means taking the implied messages for granted. It might be nice to major in ceramics, but a lot nicer to own a luxury car. Wealth trumps art. The successful person buys luxury goods. The dreamer has nothing. Challenging the story starts by recognizing it as a cleverly designed television commercial to sell luxury cars. The message is there in one's dorm room or living room because millions of dollars have been spent producing and broadcasting it. The opposing message about art or the simple life devoted to helping others is not there. The television industry depends on sponsoring commercials that encourage people to want things they cannot afford. Any schoolchild has grasped this at least well enough to be somewhat cynical about television and the products it advertises. However, reflection goes beyond cynicism. It requires probing deeper into the narratives about individuality and success on which our way of life is based. Reflection requires considering the story critically, thinking about what kind of message is being presented, and knowing what kind of society the message implies. That is the choice.

The New Elites Project, from which some information is presented in chapters 2, 3, 4, 5, and 6, was conceived in July 2001 and conducted between August 2001 and July 2003. The purpose of the project was to identify and conduct in-depth qualitative interviews with first- or second-generation immigrants who had distinguished themselves in their given occupations. In all, 200 interviews were completed, 192 of which focused on patterns of success, while 8 were pilot interviews that included a wider range of topics. Each interview lasted approximately one and one-half hours. The interviews were semistructured, meaning that a prespecified menu of topics was included, but that interviewees were given the opportunity to respond in their own words and were encouraged to tell stories or otherwise amplify on their responses. The topics included the trajectory of interviewees' education, work history, and work patterns; family background and values; the timing and reasons for their coming to the United States; issues of ethnic identity, discrimination, and the role of ethnicity in work and social life; and issues of religious beliefs and practices, family values, and relationships with parents, siblings, and children. The interviews were conducted by professional interviewers with extensive training and experience in elite interviewing. Each interview was transcribed, each transcript was verified for accuracy, and when possible, interviewees were given copies of the transcripts and asked to make corrections. Interviewees were asked whether they preferred to be identified by their real names or by pseudonyms. In nearly all cases, interviewees approved the use of their real names; however, because of the personal nature of the material pseudonyms have been used or identifying information has been withheld.

Interviewees were selected on the basis of a quota design that was established to ensure a maximum of variation among a number of the key characteristics of interest. Because one aim was to include comparisons among people from different religious traditions, five major ethno-religious groups were selected and approximately equal numbers of interviewees were sought from each group: Muslim Americans, Hindu Americans, Buddhist Americans, Asian American Christians, and Hispanic or Latino Christians. For a respondent to be eligible, it was not necessary for him or her to be actively religious or to regard himself or herself as a follower of a particular religious tradition, only to have been reared in one or another of these traditions. Of the 192 interviewees who received the standard questions, 36 were from Muslim backgrounds, 35 were from Hindu backgrounds, 37 were from Buddhist backgrounds, 40 were from Asian or Asian American Christian backgrounds, 36 were from Hispanic or Latino Christian backgrounds, and the remaining 8 were from Sikh, Jain, Orthodox Christian, or other backgrounds. In addition, the quota design stipulated that approximately two-thirds of the respondents be first-generation immigrants and that the remainder be second-generation immigrants. Of the 192 interviewees, 66 percent were in fact first-generation immigrants. The quota design also called for as much diversity as possible on other factors, such as country of origin and current residence. The 192 interviewees came from 42 different countries and currently lived in 25 different states. They also represented a wide range of occupations: entrepreneurship, computer hardware and software, venture capital, construction, law, government, medicine, professional athletics, journalism, music, finance, science, and engineering, among others.

The interviewees were identified through a strategy of multiple starting points to ensure diversity and avoid restricting potential participants to particular social networks or locations. Two extensive searches of on-line sources were conducted, one at the start of the project and one approximately a year and a half later. These searches included on-line national and local newspapers, individual Web sites, Web sites of ethnic associations, and Web sites of professional associations and organizations granting awards to distinguished individuals. Keywords were used to identify potential respondents who were immigrants or who belonged to particular ethnic or ethnoreligious groups and who had distinguished themselves by achieving awards or occupational success. Eighty-seven of the interviewees were identified in this way. Once the interviewing began, a snowball technique was used to identify additional respondents.

This involved asking interviewees to nominate others they knew, or knew of, who had achieved distinction in various fields. Fifty-nine interviewees were selected this way. Through interviews with clergy, community leaders, and leaders of ethnic organizations conducted as part of a previous study, referrals were received that resulted in 35 other interviews. And the remaining 11 respondents were identified in other ways, such as Listserves and personal contacts.

# Notes

## Introduction

1. Arguably, it might be more accurate to say "mythoi," because American culture is composed of diverse narratives and diverse interpretations of core narratives. As we shall see, however, the American mythos is sufficiently shared that it often emerges in unexpected places (such as the stories of immigrants from widely divergent backgrounds).

2. On human agency, a useful bibliography is included in Mustafa Emirbayer and Ann Mische, "What Is Agency?" *American Journal of Sociology* 103, no. 4 (January 1998): 962–1023. One of the more imaginative attempts to bring agency back into sociological investigation is William F. Sewell, "A Theory of Structure: Duality, Agency, and Transformation," *American Journal of Sociology* 98, no. 1 (July 1992): 1–29.

3. See the appendix for more details about the New Elites Project.

## Chapter 1
### Deep Culture and Democratic Renewal

1. Horace Greeley, *Miscellanies* (New York: J. B. Ford, 1869), 526.

2. R.W.B. Lewis, *The American Adam: Innocence, Tragedy and Tradition in the Nineteenth Century* (Chicago: University of Chicago Press, 1955), ix.

3. A largely forgotten book that usefully delineates broader concerns about societal values from more specific (norm-oriented) reform movements is Neil J. Smelser, *Theory of Collective Behavior* (New York: Free Press, 1962).

4. Jimmy Carter, "Crisis of Confidence Speech," July 15, 1979; on-line at www.pbs.org.

5. Robert N. Bellah, Richard Madsen, William M. Sullivan, Ann Swidler, and Steven M. Tipton, *Habits of the Heart: Individualism and Commitment in American Life* (Berkeley and Los Angeles: University of California Press, 1985; rev. ed., 1996).

6. Robert D. Putnam, *Bowling Alone: The Collapse and Revival of American Community* (New York: Simon & Schuster, 2000).

7. For instance, see Andrew Kohut, *Views of a Changing World* (Washington, D.C.: Pew Research Center for the People and the Press, 2003); on-line at www.people-press.org.

8. Melani McAlister, *Epic Encounters: Culture, Media, and U.S. Interests in the Middle East, 1945–2000* (Berkeley and Los Angeles: University of California Press, 2001).

9. This point has been made recently by Amitai Etzioni, "How Liberty Is Lost," *Society* 40 (July/August 2003), 44–51: Etzioni suggests that Weimar is the only example, and questions whether democracy there was well established.

10. Plato, *The Republic of Plato*, trans. Francis Cornford (New York: Oxford University Press, 1945), bk. 8. My intention here, of course, is not to depict Plato as an advocate of democracy, which he certainly was not, but to show his emphasis on the frailty of democracy.

11. John Adams, "Letter to John Taylor, April 15, 1814," in *The Works of John Adams, Second President of the United States: With a Life of the Author, Notes and Illustrations*, ed. Charles Francis Adams (Boston: Little Brown, 1851), 6:484.

12. James Madison, "The Union as a Safeguard against Domestic Faction and Insurrection—Continued: Federalist Paper No. 10," *Daily Advertiser*, November 22, 1787.

13. Thomas Jefferson, "First Inaugural Address," March 4, 1801.

14. Alexis de Tocqueville, *Democracy in America* (New York: Knopf, 1945).

15. Jean Bethke Elshtain, *Democracy on Trial* (New York: Basic Books, 1995), 1–2.

16. John Dewey, "The School as a Means of Developing a Social Consciousness and Social Ideals in Children," *Journal of Social Forces* 1 (September 1923): 513–17; the quotation is on 514.

17. Peter L. Berger and Richard John Neuhaus, *To Empower People: The Role of Mediating Structures in Public Policy* (Boston: Rowman & Littlefield, 1977).

18. Émile Durkheim, *The Elementary Forms of Religious Life* (1912), trans. Carol Cosman, introd. Mark Sydney Cladis (New York: Oxford University Press, 2001; Robert N. Bellah's introduction to Émile Durkheim, *On Morality and Society: Selected Writings*, ed. Robert N. Bellah, The Heritage of Sociology (Chicago: University of Chicago Press, 1973), is, in my view, the single most helpful source for an understanding of the larger significance of Durkheim's work on culture and moral community.

19. For instance, the essays included in Jeffrey C. Alexander, *Durkheimian Sociology: Cultural Studies* (Cambridge: Cambridge University Press, 1990).

20. Michael J. Sandel, *Democracy's Discontent: America in Search of a Public Philosophy* (Cambridge, Mass.: Harvard University Press, 1996), 4. In quoting Sandel I do not mean to imply that culture as deep meaning can be regarded as a form of public philosophy; that focuses too much attention on theorized knowledge and not enough on tacit understanding.

21. Readers of my earlier work on this topic (especially *Meaning and Moral Order: Explorations in Cultural Analysis* [Berkeley and Los Angeles: University of California Press, 1987]) have sometimes mistakenly concluded that I was arguing against any emphasis on meaning in the study of culture; my argument was rather that cultural analysts need to be cautious about asserting that they have deciphered *the* meaning of any particular symbolic-expressive act or object.

22. Francis Fukuyama, *Trust: The Social Virtues and the Creation of Prosperity* (New York: Free Press, 1995), and Adam Seligman, *The Problem of Trust* (Princeton, N.J.: Princeton University Press, 1997); both constructively illuminate the deeper cultural meanings with which trust is associated.

23. Michael Schudson, "How People Learn to Be Civic," in *United We Serve: National Service and the Future of Citizenship*, ed. E. J. Dionne Jr., Kayla Meltzer Drogosz, and Robert E. Litan (Washington, D.C.: Brookings Institution Press, 2003), 263–77; the quotation is on 263.

24. The distinction between Dionysian and Apollonian cultures was propounded in Ruth Benedict, *Patterns of Culture* (New York: Mentor Books, 1960).

25. This point has also been made recently in a quite different context by Lawrence E. Harrison, introduction to *Culture Matters: How Values Shape Human Progress*, ed. Lawrence E. Harrison and Samuel P. Huntington (New York: Basic Books, 2000), xvi.

26. Ann Swidler, "Culture in Action: Symbols and Strategies," *American Sociological Review* 51 (April 1986): 273–86; see also Ann Swidler, *Talk of Love: How Culture Matters* (Chicago: University of Chicago Press, 2001).

27. My criticism of this tendency in cultural studies should not be taken as a blanket indictment of recent work in cultural sociology, which includes many examples of studies concerned with such enduring issues as national identity, good and evil, love, morality, and empowerment; see, for instance, the essays in *Culture in Mind: Toward a Sociology of Culture and Cognition*, ed. Karen A. Cerulo (New York: Routledge, 2002).

28. Jeffrey C. Alexander, *The Meanings of Social Life: A Cultural Sociology* (Cambridge: Cambridge University Press, 2003), 121.

29. Nathan O. Hatch, "The Democratization of Christianity and the Character of American Politics," in *Religion and American Politics: From the Colonial Period to the 1980s*, ed. Mark A. Noll (New York: Oxford University Press, 1990), 92–120; the quotation is on 93. See also Nathan O. Hatch, *The Democratization of American Christianity* (New Haven: Yale University Press, 1990).

30. Donald G. Mathews, "The Second Great Awakening as an Organizing Process, 1780–1830: An Hypothesis," *American Quarterly* 21 (1969): 23–43.

31. My discussion of commonsense morality follows the very thorough account of the intellectual history of the early nineteenth century in Mark A. Noll, *America's God: From Jonathan Edwards to Abraham Lincoln* (New York: Oxford University Press, 2002), especially chapters 4 through 17.

32. Michael P. Young, "Confessional Protest: The Religious Birth of U.S. National Social Movements," *American Sociological Review* 67 (October 2002): 660–88; the quotation is on 660.

33. John L. Hammond, *The Politics of Benevolence: Revival Religion and American Voting Behavior* (Norwood, N.J.: Ablex, 1979).

34. Noll, *America's God*, 440; the phrase Noll quotes is from John M. Murrin, "Self-Interest Conquers Patriotism: Republicanism, Liberals, and Indians Reshape

the Nation," in *The American Revolution: Its Character and Limits*, ed. Jack P. Greene (New York: New York University Press, 1987), 227.

35. Noll, *America's God*, 445.

36. Claude S. Fischer, *America Calling: A Social History of the Telephone to 1940* (Berkeley and Los Angeles: University of California Press, 1992), traces the social significance of some of these developments in communication.

37. On the growth of nationally centralized religious organizations, see Ben Primer, *Protestants and American Business Methods* (Ann Arbor, Mich.: UMI Research Press, 1979), and Mark Chaves and John R. Sutton, "Organizational Consolidation in American Protestant Denominations, 1890–1990," *Journal for the Scientific Study of Religion* 43 (2004): 1–23. According to Theda Skocpol, "How Americans Became Civic," in *Civic Engagement in American Democracy*, ed. Theda Skocpol and Morris P. Fiorina (Washington, D.C.: Brookings Institution Press; New York: Russell Sage Foundation, 1999), 27–80, the number of national voluntary associations with memberships exceeding 1 percent of the population grew steadily between the 1860s and 1920s (see p. 54, fig. 2-3). See also William Pencak, *For God and Country: The American Legion, 1919–1941* (Boston: Northeastern University Press, 1989). On magazines and advertising, see Christopher P. Wilson, "The Rhetoric of Consumption: Mass-Market Magazines and the Demise of the Gentle Reader, 1880–1920," in *The Culture of Consumption: Critical Essays in American History, 1880–1980*, ed. Richard Wightman Fox and T. J. Jackson Lears (New York: Pantheon, 1983), 39–64.

38. Deward Clayton Brown, *Electricity for Rural America: The Fight for the REA* (Westport, Conn.: Greenwood Press, 1980).

39. William Foote Whyte, *Street Corner Society: The Social Structure of an Italian Slum* (Chicago: University of Chicago Press, 1943), 273.

40. Louis Wirth, "Localism, Regionalism, and Centralization," *American Sociological Review* 42 (January 1937): 493–509; the quotation is on 495–96.

41. Approximately 10 million were drafted and 6 million joined voluntarily (all but 2 percent of military personnel in World War II were male); the 1940 male population age 15 through 44 totaled 32 million; the 1940 male population age 15 through 34 totaled 24 million.

42. Harold G. Vatter, *The U.S. Economy in World War II* (New York: Columbia University Press, 1985).

43. "Income Tax," in *Houghton Mifflin Reader's Companion to American History*; on-line at http://college.hmco.com/history/readerscomp.

44. Ronald Tobey, Charles Wetherell, and Jay Brigham, "Moving Out and Settling In: Residential Mobility, Home Owning, and the Public Enframing of Citizenship, 1921–1950," *American Historical Review* 95 (December 1990): 1414; David M. Kennedy, *Freedom from Fear: The American People in Depression and War, 1929–1945* (New York: Oxford University Press, 1999).

45. On the cultural significance of the interstate highway system, see David Halberstam, *The Fifties* (New York: Fawcett, 1993).

46. Quoted in Stephen J. Whitfield, *The Culture of the Cold War* (Baltimore: Johns Hopkins University Press, 1991), 81.

47. C. Wright Mills, *White Collar: The American Middle Classes* (New York: Oxford University Press, 1951), xii.

48. Putnam, *Bowling Alone*, 253–54.

49. Quoted in William H. Whyte Jr., *The Organization Man* (Garden City, N.Y.: Doubleday, 1956), 51.

50. Herbert J. Gans, *The Levittowners: Ways of Life and Politics in a New Suburban Community* (New York: Pantheon, 1967).

51. The definitive examination of the rights revolution, in my view, is John D. Skrentny, *The Minority Rights Revolution* (Cambridge, Mass.: Harvard University Press, 2002).

52. David Brooks, "Refuting the Cynics," *New York Times*, November 25, 2003.

CHAPTER 2

QUANDARIES OF INDIVIDUALISM

1. My thinking on this topic is especially indebted to Wilfred M. McClay, *The Masterless: Self and Society in Modern America* (Chapel Hill: University of North Carolina Press, 1994), which, in my opinion, is the most valuable treatment of changes in popular discourse about the balance of individuals and communities.

2. George Kateb, *The Inner Ocean: Individualism and Democratic Culture* (Ithaca, N.Y.: Cornell University Press, 1992), 83.

3. I especially have in mind the work of Erik Erikson, for instance, *Identity and the Life Cycle*, Psychological Monographs, vol. 1 (New York: International Universities Press, 1959); and more recent work in this tradition, such as Mihaly Csikszentmihalyi, *Finding Flow* (New York: Basic Books, 1997).

4. Robert A. Nisbet, "Conservatism and Sociology," *American Journal of Sociology* 58 (September 1952): 167–75; the quotation is on 167.

5. Ibid., 168.

6. Erich Fromm, *Escape from Freedom* (New York: Farrar & Rinehart, 1941), 283.

7. David Riesman, *The Lonely Crowd* (New Haven: Yale University Press, 1950).

8. Whyte, *Organization Man*, 7.

9. Ibid., 6.

10. Mills, *White Collar*, 189.

11. C. Wright Mills, "The Structure of Power in American Society," *British Journal of Sociology* 9 (March 1958): 29–41; the quotation is on 29.

12. Ralph Linton, *The Cultural Background of Personality* (New York: Appleton-Century, 1945), 26–27.

13. Mills, *White Collar*, 10.

14. Amitai Etzioni, "Too Many Rights, Too Few Responsibilities," in *Toward a Global Civil Society*, ed. Amitai Etzioni (Providence, R.I.: Berghahn Books, 1995), 95–105; the quotation is on 95.

15. James Davison Hunter, *The Death of Character: Moral Education in an Age without Good or Evil* (New York: Basic Books, 2000).

16. Bellah et al., *Habits of the Heart*, 221.

17. David Herbert Lawrence, *Selected Essays* (Baltimore: Penguin, 1950), 231.

18. My reference to the therapeutic state is to the very insightful book on this topic by James L. Nolan Jr., *The Therapeutic State: Justifying Government at Century's End* (New York: New York University Press, 1998).

19. Louis A. Zurcher, *The Mutable Self: A Self-Concept for Social Change* (Beverly Hills, Calif.: Sage, 1977).

20. Robert M. Orrange, "The Emerging Mutable Self: Gender Dynamics and Creative Adaptations in Defining Work, Family, and the Future," *Social Forces* 82 (September 2003): 1–34; the quotation is on 15.

21. Paul Leinberger and Bruce Tucker, *The New Individualists: The Generation after the Organization Man* (New York: HarperCollins, 1991), 21.

22. Alan Ehrenhalt, *The Lost City: The Forgotten Virtues of Community in America* (New York: Basic Books, 1995), 25.

23. James Ishmael Ford, "The Gathered Community," on-line at www.vuu.org.

24. On this aspect of moral conviction, see Bernard Williams, *Problems of the Self: Philosophical Papers, 1956–1972* (Cambridge: Cambridge University Press, 1973), 207–29.

25. John Barth, *Lost in the Funhouse* (New York: Doubleday, 1988), 3.

26. John Kekes, *Moral Tradition and Individuality* (Princeton, N.J.: Princeton University Press, 1989), 106.

27. I am here following the very insightful argument presented in Richard Sennett, *The Fall of Public Man* (New York: Norton, 1992).

28. Michael J. Sandel, "The Procedural Republic and the Unencumbered Self," *Political Theory* 12 (February 1984): 81–96; the quotation is on 94.

29. Alejandro Portes, "Social Capital: Its Origins and Applications in Modern Sociology," *Annual Review of Sociology* 24, no. 2 (1998): 1–24; Nan Lin, *Social Capital: A Theory of Social Structure and Action* (Cambridge: Cambridge University Press, 2002); Stephen Baron, John Field, and Tom Schuller, eds., *Social Capital: Critical Perspectives* (New York: Oxford University Press, 2001).

30. William Julius Wilson, *When Work Disappears: The World of the New Urban Poor* (New York: Viking, 1997).

31. Amitai Etzioni, "The Responsive Community: A Communitarian Perspective," *American Sociological Review* 61 (February 1996): 1–11; the quotation is on 10.

32. Anthony Giddens, *Modernity and Self-Identity: Self and Society in the Late Modern Age* (Stanford, Calif.: Stanford University Press, 1991), 53.

33. Michael J. Sandel, *Liberalism and the Limits of Justice* (New York: Cambridge University Press, 1982), 179.

34. Kekes, *Moral Tradition and Individuality*, 114.

35. Dan P. McAdams, *The Stories We Live By: Personal Myths and the Making of the Self* (New York: Guilford Press, 1993), 12.

36. Fatima Akhtar (a pseudonym) was one of the persons with whom a pilot interview for the New Elites Project was conducted; see the appendix for further details.

37. The usefulness of examining accounts was first proposed in sociology by Marvin B. Scott and Sanford M. Lyman, "Accounts," *American Sociological Review* 33 (February 1968): 46–62; for a helpful overview of the recent literature, see Terri L. Orbuch, "People's Accounts Count: The Sociology of Accounts," *Annual Review of Sociology* 23 (1997): 445–78.

38. Orbuch, "People's Accounts Count," 459.

39. Charlotte Linde, *Life Stories: The Creation of Coherence* (New York: Oxford University Press, 1993).

40. Christian Smith, *Moral, Believing Animals: Human Personhood and Culture* (New York: Oxford University Press, 2003), 75; Smith's book is worth reading in full for its brilliant analysis of the role of narratives.

41. Ibid., chapter 4, provides several examples of grand narratives; see also Peter L. Berger and Thomas Luckmann, *The Social Construction of Reality: A Treatise in the Sociology of Knowledge* (New York: Doubleday, 1966), on "symbolic universes."

42. Analysis of ordinary narratives can illuminate the underlying assumptions about moral ontology that are widely shared in the culture, but that is different from arguing that particular individuals are guided by single grand narratives. "The moral ontology behind any person's views can remain largely implicit. Indeed, it usually does," writes Charles Taylor, *Sources of the Self: The Making of the Modern Identity* (Cambridge, Mass.: Harvard University Press, 1989), 9.

43. On the narratives of working scientists, Bruno Latour, *Laboratory Life* (Princeton, N.J.: Princeton University Press, 1986), and G. Nigel Gilbert and Michael Mulkay, *Opening Pandora's Box: A Sociological Analysis of Scientists' Discourse* (Cambridge: Cambridge University Press, 1984), are especially useful; delimited narratives that focus on specific events and roles are also emphasized in Swidler, *Talk of Love*, and Nina Eliasoph and Paul Lichterman, "Culture in Interaction," *American Journal of Sociology* 108 (January 2003): 735–94. These publications include extensive references to other sources.

44. Walker Percy, *The Last Gentleman* (New York: Ivy Books, 1966), 16.

45. Riesman, *Lonely Crowd*, 85.

46. George Ritzer, *The McDonaldization of Society* (Thousand Oaks, Calif.: Pine Forge Press, 1993).

47. Robert Wuthnow, *Sharing the Journey: Support Groups and America's New Quest for Community* (New York: Free Press, 1994), especially chapter 10.

48. R. Marie Griffith, *God's Daughters: Evangelical Women and the Power of Submission* (Berkeley and Los Angeles: University of California Press, 1997), provides one of the best ethnographic analyses of this process of empowerment in prayer groups.

49. Clifford Geertz, *The Interpretation of Cultures* (New York: Basic Books, 1973), 79–93.

50. Stereotypic characters and patterned transformations are insightfully discussed in Sidonie Smith and Julia Watson, *Reading Autobiography: A Guide for Interpreting Life Narratives* (Minneapolis: University of Minnesota Press, 2001).

CHAPTER 3
THE JUSTICE OF PRIVILEGE

1. Walt Whitman, "Preface, 1872, to 'As a Strong Bird on Pinions Free,' " in *Prose Works* (Philadelphia: David McKay, 1892); Bartleby.com, 2000; www.bartleby.com/229.

2. Elaine Sciolino, "Understanding Why 'They' Hate Us," *New York Times*, September 23, 2001.

3. *Newsweek*, October 7, 2001.

4. Quoted in Peter Vilbig, "Why Do They Hate America?" *New York Times*, October 15, 2001, 10.

5. CNN/Gallup Poll, March 5, 2002; *Public Opinion Online* (available through Lexis-Nexis).

6. Each of these meanings is suggested in the *Oxford English Dictionary* definition of arrogance: "The taking of too much upon oneself as one's right; the assertion of unwarrantable claims in respect of one's own importance; undue assumption of dignity, authority, or knowledge; aggressive conceit, presumption, or haughtiness" (*Oxford English Dictionary*, 2nd ed., 1989; on-line).

7. Berger and Luckmann, *Social Construction of Reality*, 93.

8. Zev Chafets, "Why They Hate: U.S. Land of the Free Seduces World's Sons and Daughters," *New York Daily News*, September 1, 2002, 43.

9. Charles William Eliot, "Five American Contributions to Civilization," in *The Oxford Book of American Essays*, ed. Brander Matthews (New York: Oxford University Press, 1914), 25.

10. Carol Aronovici, "Americanization: Its Meaning and Function," *American Journal of Sociology* 25 (May 1920): 695–730; the quotation is on 701.

11. Robert N. Bellah, *The Broken Covenant: American Civil Religion in Time of Trial* (New York: Seabury, 1975), 88.

12. Robert Wuthnow, Religion and Diversity Survey, conducted among 2,910 persons between September 2002 and February 2003 (Princeton, N.J.: Princeton University, Department of Sociology, 2003 [machine-readable datafile]).

13. Oscar Handlin, *The Uprooted: The Epic Story of the Great Migrations That Made the American People* (New York: Grosset & Dunlap, 1951), 38.

14. Seymour Rechtzeit, "A Boy's Journey," *Scholastic* (2003); on-line at teacher.scholastic.com/immigrat.

15. Edward Marshall, "Makes Six Ocean Trips to Study Steerage Reform: Ernest C. Cotterill Reports on the Bad State of Affairs among the Immigrants on Some Ships and Offers Recommendations for the Improvement of Conditions," *New York Times*, November 30, 1913, 10.

16. Durkheim, *On Morality and Society*, 189.

17. Norman O. Brown, *Love's Body* (New York: Vintage, 1966), 247.

18. Harold Garfinkel, "Conditions of Successful Degradation Ceremonies," *American Journal of Sociology* 61 (1956): 420–24.

19. Handlin, *The Uprooted*, 304.

20. Carlos Cortez, "The Immigrant in Film: Evolution of an Illuminating Icon," in *Beyond the Stars: Stock Characters in American Popular Film*, ed. Paul Loukides and Linda K. Fuller (Bowling Green, Ohio: Bowling Green University Popular Press, 1990), 23–34.

21. Seth Stern, "At Home in Justice," *Harvard Law Bulletin*, Fall 2002, on-line at www.law.harvard.edu/alumni/bulletin/2002/fall.

22. Maya Blackmun, "Home at Last—after 14 Years," *Portland Oregonian*, September 14, 1992, B1.

23. Anthony Lewis, "Boat People Helping to Build Our Future," *San Francisco Chronicle*, November 29, 2003, A18.

24. Seth Stern, "From Boat Person to Terror War Point Man," *Christian Science Monitor*, June 9, 2003; on-line at www.csmonitor.com/2003/0609.

25. Dena Bunis and Anh Do, "Ex-Refugee Is Nominated for Justice Post: Immigrants, A Fullerton High Grad Gets Praise at His Senate Confirmation Hearing," *Orange County Register*, May 10, 2001, 1.

26. Nancy Foner, *From Ellis Island to JFK: New York's Two Great Waves of Immigration* (New Haven: Yale University Press; New York: Russell Sage Foundation, 2000), 10.

27. See the appendix for further details about this study.

28. Of the 192 people in the New Elites Project who told stories about themselves or their parents coming to America, only one—the son of a Cuban immigrant whose father had been temporarily detained in Haiti—described the trip itself as a time of trial.

29. Foner, *From Ellis Island to JFK*, 34–35.

30. Rob Nixon, "From *Dreambirds: The Strange History of the Ostrich in Fashion, Food, and Fortune*," in *Crossing into America: The New Literature of Immigration*, ed. Louis Mendoza and S. Shankar (New York: New Press, 2003), 68–71; the quotation is on 69–70.

31. Peter G. Stromberg, *Language and Self-Transformation: A Study of the Christian Conversion Narrative* (New York: Cambridge University Press, 1993). This remains one of the most useful sources on conversation narratives.

CHAPTER 4

SELF-MADE MEN AND WOMEN

1. "Penniless Immigrants Who Have Made Millions," *New York Times*, November 2, 1913, 12.

2. Ruth Miller Elson, *Guardians of Tradition: American Schoolbooks of the Nineteenth Century* (Lincoln: University of Nebraska Press, 1964), 189–95.

3. Quentin Reynolds, *The Fiction Factory; or from Pulp Row to Quality Street* (New York: Random House, 1955).

4. Irvin G. Wyllie, *The Self-Made Man in America: The Myth of Rags to Riches* (New York: Free Press, 1954), 6.

5. Of particular interest are Jeffrey Louis Decker, *Made in America: Self-Styled Success from Horatio Alger to Oprah Winfrey* (Minneapolis: University of Minnesota Press, 1997); and James V. Catano, *Ragged Dicks: Masculinity, Steel, and the Rhetoric of the Self-Made Man* (Carbondale: Southern Illinois University Press, 2001).

6. Horatio Alger Association of Distinguished Americans (www.horatioalger.com).

7. This aspect of her story is mentioned in a biographical account for the Colorado Women's Hall of Fame; on-line at www.cogreatwomen.org.

8. Andrea Rabin, "The Last 'Women in Business' Story," *Denver Business*, June 1, 1985, 16.

9. "Three Coloradans Ranked among Richest Hispanics," *Rocky Mountain News*, March 17, 1995, 48A.

10. Additional information from an interview with Linda Alvarado, October 2, 2002, and from the following news articles: "Linda Alvarado Honored," *Denver Business Journal*, December 6, 2000, on-line at www.bizjournals.com/denver/stories/2000; Deborah Prussel, "Linda Alvarado: Women in Construction," *IMDiversity*, on-line at www.imdiversity.com/villages/woman; and "Constructing a Better America: Linda Alvarado," *American Dreams*, on-line at www.usdreams.com.

11. Though more inclusive, recent stories about self-made Americans still focus overwhelmingly on white males; for instance, of the one hundred Horatio Alger awards given between 1995 and 2004, only eleven went to women.

12. Wyllie, *Self-Made Man*, 7.

13. Roland Barthes, *Mythologies* (1957) (New York: Hill and Wang, 1972), 124.

14. Ibid.

15. George W. Bush, "Remarks by the President at Horatio Alger Awards" (April 6, 2001), www.whitehouse.gov.

16. Dahlia Jean Weinstein, "Chamber Fiesta Pays Tribute to Five Hispanic Pioneers," *Rocky Mountain News*, October 29, 2001, 14D.

17. "Hispanic Trailblazer Breaks All the Barriers," *American Dreams*; on-line at www.usdreams.com.

18. According to data collected in 1997 by the U.S. Bureau of Labor Statistics, only 10 percent of employed men worked 55 hours a week or more; among men employed as executives, officials, or managers, 20 percent did; and among professionals, 15 percent did. Male physicians and clergy had the longest work weeks, averaging 52 hours; women lawyers and teachers had the longest work weeks among women, averaging 46 and 45 hours, respectively. Daniel Hecker, "How Hours of Work Affect Occupational Earnings," *Monthly Labor Review*, October 1998, 8–18; on-line at www.bls.gov/opub/mlr/1998. For all nonagricultural workers who "usually work full time," the average number of hours worked per week in 2002 was 42.8 (www.bls.gov/cps/cpsaat20.pdf).

19. Money and the American Family Survey, conducted among 2,366 respondents between January 23 and February 21, 2000, by Research, Strategy, Management and Belden Russonello and Stewart for the American Association of Retired Persons; available through Lexis-Nexis.

20. Values Update Survey, conducted among 2,528 respondents between July 14 and August 5, 2003, by Princeton Survey Research Associates for the Pew Research Center for People and the Press; available through Lexis-Nexis.

21. General Social Survey 2000, conducted among 2,817 respondents, 1,861 of whom were asked this particular question, by the National Opinion Research Center at the University of Chicago, machine-readable data analysis; dataset available online at www.icpsr/gss.

22. General Social Survey 2000; my analysis, using the "SEI" measure of social status.

23. The relevant figures, respectively, for those who attributed getting ahead to hard work or to luck were as follows: agreeing that in America "People get rewarded for their intelligence and skills," 73 percent versus 49 percent; agreeing that "The way things are in America, people like me and my family have a good chance of improving our standard of living," 81 percent versus 68 percent; and disagreeing that "Inequality continues to exist because it benefits the rich and powerful," 22 percent versus 12 percent.

24. Decker, *Made in America*, xvi.

25. Hecker, "How Hours of Work Affect Occupational Earnings."

26. "Billboards Marketing Virtues We Can Use Now," *St. Petersburg Times*, February 2, 2002.

27. Among recent studies that also provide useful overviews of the research literature, see especially Reynolds Farley and Richard Alba, "The New Second Generation in the United States," *International Migration Review* 36, no. 3 (2002): 669–701; V. Louie, "Parents' Aspirations and Investment: The Role of Social Class in the Educational Experiences of 1.5- and Second-Generation Chinese Americans," *Harvard Educational Review* 71, no. 3 (2001): 438–74; Alejandro Portes and Dag MacLeod, "Educational Progress of Children of Immigrants: The Roles of Class, Ethnicity, and School Context," *Sociology of Education* 69, no. 4 (1996): 255–75; Alejandro Portes and Dag MacLeod, "Educating the Second Generation: Determinants of Academic Achievement among Children of Immigrants in the United States," *Journal of Ethnic and Migration Studies* 25, no. 3 (1999): 373–96; and Wendy Schwartz, *Immigrants and Their Educational Attainment: Some Facts and Findings* (New York: ERIC Clearinghouse on Urban Education, 1996).

28. Horatio Alger Association, www.horatioalger.com/members.

29. "Army Supports Full Claim in Gas-Test Death of Sheep," *New York Times*, August 21, 1968, 7; "Who Is Philip Anschutz," *Denver Post*, August 18, 2002; online at www.uswestretiree.org.

30. Ken Schallenkamp, "Contemporary Honors Award Recipient: Philip Anschutz 2000 Art, Oil, Sports, Railroads, Real Estate, Fiber-Optics, Agriculture, Telecommunications and Philanthropy," *Kansas Business Hall of Fame*, www.emporia.edu/kbhf/Contemporary/anschutz.

31. *Fortune*, September 6, 1999; quoted in ibid.

32. Mark Gimein, "The Greedy Bunch," *Fortune*, August 13, 2002.

33. "Unearned Break for Qwest Execs," *Rocky Mountain News,* January 17, 2004; "Corporate Scandals," *Atlanta Journal Constitution,* December 28, 2003.

34. Christopher Thorne, "Interior Department Says It Will Protect Sacred Indian Lands, but Tribal Leaders Skeptical," *Alliance of California Tribes News,* March 20, 2002; on-line at www.allianceofcatribes.org.

35. "Anschutz Reacts to 'Greediest Executive' Moniker," *Denver Business Journal,* August 13, 2002; on-line at www.bizjournals.com/denver.

36. Most accounts say that Mr. Anschutz was raised in Russell, Kansas, the hometown of Senator Bob Dole, a farming and oil-drilling community of about 6,000 people; others locate Mr. Anschutz's childhood in Hays, Kansas, population 11,947 in 1960.

37. Lewis MacAdams, "The Invisible Man: Billionaire Philip Anschutz Is Virtually Unknown to the Public," *Los Angeles Magazine,* October 1998, www.findarticles.com.

CHAPTER 5
IN AMERICA, ALL RELIGIONS ARE TRUE

1. Tocqueville, *Democracy in America,* vol. 2.

2. Will Herberg, *Protestant-Catholic-Jew: An Essay in American Religious Sociology* (Garden City, N.Y.: Doubleday, 1955).

3. One of the most useful overviews of American religion during the 1950s is Robert S. Ellwood, *The Fifties Spiritual Marketplace: American Religion in a Decade of Conflict* (New Brunswick, N.J.: Rutgers University Press, 1997); Ellwood's *1950: Crossroads of American Religious Life* (Louisville, Ky.: Westminster John Knox, 2000), is also helpful and covers a wider period than its title suggests. I have written about the 1950s as background to the subsequent changes in American public religion in my book *The Restructuring of American Religion: Society and Faith since World War II* (Princeton, N.J.: Princeton University Press, 1988), and as staging ground for later shifts in private spirituality in *After Heaven: Spirituality in America since the 1950s* (Berkeley and Los Angeles: University of California Press, 1998).

4. Diana Eck, "E Pluribus Unum: A New Religious America," *Humanities* 23 (September/October 2002): 24–26.

5. Ihsan Babgy, Paul M. Perl, and Bryan T. Froehle, *The Mosque in America: A National Portrait. A Report from the Mosque Study Project* (Washington, D.C.: Council on American-Islamic Relations, 2001).

6. Edwin Scott Gaustad and Philip L. Barlow, *New Historical Atlas of Religion in America* (New York: Oxford University Press, 2000), 268–74.

7. *Pluralism Project Directory*; on-line at www.pluralism.org.

8. James W. Coleman, *The New Buddhism: The Western Transformation of an Ancient Tradition* (New York: Oxford University Press, 2001).

9. Don Morreale, ed., *The Complete Guide to Buddhist America* (Boston: Shambala, 1998).

10. The Gallup information is summarized in a very useful paper by Michael Hout and Claude S. Fischer, "Religious Diversity in America, 1940–2000" (presented at the annual meeting of the American Sociological Association, Chicago, August 2001).

11. Guillermina Jasso, Douglas S. Massey, Mark R. Rosenzweig, and James P. Smith, "Exploring the Religious Preference of Recent Immigrants to the United States: Evidence from the New Immigrant Survey Pilot," in *Religion and Immigration: Christian, Jewish, and Muslim Experiences in the United States*, ed. Yvonne Haddad, Yazbeck Haddad, Jane I. Smith, and John L. Esposito (Walnut Creek, Calif.: AltaMira, 2003), 217–53.

12. Gaston Espinosa, Virgilio Elizondo, and Jesse Miranda, *Hispanic Churches in American Public Life: Summary of Findings* (Notre Dame, Ind.: University of Notre Dame, Institute for Latino Studies, 2003).

13. Arthur N. Tafoya, *Hispanic Ministry at the Turn of the New Millennium* (Washington, D.C.: United States Conference of Catholic Bishops, 2000).

14. Espinosa, Elizondo, and Miranda, *Hispanic Churches in American Public Life*, 16; figures obtained in the mid-1990s on Latino parishes and congregations are also reported in R. Stephen Warner, "Approaching Religious Diversity: Barriers, Byways, and Beginnings," *Sociology of Religion* 59 (Fall 1998): 193–215.

15. General Board of Discipleship, *Comprehensive Plans for Hispanic/Latino Ministries* (Nashville, Tenn.: United Methodist Church, 2000).

16. Michael Luo, "For Asian-American Churches, Integration Proves Complicated," *Associated Press*, June 2000; on-line at www.imdiversity.com.

17. George Gallup Jr. and D. Michael Lindsay, *Surveying the Religious Landscape* (Harrisburg, Pa.: Morehouse, 1999).

18. R. Stephen Warner, "Work in Progress toward a New Paradigm for the Sociological Study of Religion in the United States," *American Journal of Sociology* 98 (1993): 1044–93.

19. Roger Finke and Rodney Stark, *The Churching of America, 1776–1990: Winners and Losers in Our Religious Economy* (New Brunswick, N.J.: Rutgers University Press, 1992).

20. Dean M. Kelley, *Why Conservative Churches Are Growing: A Study in the Sociology of Religion* (New York: Harper & Row, 1972).

21. Laurence R. Iannaccone, "Why Strict Churches Are Strong," *American Journal of Sociology* 99 (1994): 1180–1211.

22. The Taiwan survey was conducted as part of the World Values Surveys and International Social Survey Program, which were carried out in more than 50 countries between 1996 and 1998; my analysis of weekly participation in religious services, based on a total of 81,492 respondents in 59 countries; data are available from the author or from the International Consortium for Political and Social Research at the University of Michigan.

23. In the World Values Surveys and International Social Survey Program, the percentages who reported attending religious services weekly in these countries were as follows: Russia, 4; Azerbaijan, 6; Belarus, 6; Croatia, 22; Estonia, 4; Serbia, 6; Slovenia, 13; and Ukraine, 10.

24. I leave aside here a number of other criticisms that could be raised about the religious markets perspective more generally, such as what exactly constitutes "competition" and whether "strict" religious groups generate vitality throughout the market or gain at the expense of less strict organizations in a kind of zero-sum game.

25. Carolyn Chen, "The Religious Varieties of Ethnic Presence: A Comparison between a Taiwanese Immigrant Buddhist Temple and an Evangelical Christian Church," *Sociology of Religion* 63 (Summer 2002): 215–38.

26. Wendy Cadge, *Heartwood: The First Generation of Theravada Buddhism in America* (Chicago: University of Chicago Press, 2005).

27. Prema Kurien, "Becoming American by Becoming Hindu: Indian Americans Take Their Place at the Multicultural Table," in *Gatherings in Diaspora: Religious Communities and the New Immigration,* ed. R. Stephen Warner and Judith G. Wittner (Philadelphia: Temple University Press, 1998), 37–70.

28. Warner, "Approaching Religious Diversity," 205.

29. Christian Smith, *American Evangelicalism: Embattled and Thriving* (Chicago: University of Chicago Press, 1998).

30. Wade Clark Roof, *A Generation of Seekers: The Spiritual Journeys of the Baby Boom Generation* (San Francisco: HarperSanFrancisco, 1993).

31. Alan Wolfe, *The Transformation of American Religion: How We Actually Live Our Faith* (New York: Free Press, 2003), especially chapter 7.

32. Theodore Caplow, Howard M. Bahr, and Bruce A. Chadwick, *All Faithful People* (Minneapolis: University of Minnesota Press, 1983), chapter 4.

33. Peter L. Berger, *The Sacred Canopy: Elements of a Sociological Theory of Religion* (Garden City, N.Y.: Doubleday, 1967).

34. It is important to note that these elites were selected because they had been reared as Muslims, Hindus, Buddhists, or Christians, but that still being actively involved in any of those traditions was not a requirement for inclusion.

35. William R. Hutchison, *Religious Pluralism in America: The Contentious History of a Founding Ideal* (New Haven: Yale University Press, 2003), 234.

36. José Casanova, *Public Religions in the Modern World* (Chicago: University of Chicago Press, 1994).

37. R. Laurance Moore, *Religious Outsiders and the Making of Americans* (New York: Oxford University Press, 1986).

38. Elaine Howard Ecklund, *Korean American Religion: Race, Ethnicity, and Civic Life* (New York: Oxford University Press, 2006).

39. Editorial, "Muslims in European Schools," *New York Times,* October 8, 2003.

40. Robert Wuthnow, Arts and Religion Survey (Princeton, N.J.: Princeton University, Department of Sociology, 1999 [machine-readable dataset]). The study was a representative survey of the adult U.S. population involving 1,530 respondents and

conducted by the Gallup Organization. Further description of the study is available in my book *All in Sync: How Music and Art Are Revitalizing American Religion* (Berkeley and Los Angeles: University of California Press, 2003). Eighty percent of foreign-born respondents said their beliefs were personal and private, compared with 72 percent of native-born respondents; 65 percent and 69 percent, respectively, agreed with the other statement. Among all respondents, 67 percent of religious conservatives agreed with the first statement, and 57 percent agreed with the second.

41. Wolfe, *The Transformation of American Religion*, especially 245–64.

42. Eck, "E Pluribus Unum," 26.

43. Kenneth Richard Samples, "Do All Religions Lead to God?" *Facts for Faith* 8 (2002): 52–58.

44. Robert N. Bellah, "Righteous Empire," *Christian Century* 120 (March 8, 2003): 20–23.

CHAPTER 6
ETHNIC TIES THAT BIND (LOOSELY)

1. Federal Bureau of Investigation, *Uniform Crime Reports* (2002); on-line at www.fbi.gov/ucr.

2. Fox News, "Opinion Dynamics Poll," conducted January 14–15, 2003, among 900 respondents; available on-line though Lexis-Nexis.

3. Wuthnow, Religion and Diversity Survey.

4. Maria Krysan, "Data Update to *Racial Attitudes in America*," an update and Web site to complement *Racial Attitudes in America: Trends and Interpretations*, rev. ed., by Howard Schuman, Charlotte Steeh, Lawrence Bobo, and Maria Krysan (Cambridge, Mass.: Harvard University Press, 1997); http://tigger.uic.edu/~krysan/racialattitudes.htm.

5. Lawrence D. Bobo, "Racial Attitudes and Relations at the Close of the Twentieth Century," in *America Becoming: Racial Trends and Their Consequences*, ed. Neil Smelser, William Julius Wilson, and Faith Mitchell (Washington, D.C.: National Academy Press, 2001), 262–99.

6. Ibid., 269.

7. Thomas C. Wilson, "Cohort and Prejudice: Whites' Attitudes toward Blacks, Hispanics, Jews, and Asians," *Public Opinion Quarterly* 60 (1996): 253–74; Wilson was also interested in the fact that the most recent cohorts were not less prejudiced than those who came of age during the 1960s, and speculated that they would have been had it not been for the more conservative climate of the Reagan era. For a review of theories of attitude formation during the civil rights movement and an examination of shifts leading up to the civil rights era, see Tacku Lee, "Black Insurgency and the Dynamics of Racial Attitudes in the United States, 1956–64" (paper presented at the annual meeting of the American Political Science Association, Washington, D.C., September 1997); on-line at www.ksg.harvard.edu/prg/lee/insurge/insurge.pdf.

8. See, for instance, Lauren M. McLaren, "Anti-Immigrant Prejudice in Europe: Contact, Threat Perception, and Preferences for the Exclusion of Migrants," *Social Forces* 81 (March 2003): 909–36.

9. The cultural roots and arguments of assimilationism have usefully been summarized in Charles Hirschman, "America's Melting Pot Reconsidered," *Annual Review of Sociology* 9 (1983): 397–423.

10. Among the ablest defenses of what I call the soft assimilationist perspective is Richard Alba and Victor Nee, *Remaking the American Mainstream: Assimilation and Contemporary Immigration* (Cambridge, Mass.: Harvard University Press, 2003); see also Richard Alba, "Immigration and the American Realities of Assimilation and Multiculturalism," *Sociological Forum* 14 (1999): 3–25. Although it relies less on the language of assimilation, this perspective is also ably defended in David A. Hollinger, *Postethnic America: Beyond Multiculturalism* (New York: Basic Books, 1995).

11. Nathan Glazer, *We Are All Multiculturalists Now* (Cambridge, Mass.: Harvard University Press, 1997).

12. A description of multiculturalism that demonstrates its differences from the view of pluralism presented here can be found in Christian Joppke, "Multiculturalism and Immigration: A Comparison of the United States, Germany, and Great Britain," *Theory and Society* 25 (August 1996): 449–500; Joppke describes multiculturalism as a world in which the individual is subordinated to groups that are inert, homogeneous, and mutually exclusive.

13. Jean Bethke Elshtain, "Review of *We Are All Multiculturalists Now*," *Civreview* 1 (May 1997), on-line at www.civnet.org/journal/issue1.

14. Alejandro Portes and Julia Sensenbrenner, "Embeddedness and Immigration: Notes on the Social Determinants of Economic Action," *American Journal of Sociology* 98 (1993): 1320–50.

15. Herbert Gans, "Symbolic Ethnicity: The Future of Ethnic Groups and Cultures in America," *Ethnic and Racial Studies* 2 (1979): 1–20.

16. This point has been nicely examined in Mary C. Waters, *Ethnic Options: Choosing Ethnic Identities in America* (Berkeley and Los Angeles: University of California Press, 1990).

17. Of course the success of ethnic business depends greatly on location and industry; for instance, see Alejandro Portes and Leif Jensen, "The Enclave and the Entrants: Patterns of Ethnic Enterprise in Miami before and after Mariel," *American Sociological Review* 54 (1989): 929–49; and John R. Logan, Richard D. Alba, and Thomas L. McNulty, "Ethnic Economies in Metropolitan Regions: Miami and Beyond," *Social Forces* 72 (1994): 691–724. The success of some ethnic businesses should not overshadow the larger point that I make in this chapter about pressures to assimilate among immigrants who wish to succeed in the wider society.

18. On the principle of parents and children sharing ethnic values, see especially Joseph Raz, *Ethics in the Public Domain* (New York: Oxford University Press, 1994).

19. The tendency to use country-of-origin labels was also evident in a national study of Latinos in which 88 percent said they use such terms to describe themselves,

compared with only 53 percent who use the term "American": Mollyann Brodie, Annie Steffenson, Jaime Valdez, Rebecca Levin, and Roberto Suro, *National Survey of Latinos* (Cambridge, Mass.: Kaiser Family Foundation, 2002).

20. Among Muslims, 66 percent helped parents financially; among Buddhists, 68 percent did. That remittances to parents were more common for groups whose parents were more likely to be in need is suggested by the fact that 73 percent of Hispanics in the study had fathers who had not graduated from college, compared with only 42 percent of Asian American Christians. However, other cultural factors are apparently involved as well, because even fewer Muslim, Hindu, and Buddhist respondents had fathers who had not graduated from college (26 percent, 35 percent, and 37 percent, respectively); i.e., in those groups, parents were more likely to have means of their own, and yet large percentages received remittances from children.

21. Peggy Levitt, "Social Remittances: A Local-Level, Migration-Driven Form of Cultural Diffusion," *International Migration Review* 32 (Winter 1999): 926–49.

22. Hispanics and Buddhists were the most likely to help siblings financially (47 percent and 49 percent, respectively, did so); Asian American Christians were least likely (18 percent did), and Muslims (42 percent) and Hindus (31 percent) were in between.

23. Feeling that one had been treated unfairly or discriminated against at work because of one's ethnicity varied from 36 percent among Muslims to 51 percent among Hindus, 56 percent among Hispanics, 65 percent among Buddhists, and 68 percent among Asian American Christians.

24. Victor Nee, Jimy M. Sanders, and Scott Sernau, "Job Transitions in an Immigrant Metropolis: Ethnic Boundaries and the Mixed Economy," *American Sociological Review* 59 (1994). 849–72.

25. Social scientists sometimes refer to this process of responding to the present through the lessons of the past as "path dependency"; for a valuable study that focuses more on the role of culture, see Frank Dobbin, *Forging Industrial Policy: The United States, Britain, and France in the Railway Age* (New York: Cambridge University Press, 1994).

26. The classic study of prejudice and discrimination against immigrants during the nineteenth and early twentieth centuries is John Higham, *Strangers in the Land: Patterns of American Nativism, 1860–1925*, 2nd ed. (New Brunswick, N.J.: Rutgers University Press, 1988).

27. Wilson, *When Work Disappears.*

28. Richard Rodriguez, "The Browning of America," *Pacific News Service*, February 23, 1998; on-line at www.pacificnews.org/jinn/stories.

29. Frank Wu, *Yellow: Race in America beyond Black and White* (New York: Basic Books, 2002).

30. Nathan Glazer, "Pluralism and the New Immigrants," *Society* 35 (January/February 1998): 232–38.

31. The other problem with the let-them-start-voluntary-associations response is that hardly anyone—only 4 percent of the public at large—seems to be involved in any kind of ethnic or nationality organization; the difficulties that all such voluntary

associations face and the reasons for their declining memberships have been extensively examined in Putnam, *Bowling Alone.*

32. Robert D. Putnam, *Making Democracy Work: Civic Traditions in Modern
Italy* (Princeton, N.J.: Princeton University Press, 1994).

33. Marcelo M. Suarez-Orozco, "Everything You Ever Wanted to Know about
Assimilation but Were Afraid to Ask," *Daedalus* 129 (Fall 2000): 1–30; the quotation
is on 23.

34. On these larger issues, see Alan Wolfe, ed., *School Choice: The Moral Debate*
(Princeton, N.J.: Princeton University Press, 2003).

35. F. L. Jones, "Convergence and Divergence in Ethnic Divorce Patterns: A Research Note," *Journal of Marriage and the Family* 58 (February 1996): 213–18.

36. Gregory Rodriguez, "Mongrel America," *Atlantic Monthly* 291 (January/
February 2003): 95–98. National figures suggesting growing preferences for interethnic marriages are contradicted by figures suggesting preferences for endogamy
in areas with higher proportions of coethnic residents: for instance, in Los Angeles
County, 85 percent of Mexican-origin women in 1990 were married to Mexican-
origin men; see David E. Hayes-Bautista, *American Dream Makers: Latino Profiles
Study Report* (Los Angeles: Loyola Marymount Center for the Study of Los Angeles,
2000). On endogamy as marital preference, see also Matthijs Kalmijn, "Assortative
Mating by Cultural and Economic Occupational Status," *American Journal of Sociology* 100 (September 1994): 422–52.

CHAPTER 7
SAVING OURSELVES FROM MATERIALISM

1. Lawrence Ferlinghetti, *A Coney Island of the Mind: Poems* (1958) (New York:
New Directions, 1974).

2. Howard Rheingold, "Look Who's Talking," *Wired Magazine* 7 (January 1999);
on-line at www.wired.com.

3. Nicolaus Mills, *The Triumph of Meanness: America's War against Its Better
Self* (New York: Houghton Mifflin, 1997).

4. Wayne Parry, "Group Promotes Muslim Values," *Grand Rapids Press*, January
4, 2003, B3.

5. A poll conducted in 1997 in North Carolina, for instance, showed that four out
of five respondents thought Hispanics were hardworking; only 8 percent thought
they were not industrious: David Williamson, "New Survey: Influx of Hispanics
Displeases Some State Residents," *UNC News*, August 26, 1997; on-line at
www.unc.edu/news.

6. Holly Marsingill, "Don't Discriminate against Hard-Working Immigrant Families," *Athens Banner-Herald*, January 21, 2003; on-line at www.onlineathens.com/
stories.

7. Huang Communications; on-line at www.huangcomm.com.

8. Mireya Navarro, "Miami's Generations of Exiles Side by Side, yet Worlds Apart," *New York Times*, February 11, 1999, A1, A25.

9. Quoted in Laura Meckler, "Bush Urges Americans to Volunteer," November 9, 2001; on-line at www.firehouse.com.

10. "State of the Union, Columbus Day Survey: Looking for America," Princeton Survey Research Associates for Wisconsin Public Television; on-line at www.pbs.org/weta.

11. During the early 1990s I directed a large research project involving hundreds of in-depth interviews with ordinary Americans in which they talked about their work, possessions, and views about money; see my book *Poor Richard's Principle: Recovering the American Dream through the Moral Dimension of Work, Business, and Money* (Princeton, N.J.: Princeton University Press, 1996).

12. Narbeth Emmanuel, "Diversity Is a Project All Should Work on Together," October 30, 1997; on-line at www.siue.edu.

13. Roberto Suro, *Strangers among Us: How Latino Immigration Is Transforming America* (New York: Knopf, 1998).

14. Jane I. Smith, quoted in Amy Miller, "Between Two Worlds: The Islamic Conversion of Mary Am Beulen," in *Race and Ethnicity in the New Urban America*; on-line at www.jrn.columbia.edu.

15. David B. Burrell, "The Attraction of Islam," *Commonweal* 130 (January 17, 2003): 17–19.

16. Daniel B. Wood, "Buddhist Practices Make Inroads in the U.S.," *Christian Science Monitor*, November 3, 1997.

17. Wuthnow, Religion and Diversity Survey.

18. I discussed these criticisms in chapter 6.

19. Suarez-Orozco, "Everything You Ever Wanted to Know about Assimilation."

20. See, for instance, Henry Nash Smith, *Virgin Land: The American West as Symbol and Myth* (Cambridge, Mass.: Harvard University Press, 1950).

21. Thomas Jefferson, "Letter to Madison" (1787), in *Thomas Jefferson: Writings*, ed. Merrill D. Peterson (New York: Library of America, 1984).

22. Rebecca Kneale Gould, "Getting (Not Too) Close to Nature: Modern Homesteading as Lived Religion in America," in *Lived Religion in America: Toward a History of Practice*, ed. David D. Hall (Princeton, N.J.: Princeton University Press, 1997), 217–42.

23. Kathleen Norris, *Dakota: A Spiritual Geography* (New York: Ticknor & Fields, 1993), 168–69.

24. John Adams, "Letter from John Adams to Abigail Adams (May 12, 1780); from the Massachusetts Historical Society Adams Papers Collection; on-line at www.masshist.org; also quoted in Richard Brookhiser, *America's First Dynasty: The Adamses, 1735–1918* (New York: Free Press, 2002).

25. Ralph Waldo Emerson, "Art," in *Essays: First Series* (London: James Fraser, 1841), essay 12.

26. Greg Glazner, *From the Iron Chair: Poems* (New York: Norton, 1992), 80.

27. Wuthnow, Arts and Religion Survey; also described in my book *All In Sync*. The statistical relationship I mention here is not attributable to more general differences in educational levels, gender, or other background characteristics between those with less and those with more exposure to the arts.

28. Among other sources see especially Nancy F. Cott, *The Bonds of Womanhood: "Woman's Sphere" in New England, 1780–1835*, 2nd ed. (New Haven: Yale University Press, 1997).

29. Thorstein Veblen, *The Theory of the Leisure Class* (1899) (New York: Viking, 1967).

30. Catharine E. Beecher, *A Treatise on Domestic Economy, for the Use of Young Ladies at Home, and at School*, rev. ed. (Boston: T. H. Webb, 1842), 137–38.

31. Norman Mailer, "The White Negro" (1957), in *Legacy of Dissent*, ed. Nicolaus Mills (New York: Touchstone, 1994), 153–74; the quotation is on 157.

32. Ibid., 153, 157.

33. Carol Stack, *All Our Kin: Strategies for Survival in a Black Community* (New York: Basic Books, 1974); the Houston report, entitled "The Black Community Today," is available on-line at www.neosoft.com/~sgriffin/houstonhistory/ethnic/history3blacks.htm.

34. Georg Simmel, *On Individuality and Social Forms* (1908), ed. Donald N. Levine (Chicago: University of Chicago Press, 1971), 145.

35. Wuthnow, Arts and Religion Survey; the difference between first-generation and other Americans was in the proportion who thought "materialism" was a "serious" problem in the United States (42 percent versus 37 percent), not in the proportion who said it was an extremely serious problem (33 percent in both cases); only 49 percent of Asian Americans thought materialism was a serious or extremely serious problem, compared with 70 percent of whites and 77 percent of African Americans.

36. Michelle Singletary, "Living above Your Means Can Put You in the Poor House," *Washington Post*, May 11, 2003.

37. Wuthnow, Arts and Religion Survey; in each instance, about half of those who thought the problem was at least "serious" said it was "extremely serious."

38. *Newsweek*, April 29, 2000, a national survey conducted among 509 parents of teenagers age 13 to 19 by Princeton Survey Research Associates; *Public Opinion Online*, available through Lexis-Nexis.

39. Robert Wuthnow, *God and Mammon in America* (New York: Free Press, 1994), 173, 181.

40. Bureau of Labor Statistics, *Consumer Expenditures in 2001* (Washington, D.C.: U.S. Department of Labor, April 2003), Report 966.

41. John de Graaf, David Wann, and Thomas H. Naylor, *Affluenza: The All-Consuming Epidemic* (San Francisco: Berrett-Koehler, 2001), 13.

42. John R. Schneider, *The Good of Affluence: Seeking God in a Culture of Wealth* (Grand Rapids, Mich.: Eerdmans, 2002).

43. Central Intelligence Agency, *The World Factbook, 2002*; on-line at www.odci.gov/cia/publications.

44. U.S. Census Bureau, *Statistical Abstract of the United States: 2002* (Washington, D.C.: Government Printing Office, 2002), p. 835, table 1321.

45. Ibid., p. 831, table 1316.

46. Central Intelligence Agency, *World Factbook, 2002.*

47. The percentages mentioned are from my own analysis of the surveys, which are known as the World Values Surveys and the European Values Surveys; further information on the surveys can be found in Loek Halman, *The European Values Study: A Third Wave* (Tilburg, Netherlands: Tilburg University Press, 2001); and on-line at www.worldvaluessurvey.org. The term "post-materialism" is from Ronald Inglehart, *Culture Shift in Advanced Industrial Society* (Princeton, N.J.: Princeton University Press, 1989).

48. The complexities of this "soft" form of American power are insightfully examined in Joseph S. Nye Jr., *The Paradox of American Power: Why the World's Only Superpower Can't Go It Alone* (New York: Oxford University Press, 2002).

49. Kohut, *Views of a Changing World;* on-line at people-press.org/reports.

50. Dora L. Costa, "American Living Standards: Evidence from Recreational Expenditures," National Bureau of Economic Research, NBER Working Papers (May 1999), No. 7148; on-line at ideas.repec.org.

51. Victor C. Strasburger, "Children and TV Advertising: Nowhere to Run, Nowhere to Hide," *Journal of Developmental and Behavioral Pediatrics* 22 (June 2001): 185–87.

52. Joseph Mercola, "Turn Off the TV and Your Kids Become Less Materialistic," *Journal of Developmental and Behavioral Pediatrics* 22 (June 2001): 179–84.

53. James B. Twitchell, *Living It Up: Our Love Affair with Luxury* (New York: Columbia University Press, 2002), 48.

54. Juliet Schor, "The New Politics of Consumption: Why Americans Want So Much More Than They Need," *Boston Review* 24 (Summer 1999); on-line at bostonreview.net.

55. An especially useful historical study that puts the recent concerns about materialism in a larger perspective is Lizabeth Cohen, *A Consumer's Republic: The Politics of Mass Consumption in Postwar America* (New York: Knopf, 2003).

56. Herberg, *Protestant-Catholic-Jew,* 186.

57. Beth Wenger, "Memory as Identity: The Invention of the Lower East Side," *American Jewish History* 85 (March 1997): 3–27; the quotation is on 3.

58. Jenna Weissman Joselit, *Wonders of America: Reinventing Jewish Culture, 1880–1950* (New York: Hill and Wang, 1994).

59. Robert Anthony Orsi, *The Madonna of 115th Street: Faith and Community in Italian Harlem, 1880–1950* (New Haven: Yale University Press, 1985).

60. M. R. Lovett, "Interview with Vito Cacciola #24, February 10, 1939," *American Life Histories: Manuscripts from the Federal Writers' Project, 1936–1940* (Washington, D.C.: Library of Congress, 1940); on-line at memory.loc.gov.

61. Gustavo Gutierrez, quoted in Daniel Hartnett, "Remembering the Poor," *America* 188 (February 3, 2003): 12–16.

62. Gary Cross, *An All-Consuming Century: Why Commercialism Won in Modern America* (New York: Columbia University Press, 2000), also stresses the relationship between immigrant Catholicism and anticommercialism.

63. Tom Hayden and Dick Flacks, "The Port Huron Statement at 40," *The Nation* 275 (August 5–12, 2002): 18–21.

64. Lee Siegel, "Seize the Day Job," *Harper's* 302 (March 2001): 75–83; quoted in Andrew Furman, "The Exaggerated Demise of the Jewish-American Writer," *Chronicle of Higher Education* 47 (July 6, 2001): B7–B9.

65. Steve McKinley, "Time's Up"; on-line at house-of-prayer.com/sermons/03/09/03_Times_Up.htm.

66. *Religion and Ethics Newsweekly* and *U.S. News and World Report*, April 26, 2002; a survey of 2,002 representative adult respondents conducted by Mitoftsky International and Edison Media Research; *Public Opinion Online*, available through Lexis-Nexis.

67. For Goodness Sake Survey, January 9, 2001, a national survey of 1,507 adults conducted for the Pew Charitable Trust by the Public Agenda Foundation; *Public Opinion Online*, available through Lexis-Nexis.

68. Wuthnow, *God and Mammon in America*, 129.

69. Harold Bloom, *The American Religion: The Emergence of the Post-Christian Nation* (New York: Simon & Schuster, 1992), 31.

70. Matt. 19:16–30; Luke 12:13–21.

71. I quote here from one of the later versions of Beecher's popular advice book: Catharine E. Beecher, *Miss Beecher's Housekeeper and Healthkeeper: Containing Five Hundred Recipes for Economical and Healthful Cooking; Also, Many Directions for Securing Health and Happiness* (New York: Harper & Brothers, 1873), 260; italics in the original.

72. Abraham Lincoln, "Second Inaugural Address," given Saturday, March 4, 1865; see especially Ronald White Jr., *Lincoln's Greatest Speech: The Second Inaugural* (New York: Simon & Schuster, 2002).

73. Noll, *America's God*, 426–38.

74. Still especially valuable on this aspect of Marx's thought is Bertell Ollman, *Alienation: Marx's Conception of Man in Capitalist Society* (Cambridge: Cambridge University Press, 1971).

75. Max Weber, *The Protestant Ethic and the Spirit of Capitalism* (1904–5), trans. Talcott Parsons (New York: Charles Scribner's Sons, 1958), 181.

76. Max Weber, *Economy and Society: An Outline of Interpretive Sociology*, ed. Guenther Roth and Claus Wittich (Berkeley and Los Angeles: University of California Press, 1978), 1:24.

77. Weber, *Protestant Ethic*, 182.

78. David Brooks, *Bobos in Paradise: The New Upper Class and How They Got There* (New York: Touchstone, 2000), 83.

79. Ole Edvart Rolvaag, *Giants in the Earth: A Saga of the Prairie*, trans. Lincoln Colcord (New York: Harper, 1927); quoted in Norris, *Dakota*, 168.

80. Richard Wightman Fox and T. J. Jackson Lears, eds., *The Culture of Consumption: Critical Essays in American History, 1880–1980* (New York: Knopf, 1983).

81. Costa, "American Living Standards," table 1.

82. Frank W. Blackmar, *Kansas: A Cyclopedia of State History, Embracing Events, Institutions, Industries, Counties, Cities, Towns, Prominent Persons, Etc.* (Chicago: Standard Pub. Co., 1912), 1:622–29; the larger history of the Farmers' Alliance is included in Lawrence Goodwyn, *The Populist Moment: A Short History of the Agrarian Revolt in America* (Oxford: Oxford University Press, 1978).

83. "To Help the Farmers: Growth of the Farmers' Alliance Throughout Kansas," *New York Times*, December 14, 1889.

84. Craig Miner, *Kansas: The History of the Sunflower State, 1854–2000* (Lawrence: University of Kansas Press, 2002).

85. Edward Wolff, "Recent Trends in Wealth Ownership, 1983–1998," Levy Institute Working Paper (2000), table 3; on income inequality, see Bureau of the Census, *Money Income in the United States* (Washington, D.C.: U.S. Department of Commerce, 1997), Current Population Reports, P60-200.

86. The Gini index for distribution of family incomes, which yields higher scores for higher levels of inequality, was 41 in the United States in 2001, 37 in England, 33 in France, and 30 in Germany; CIA, *World Factbook 2002*.

87. Wade Clark Roof, *Spiritual Marketplace: Baby Boomers and the Remaking of American Religion* (Princeton, N.J.: Princeton University Press, 1999).

88. Murray Joseph Haar, "Self-Serving Redemptionism: A Jewish-Christian Lament," *Theology Today* 52 (April 1995): 108–12.

89. Juliet Schor, *The Overspent American: Why We Want What We Don't Need* (New York: Harper Perennial, 1999).

90. Wuthnow, *Poor Richard's Principle*, chapters 6 and 7.

91. On shopping, national transportation data indicate that travel in the United States involving "consumer activities" grew from 29.3 percent of all travel in 1969 to 44.3 percent in 1995: Johanna P. Zmud and Carlos H. Arce, "Influence of Consumer Culture and Race on Travel Behavior," *TRB Transportation Research Circular E-C926—Personal Travel: The Long and Short of It*; available on-line at gulliver.trb.org/publications.

92. Lawrence Ferlinghetti, "To the Oracle at Delphi," in *San Francisco Poems* (San Francisco: City Lights Foundation, 2001).

CHAPTER 8
VENUES FOR REFLECTIVE DEMOCRACY

1. Jeffrey Stout, *Democracy and Tradition* (Princeton, N.J.: Princeton University Press, 2003), is especially helpful in showing the continuing relevance of tradition, and of discourse rooted in tradition, to democracy.

2. The importance of reflection, and of alone-time spent reflecting, has valuably been emphasized by Robert Goodin, *Reflective Democracy* (Oxford: Oxford University Press, 2003); however, it seems to me that Goodin stops short of recognizing the full implications of such reflection insofar as he writes too much within the framework of rational political theory and thus focuses almost entirely on thoughts about arguments, reasons, and expressed preferences.

3. Jürgen Habermas, *The Theory of Communicative Action*, vol. 1, *Reason and the Rationalization of Society* (Boston: Beacon, 1981), and *The Theory of Communicative Action*, vol. 2, *Lifeworld and System: A Critique of Functionalist Reason* (Boston: Beacon, 1987); Habermas's concern with the lifeworld as context in which rational communicative action occurs is another point at which his arguments intersect with my emphasis on the ambience of deep cultural assumptions.

4. Paul Lichterman, *Elusive Togetherness: Religious Groups and Civic Engagement in America* (Princeton, N.J.: Princeton University Press, 2005).

5. Judith Rodin, "The University as Discourse Community," in *Public Discourse in America: Conversation and Community in the Twenty-First Century*, ed. Judith Rodin and Stephen P. Steinberg (Philadelphia: University of Pennsylvania Press, 2003), 232–36; the quotation is on 235.

6. Paul Ricoeur, *Freud and Philosophy: An Essay on Interpretation* (New Haven: Yale University Press, 1970). Useful secondary sources include David Stewart, "The Hermeneutics of Suspicion," *Journal of Literature and Theology* 3 (1989): 296–307; and Anthony Thisleton, *New Horizons in Hermeneutics* (Grand Rapids, Mich.: Zondervan, 1992).

7. Besides Ricoeur, one thinks especially of Louis Althusser, Hannah Arendt, Viktor Frankl, Eric Fromm, Jacques Lacan, Herbert Marcuse, and Theodor Adorno.

# SELECTED BIBLIOGRAPHY

Adams, John. "Letter to John Taylor, April 15, 1814." In *The Works of John Adams, Second President of the United States: With a Life of the Author, Notes and Illustrations*, edited by Charles Francis Adams, 6:484–85. Boston: Little Brown, 1851.

Alba, Richard. "Immigration and the American Realities of Assimilation and Multiculturalism." *Sociological Forum* 14 (1999): 3–25.

Alba, Richard, and Victor Nee. *Remaking the American Mainstream: Assimilation and Contemporary Immigration*. Cambridge, Mass.: Harvard University Press, 2003.

Alexander, Jeffrey C. *Durkheimian Sociology: Cultural Studies*. Cambridge: Cambridge University Press, 1990.

———. *The Meanings of Social Life: A Cultural Sociology*. Cambridge: Cambridge University Press, 2003.

Aronovici, Carol. "Americanization: Its Meaning and Function." *American Journal of Sociology* 25 (May 1920): 695–730.

Babgy, Ihsan, Paul M. Perl, and Bryan T. Froehle. *The Mosque in America: A National Portrait. A Report from the Mosque Study Project*. Washington, D.C.: Council on American-Islamic Relations, 2001.

Baron, Stephen, John Field, and Tom Schuller, eds. *Social Capital: Critical Perspectives*. New York: Oxford University Press, 2001.

Barth, John. *Lost in the Funhouse*. New York: Doubleday, 1988.

Barthes, Roland. *Mythologies*. New York: Hill and Wang, 1972.

Beecher, Catharine E. *Miss Beecher's Housekeeper and Healthkeeper: Containing Five Hundred Recipes for Economical and Healthful Cooking; Also, Many Directions for Securing Health and Happiness*. New York: Harper & Brothers, 1873.

———. *A Treatise on Domestic Economy, for the Use of Young Ladies at Home, and at School*. Rev. ed. Boston: T. H. Webb, 1842.

Bellah, Robert N. *The Broken Covenant: American Civil Religion in Time of Trial*. New York: Seabury, 1975.

———. "Righteous Empire." *Christian Century* 120 (March 8, 2003): 20–23.

Bellah, Robert N., Richard Madsen, William M. Sullivan, Ann Swidler, and Steven M. Tipton. *Habits of the Heart: Individualism and Commitment in American Life*. Berkeley and Los Angeles: University of California Press, 1985; rev. ed., 1996.

Benedict, Ruth. *Patterns of Culture*. New York: Mentor Books, 1960.

Berger, Peter L. *The Sacred Canopy: Elements of a Sociological Theory of Religion.* Garden City, N.Y.: Doubleday, 1967.

Berger, Peter L., and Thomas Luckmann. *The Social Construction of Reality: A Treatise in the Sociology of Knowledge.* New York: Doubleday, 1966.

Berger, Peter L., and Richard John Neuhaus. *To Empower People: The Role of Mediating Structures in Public Policy.* Boston: Rowman & Littlefield, 1977.

Blackmar, Frank W. *Kansas: A Cyclopedia of State History, Embracing Events, Institutions, Industries, Counties, Cities, Towns, Prominent Persons, Etc.* Chicago: Standard Pub. Co, 1912.

Blackmun, Maya. "Home at Last—after 14 Years." *Portland Oregonian,* September 14, 1992, B1.

Bloom, Harold. *The American Religion: The Emergence of the Post-Christian Nation.* New York: Simon & Schuster, 1992.

Bobo, Lawrence. "Racial Attitudes and Relations at the Close of the Twentieth Century." In *America Becoming: Racial Trends and Their Consequences,* edited by Neil J. Smelser, William Julius Wilson, and Faith Mitchell. Washington, D.C.: National Academy Press, 2001.

Brodie, Mollyann, Annie Steffenson, Jaime Valdez, Rebecca Levin, and Roberto Suro. *National Survey of Latinos.* Cambridge, Mass.: Kaiser Family Foundation, 2002.

Brookhiser, Richard. *America's First Dynasty: The Adamses, 1735–1918.* New York: Free Press, 2002.

Brooks, David. *Bobos in Paradise: The New Upper Class and How They Got There.* New York: Touchstone, 2000.

———. "Refuting the Cynics." *New York Times,* November 25, 2003.

Brown, Deward Clayton. *Electricity for Rural America: The Fight for the REA.* Westport, Conn.: Greenwood Press, 1980.

Brown, Norman O. *Love's Body.* New York: Vintage, 1966.

Bunis, Dena, and Anh Do. "Ex-Refugee Is Nominated for Justice Post: Immigrants, a Fullerton High Grad Gets Praise at His Senate Confirmation Hearing." *Orange County Register,* May 10, 2001.

Bureau of Labor Statistics. *Consumer Expenditures in 2001.* Washington, D.C.: U.S. Department of Labor, 2003.

Burrell, David B. "The Attraction of Islam." *Commonweal* 130 (January 17, 2003): 17–19.

Cadge, Wendy. *Heartwood: The First Generation of Theravada Buddhism in America.* Chicago: University of Chicago Press, 2005.

Caplow, Theodore, Howard M. Bahr, and Bruce A. Chadwick. *All Faithful People.* Minneapolis: University of Minnesota Press, 1983.

Casanova, José. *Public Religions in the Modern World.* Chicago: University of Chicago Press, 1994.

Catano, James V. *Ragged Dicks: Masculinity, Steel, and the Rhetoric of the Self-Made Man.* Carbondale: Southern Illinois University Press, 2001.

Cerulo, Karen A., ed. *Culture in Mind: Toward a Sociology of Culture and Cognition.* New York: Routledge, 2002.

Chafets, Zev. "Why They Hate: U.S. Land of the Free Seduces World's Sons and Daughters." *New York Daily News,* September 1, 2002.

Chaves, Mark, and John R. Sutton. "Organizational Consolidation in American Protestant Denominations, 1890–1990." *Journal for the Scientific Study of Religion* 43 (2004): 1–23.

Chen, Carolyn. "The Religious Varieties of Ethnic Presence: A Comparison between a Taiwanese Immigrant Buddhist Temple and an Evangelical Christian Church." *Sociology of Religion* 63 (Summer 2002): 215–38.

Cohen, Lizabeth. *A Consumer's Republic: The Politics of Mass Consumption in Postwar America.* New York: Knopf, 2003.

Coleman, James W. *The New Buddhism: The Western Transformation of an Ancient Tradition.* New York: Oxford University Press, 2001.

Cortez, Carlos. "The Immigrant in Film: Evolution of an Illuminating Icon." In *Beyond the Stars: Stock Characters in American Popular Film,* edited by Paul Loukides and Linda K. Fuller. Bowling Green, Ohio: Bowling Green University Popular Press, 1990.

Cott, Nancy F. *The Bonds of Womanhood: "Woman's Sphere" in New England, 1780–1834.* 2nd ed. New Haven: Yale University Press, 1997.

Cross, Gary. *An All-Consuming Century: Why Commercialism Won in Modern America.* New York: Columbia University Press, 2000.

Csikszentmihalyi, Mihaly. *Finding Flow.* New York: Basic Books, 1997.

Decker, Louis. *Made in America: Self-Styled Success from Horatio Alger to Oprah Winfrey.* Minneapolis: University of Minnesota Press, 1997.

Dewey, John. "The School as a Means of Developing a Social Consciousness and Social Ideals in Children." *Journal of Social Forces* 1 (September 1923): 513–17.

Dobbin, Frank. *Forging Industrial Policy: The United States, Britain, and France in the Railway Age.* New York: Cambridge University Press, 1994.

Durkheim, Émile. *The Elementary Forms of Religious Life.* Translated by Carol Cosman. Introduction by Mark Sydney Cladis. New York: Oxford University Press, 2001.

———. *On Morality and Society: Selected Writings.* Edited by Robert N. Bellah. The Heritage of Sociology. Chicago: University of Chicago Press, 1973.

Eck, Diana. "E Pluribus Unum: A New Religious America." *Humanities* 23 (September/October 2002): 24–26.

Ecklund, Elaine Howard. *Korean American Religion: Race, Ethnicity, and Civic Life.* New York: Oxford University Press, 2006.

Ehrenhalt, Alan. *The Lost City: The Forgotten Virtues of Community in America.* New York: Basic Books, 1995.

Eliasoph, Nina, and Paul Lichterman. "Culture in Interaction." *American Journal of Sociology* 108 (January 2003): 735–94.

Eliot, Charles William. "Five American Contributions to Civilization." In *The Oxford Book of American Essays,* edited by Brander Matthews. New York: Oxford University Press, 1914.

Ellwood, Robert S. *The Fifties Spiritual Marketplace: American Religion in a Decade of Conflict*. New Brunswick, N.J.: Rutgers University Press, 1997.

———. *1950: Crossroads of American Religious Life*. Louisville, Ky.: Westminster John Knox, 2000.

Elshtain, Jean Bethke. *Democracy on Trial*. New York: Basic Books, 1995.

———. "Review of *We Are All Multiculturalists Now*." *Civreview* 1 (May 1997).

Elson, Ruth Miller. *Guardians of Tradition: American Schoolbooks of the Nineteenth Century*. Lincoln: University of Nebraska Press, 1964.

Emerson, Ralph Waldo. "Art." In *Essays: First Series*, essay 12. London: James Fraser, 1841.

Emirbayer, Mustafa, and Ann Mische. "What Is Agency?" *American Journal of Sociology* 103, no. 4 (January 1998): 962–1023.

Erikson, Erik. *Identity and the Life Cycle*. Psychological Monographs, vol. 1, New York: International Universities Press, 1959.

Espinosa, Gaston, Virgilio Elizondo, and Jesse Miranda. *Hispanic Churches in American Public Life: Summary of Findings*. Notre Dame, Ind.: University of Notre Dame Institute for Latino Studies, 2003.

Etzioni, Amitai. "How Liberty Is Lost." *Society* 40 (July/August 2003): 44–51.

———. "The Responsive Community: A Communitarian Perspective." *American Sociological Review* 61 (February 1996): 1–11.

———. "Too Many Rights, Too Few Responsibilities." In *Toward a Global Civil Society*, edited by Amitai Etzioni, 95–105. Providence, R.I.: Berghahn Books, 1995.

Farley, Reynolds, and Richard Alba. "The New Second Generation in the United States." *International Migration Review* 36, no. 3 (2002): 669–701.

Ferlinghetti, Lawrence. *A Coney Island of the Mind: Poems*. New York: New Directions, 1974.

———. *San Francisco Poems*. San Francisco: City Lights Foundation, 2001.

Finke, Roger, and Rodney Stark. *The Churching of America, 1776–1990: Winners and Losers in Our Religious Economy*. New Brunswick, N.J.: Rutgers University Press, 1992.

Fischer, Claude S. *America Calling: A Social History of the Telephone to 1940*. Berkeley and Los Angeles: University of California Press, 1992.

Foner, Nancy. *From Ellis Island to JFK: New York's Two Great Waves of Immigration*. New Haven: Yale University Press; New York: Russell Sage Foundation, 2000.

Fox, Richard Wightman, and T. J. Jackson Lears, eds. *The Culture of Consumption: Critical Essays in American History, 1880–1980*. New York: Knopf, 1983.

Fromm, Erich. *Escape from Freedom*. New York: Farrar & Rinehart, 1941.

Fukuyama, Francis. *Trust: The Social Virtues and the Creation of Prosperity*. New York: Free Press, 1995.

Furman, Andrew. "The Exaggerated Demise of the Jewish-American Writer." *Chronicle of Higher Education* 47 (July 6 2001): B7–B9.

Gallup, George, Jr., and Michael Lindsay. *Surveying the Religious Landscape*. Harrisburg, Pa.: Morehouse, 1999.

Gans, Herbert J. *The Levittowners: Ways of Life and Politics in a New Suburban Community*. New York: Pantheon, 1967.

———. "Symbolic Ethnicity: The Future of Ethnic Groups and Cultures in America." *Ethnic and Racial Studies* 2 (1979): 1–20.

Garfinkel, Harold. "Conditions of Successful Degradation Ceremonies." *American Journal of Sociology* 61 (1956): 420–24.

Gaustad, Edwin Scott, and Philip L. Barlow. *New Historical Atlas of Religion in America*. New York: Oxford University Press, 2000.

Geertz, Clifford. *The Interpretation of Cultures*. New York: Basic Books, 1973.

General Board of Discipleship. *Comprehensive Plans for Hispanic/Latino Ministries*. Nashville, Tenn.: United Methodist Church, 2000.

Giddens, Anthony. *Modernity and Self-Identity: Self and Society in the Late Modern Age*. Stanford, Calif.: Stanford University Press, 1991.

Gilbert, G. Nigel, and Michael Mulkay. *Opening Pandora's Box: A Sociological Analysis of Scientists' Discourse*. Cambridge: Cambridge University Press, 1984.

Glazer, Nathan. "Pluralism and the New Immigrants." *Society* 35 (January/February 1998): 232–38.

———. *We Are All Multiculturalists Now*. Cambridge, Mass.: Harvard University Press, 1997.

Glazner, Greg. *From the Iron Chair: Poems*. New York: Norton, 1992.

Goodin, Robert. *Reflective Democracy*. Oxford: Oxford University Press, 2003.

Goodwyn, Lawrence. *The Populist Moment: A Short History of the Agrarian Revolt in America*. Oxford: Oxford University Press, 1978.

Gould, Rebecca Kneale. "Getting (Not Too) Close to Nature: Modern Homesteading as Lived Religion in America." In *Lived Religion in America: Toward a History of Practice*, edited by David D. Hall, 217–42. Princeton, N.J.: Princeton University Press, 1997.

Graaf, John de, David Wann, and Thomas H. Naylor. *Affluenza: The All-Consuming Epidemic*. San Francisco: Berrett-Koehler, 2001.

Greeley, Horace. *Miscellanies*. New York: J. B. Ford, 1869.

Griffith, R. Marie. *God's Daughters: Evangelical Women and the Power of Submission*. Berkeley and Los Angeles: University of California Press, 1997.

Haar, Murray Joseph. "Self-Serving Redemptionism: A Jewish-Christian Lament." *Theology Today* 52 (April 1995): 108–12.

Habermas, Jürgen. *The Theory of Communicative Action*. Vol. 1, *Reason and the Rationalization of Society*. Boston: Beacon, 1981.

———. *The Theory of Communicative Action*. Vol. 2, *Lifeworld and System: A Critique of Functionalist Reason*. Boston: Beacon, 1987.

Halberstam, David. *The Fifties*. New York: Fawcett, 1993.

Halman, Loek. *The European Values Study: A Third Wave*. Tilburg, Netherlands: Tilburg University Press, 2001.

Hammond, John L. *The Politics of Benevolence: Revival Religion and American Voting Behavior*. Norwood, N.J.: Ablex, 1979.

Handlin, Oscar. *The Uprooted: The Epic Story of the Great Migrations That Made the American People.* New York: Grosset & Dunlap, 1951.

Harrison, Lawrence E. "Culture Matters: How Values Shape Human Progress." In *Culture Matters: How Values Shape Human Progress,* edited by Lawrence E. Harrison and Samuel P. Huntington. New York: Basic Books, 2000.

Hartnett, Daniel. "Remembering the Poor." *America* 188 (February 3, 2003): 12–16.

Hatch, Nathan O. *The Democratization of American Christianity.* New Haven: Yale University Press, 1990.

———. "The Democratization of Christianity and the Character of American Politics." In *Religion and American Politics: From the Colonial Period to the 1980s,* edited by Mark A. Noll, 92–120. New York: Oxford University Press, 1990.

Hayden, Tom, and Dick Flacks. "The Port Huron Statement at 40." *The Nation* 275 (August 5–12, 2002): 18–21.

Hayes-Bautista, David E. *American Dream Makers: Latino Profiles Study Report.* Los Angeles: Loyola Marymount Center for the Study of Los Angeles, 2000.

Hecker, Daniel. "How Hours of Work Affect Occupational Earnings." *Monthly Labor Review,* October 1998, 8–18.

Herberg, Will. *Protestant-Catholic-Jew: An Essay in American Religious Sociology.* Garden City, N.Y.: Doubleday, 1955.

Higham, John. *Strangers in the Land: Patterns of American Nativism, 1860–1925.* 2nd ed. New Brunswick, N.J.: Rutgers University Press, 1988.

Hirschman, Charles. "America's Melting Pot Reconsidered." *Annual Review of Sociology* 9 (1983): 397–423.

Hollinger, David A. *Postethnic America: Beyond Multiculturalism.* New York: Basic Books, 1995.

Hout, Michael, and Claude S. Fischer. "Religious Diversity in America, 1940–2000." Paper presented at the annual meeting of the American Sociological Association, Chicago, August 2001.

Hunter, James Davison. *The Death of Character: Moral Education in an Age without Good or Evil.* New York: Basic Books, 2000.

Hutchison, William R. *Religious Pluralism in America: The Contentious History of a Founding Ideal.* New Haven: Yale University Press, 2003.

Iannaccone, Laurence R. "Why Strict Churches Are Strong." *American Journal of Sociology* 99 (1994): 1180–1211.

Inglehart, Ronald. *Culture Shift in Advanced Industrial Society.* Princeton, N.J.: Princeton University Press, 1989.

Jasso, Guillermina, Douglas S. Massey, Mark R. Rosenzweig, and James P. Smith. "Exploring the Religious Preference of Recent Immigrants to the United States: Evidence from the New Immigrant Survey Pilot." In *Religion and Immigration: Christian, Jewish, and Muslim Experiences in the United States,* edited by Yvonne Haddad, Yazbeck Haddad, Jane I. Smith, and John L. Esposito, 217–53. Walnut Creek, Calif.: AltaMira, 2003.

Jefferson, Thomas. "First Inaugural Address." March 4, 1801.

————. "Letter to Madison (1787)." In *Thomas Jefferson: Writings*, edited by Merrill D. Peterson. New York: Library of America, 1984.

Jones, F. L. "Convergence and Divergence in Ethnic Divorce Patterns: A Research Note." *Journal of Marriage and the Family* 58 (February 1996): 213–18.

Joppke, Christian. "Multiculturalism and Immigration: A Comparison of the United States, Germany, and Great Britain." *Theory and Society* 25 (August 1996): 449–500.

Joselit, Jenna Weissman. *Wonders of America: Reinventing Jewish Culture, 1880–1950*. New York: Hill and Wang, 1994.

Kalmign, Matthijs. "Assortative Mating by Cultural and Economic Occupational Status." *American Journal of Sociology* 100 (September 1994): 422–52.

Kateb, George. *The Inner Ocean: Individualism and Democratic Culture*. Ithaca, N.Y.: Cornell University Press, 1992.

Kekes, John. *Moral Tradition and Individuality*. Princeton, N.J.: Princeton University Press, 1989.

Kelley, Dean M. *Why Conservative Churches Are Growing: A Study in the Sociology of Religion*. New York: Harper & Row, 1972.

Kennedy, David M. *Freedom from Fear: The American People in Depression and War, 1929–1945*. New York: Oxford University Press, 1999.

Kohut, Andrew. *Views of a Changing World*. Washington, D.C.: Pew Research Center for the People and the Press, 2003.

Kurien, Prema. "Becoming American by Becoming Hindu: Indian Americans Take Their Place at the Multicultural Table." In *Gatherings in Diaspora: Religious Communities and the New Immigrants*, edited by R. Stephen Warner and Judith G. Wittner, 37–70. Philadelphia: Temple University Press, 1998.

Latour, Bruno. *Laboratory Life*. Princeton, N.J.: Princeton University Press, 1986.

Lawrence, David Herbert. *Selected Essays*. Baltimore: Penguin, 1950.

Lee, Tacku. "Black Insurgency and the Dynamics of Racial Attitudes in the United States, 1956–64." Paper presented at the annual meeting of the American Political Science Association, Washington, D.C., September 1997.

Leinberger, Paul, and Bruce Tucker. *The New Individualists: The Generation after the Organization Man*. New York: HarperCollins, 1991.

Levitt, Peggy. "Social Remittances: A Local-Level, Migration-Driven Form of Cultural Diffusion." *International Migration Review* 32 (Winter 1999): 926–49.

Lewis, Anthony. "Boat People Helping to Build Our Future." *San Francisco Chronicle*, November 29, 2003, A18.

Lewis, R.W.B. *The American Adam: Innocence, Tragedy and Tradition in the Nineteenth Century*. Chicago: University of Chicago Press, 1955.

Lichterman, Paul. *Elusive Togetherness: Religious Groups and Civic Engagement in America*. Princeton, N.J.: Princeton University Press, 2005.

Lin, Nan. *Social Capital: A Theory of Social Structure and Action*. Cambridge: Cambridge University Press, 2002.

Linde, Charlotte. *Life Stories: The Creation of Coherence*. New York: Oxford University Press, 1993.

Linton, Ralph. *The Cultural Background of Personality*. New York: Appleton-Century, 1945.

Logan, John R., Richard D. Alba, and Thomas L McNulty. "Ethnic Economies in Metropolitan Regions: Miami and Beyond." *Social Forces* 72 (1994): 691–724.

Louie, V. "Parents' Aspirations and Investment: The Role of Social Class in the Educational Experiences of 1.5- and Second-Generation Chinese Americans." *Harvard Educational Review* 71, no. 3 (2001): 438–74.

Lovett, M. R. "Interview with Vito Cacciola #24, February 10, 1939." *American Life Histories: Manuscripts from the Federal Writers' Project, 1936–1940*. Washington, D.C.: Library of Congress, 1940.

Madison, James. "The Union as a Safeguard against Domestic Faction and Insurrection—Continued: Federalist Paper No. 10." *Daily Advertiser*, November 22, 1787, n.p.

Mailer, Norman. "The White Negro." In *Legacy of Dissent*, edited by Nicolaus Mills, 153–74. New York: Touchstone, 1994.

Marshall, Edward. "Makes Six Ocean Trips to Study Steerage Reform: Ernest C. Cotterill Reports on the Bad State of Affairs among the Immigrants on Some Ships and Offers Recommendations for the Improvement of Conditions." *New York Times*, November 30, 1913, 10.

Marsingill, Holly. "Don't Discriminate against Hard-Working Immigrant Families." *Athens Banner-Herald*, January 21, 2003.

Mathews, Donald G. "The Second Great Awakening as an Organizing Process, 1780–1830: An Hypothesis." *American Quarterly* 21 (1969): 23–43.

McAdams, Dan P. *The Stories We Live By: Personal Myths and the Making of the Self*. New York: Guilford Press, 1993.

McAlister, Melani. *Epic Encounters: Culture, Media, and U.S. Interests in the Middle East, 1945–2000*. Berkeley and Los Angeles: University of California Press, 2001.

McClay, Wilfred M. *The Masterless: Self and Society in Modern America*. Chapel Hill: University of North Carolina Press, 1994.

McLaren, Lauren M. "Anti-Immigrant Prejudice in Europe: Contact, Threat Perception, and Preferences for the Exclusion of Migrants." *Social Forces* 81 (March 2003): 909–36.

Mercola, Joseph. "Turn Off the TV and Your Kids Become Less Materialistic." *Journal of Developmental and Behavioral Pediatrics* 22 (June 2001): 179–84.

Mills, C. Wright. "The Structure of Power in American Society." *British Journal of Sociology* 9 (March 1958): 29–41.

———. *White Collar: The American Middle Classes*. New York: Oxford University Press, 1951.

Mills, Nicolaus. *The Triumph of Meanness: America's War against Its Better Self*. New York: Houghton Mifflin, 1997.

Miner, Craig. *Kansas: The History of the Sunflower State, 1854–2000*. Lawrence: University of Kansas Press, 2002.

Moore, R. Laurance. *Religious Outsiders and the Making of Americans*. New York: Oxford University Press, 1986.

Morreale, Don, ed. *The Complete Guide to Buddhist America*. Boston: Shambala, 1998.

Murrin, John M. "Self-Interest Conquers Patriotism: Republicanism, Liberals, and Indians Reshape the Nation." In *The American Revolution: Its Character and Limits*, edited by Jack P. Greene, 225–44. New York: New York University Press, 1987.

Navarro, Mireya. "Miami's Generations of Exiles Side by Side, yet Worlds Apart." *New York Times*, February 11, 1999, A1, A25.

Nee, Victor, Jimy M. Sanders, and Scott Sernau. "Job Transitions in an Immigrant Metropolis: Ethnic Boundaries and the Mixed Economy." *American Sociological Review* 59 (1994): 849–72.

Nisbet, Robert A. "Conservatism and Sociology." *American Journal of Sociology* 58 (September 1952): 167–75.

Nixon, Rob. "From *Dreambirds: The Strange History of the Ostrich in Fashion, Food, and Fortune*." In *Crossing into America: The New Literature of Immigration*, edited by Louis Mendoza and S. Shankar. New York: New Press, 2003.

Nolan, James L., Jr. *The Therapeutic State: Justifying Government at Century's End*. New York: New York University Press, 1998.

Noll, Mark A. *America's God: From Jonathan Edwards to Abraham Lincoln*. New York: Oxford University Press, 2002.

Norris, Kathleen. *Dakota: A Spiritual Geography*. New York: Ticknor & Fields, 1993.

Nye, Joseph S., Jr. *The Paradox of American Power: Why the World's Only Superpower Can't Go It Alone*. New York: Oxford University Press, 2002.

Ollman, Bertell. *Alienation: Marx's Conception of Man in Capitalist Society*. Cambridge: Cambridge University Press, 1971.

Orbuch, Terri L. "People's Accounts Count: The Sociology of Accounts." *Annual Review of Sociology* 23 (1997): 445–78.

Orrange, Robert M. "The Emerging Mutable Self: Gender Dynamics and Creative Adaptations in Defining Work, Family, and the Future." *Social Forces* 82 (September 2003): 1–34.

Orsi, Robert Anthony. *The Madonna of 115th Street: Faith and Community in Italian Harlem, 1880–1950*. New Haven: Yale University Press, 1985.

Parry, Wayne. "Group Promotes Muslim Values." *Grand Rapids Press*, January 4, 2003, B3.

Pencak, William. *For God and Country: The American Legion, 1919–1941*. Boston: Northeastern University Press, 1989.

Percy, Walker. *The Last Gentleman*. New York: Ivy Books, 1966.

Plato. *The Republic of Plato*. Translated by Francis Cornford. New York: Oxford University Press, 1945.

Portes, Alejandro. "Social Capital: Its Origins and Applications in Modern Sociology." *Annual Review of Sociology* 24, no. 2 (1998): 1–24.

Portes, Alejandro, and Leif Jensen. "The Enclave and the Entrants: Patterns of Ethnic Enterprise in Miami before and after Mariel." *American Sociological Review* 54 (1989): 929–49.

Portes, Alejandro, and Dag MacLeod. "Educating the Second Generation: Determinants of Academic Achievement among Children of Immigrants in the United States." *Journal of Ethnic and Migration Studies* 25, no. 3 (1999): 373–96.

———. "Educational Progress of Children of Immigrants: The Roles of Class, Ethnicity, and School Context." *Sociology of Education* 69, no. 4 (1996): 255–75.

Portes, Alejandro, and Julia Sensenbrenner. "Embeddedness and Immigration: Notes on the Social Determinants of Economic Action." *American Journal of Sociology* 98 (1993): 1320–50.

Primer, Ben. *Protestants and American Business Methods.* Ann Arbor, Mich.: UMI Research Press, 1979.

Putnam, Robert D. *Bowling Alone: The Decline and Renewal of American Communities.* New York: Simon & Schuster, 2000.

———. *Making Democracy Work: Civic Traditions in Modern Italy.* Princeton, N.J.: Princeton University Press, 1994.

Rabin, Andrea. "The Last 'Women in Business' Story." *Denver Business,* June 1, 1985.

Raz, Joseph. *Ethics in the Public Domain.* New York: Oxford University Press, 1994.

Reynolds, Quentin. *The Fiction Factory; or from Pulp Row to Quality Street.* New York: Random House, 1955.

Rheingold, Howard. "Look Who's Talking." *Wired Magazine* 7 (January 1999).

Ricoeur, Paul. *Freud and Philosophy: An Essay on Interpretation.* New Haven: Yale University Press, 1970.

Riesman, David. *The Lonely Crowd.* New Haven: Yale University Press, 1950.

Ritzer, George. *The McDonaldization of Society.* Thousand Oaks, Calif.: Pine Forge Press, 1993.

Rodin, Judith. "The University as Discourse Community." In *Public Discourse in America: Conversation and Community in the Twenty-First Century,* edited by Judith Rodin and Stephen P. Steinberg, 232–36. Philadelphia: University of Pennsylvania Press, 2003.

Rodriguez, Gregory. "Mongrel America." *Atlantic Monthly* 291 (January/February 2003): 95–98.

Rodriguez, Richard. "The Browning of America." *Pacific News Service,* February 23, 1998.

Rolvaag, Ole Edvart. *Giants in the Earth: A Sage of the Prairie.* Translated by Lincoln Colcord. New York: Harper, 1927.

Roof, Wade Clark. *A Generation of Seekers: The Spiritual Journeys of the Baby Boom Generation.* San Francisco: HarperSanFrancisco, 1993.

———. *Spiritual Marketplace: Baby Boomers and the Remaking of American Religion.* Princeton, N.J.: Princeton University Press, 1999.

Samples, Kenneth Richard. "Do All Religions Lead to God?" *Facts for Faith* 8 (2002): 52–58.

Sandel, Michael J. *Democracy's Discontent: America in Search of a Public Philosophy.* Cambridge, Mass.: Harvard University Press, 1996.

———. *Liberalism and the Limits of Justice.* New York: Cambridge University Press, 1982.

————. "The Procedural Republic and the Unencumbered Self." *Political Theory* 12 (February 1984): 81–96.

Schneider, John R. *The Good of Affluence: Seeking God in a Culture of Wealth.* Grand Rapids, Mich.: Eerdmans, 2002.

Schor, Juliet. "The New Politics of Consumption: Why Americans Want So Much More Than They Need." *Boston Review* 24 (Summer 1999).

————. *The Overspent American: Why We Want What We Don't Need.* New York: Harper Perennial, 1999.

Schudson, Michael. "How People Learn to Be Civic." In *United We Serve: National Service and the Future of Citizenship,* edited by E. J. Dionne Jr., Kayla Meltzer Drogosz, and Robert E. Litan. Washington, D.C.: Brookings Institution Press, 2003.

Schuman, Howard, Charlotte Steeh, Lawrence Bobo, and Maria Krysan. *Racial Attitudes in America: Trends and Interpretations.* Rev. ed. Cambridge, Mass.: Harvard University Press, 1997.

Schwartz, Wendy. *Immigrants and Their Educational Attainment: Some Facts and Findings.* New York: ERIC Clearinghouse on Urban Education, 1996.

Sciolino, Elaine. "Understanding Why 'They' Hate Us." *New York Times,* September 23, 2001.

Scott, Marvin B,. and Sanford M. Lyman. "Accounts." *American Sociological Review* 33 (February 1968): 46–62.

Seligman, Adam. *The Problem of Trust.* Princeton, N.J.: Princeton University Press, 1997.

Sennett, Richard. *The Fall of Public Man.* New York: Norton, 1992.

Sewell, William F. "A Theory of Structure: Duality, Agency, and Transformation." *American Journal of Sociology* 98, no. 1 (July 1992): 1–29.

Siegel, Lee. "Seize the Day Job." *Harper's* 302 (March 2001): 75–83.

Simmel, Georg. *On Individuality and Social Forms.* Edited by Donald N. Levine. Chicago: University of Chicago Press, 1971.

Singletary, Michelle. "Living above Your Means Can Put You in the Poor House." *Washington Post,* May 11, 2003.

Skocpol, Theda. "How Americans Became Civic." In *Civic Engagement in American Democracy,* edited by Theda Skocpol and Morris P. Fiorina, 27–80. Washington, D.C.: Brookings Institution Press; New York: Russell Sage Foundation, 1999.

Skrentny, John D. *The Minority Rights Revolution.* Cambridge, Mass.: Harvard University Press, 2002.

Smelser, Neil J. *Theory of Collective Behavior.* New York: Free Press, 1962.

Smith, Christian. *American Evangelicalism: Embattled and Thriving.* Chicago: University of Chicago Press, 1998.

————. *Moral, Believing Animals: Human Personhood and Culture.* New York: Oxford University Press, 2003.

Smith, Henry Nash. *Virgin Land: The American West as Symbol and Myth.* Cambridge, Mass.: Harvard University Press, 1950.

Smith, Sidonie, and Julia Watson. *Reading Autobiography: A Guide for Interpreting Life Narratives.* Minneapolis: University of Minnesota Press, 2001.

Stack, Carol. *All Our Kin: Strategies for Survival in a Black Community*. New York: Basic Books, 1974.

Stern, Seth. "From Boat Person to Terror War Point Man." *Christian Science Monitor*, June 9, 2003.

Stewart, David. "The Hermeneutics of Suspicion." *Journal of Literature and Theology* 3 (1989): 296–307.

Stout, Jeffrey. *Democracy and Tradition*. Princeton, N.J.: Princeton University Press, 2003.

Strasburger, Victor C. "Children and TV Advertising: Nowhere to Run, Nowhere to Hide." *Journal of Developmental and Behavioral Pediatrics* 22 (June 2001): 185–87.

Stromberg, Peter G. *Language and Self-Transformation: A Study of the Christian Conversion Narrative*. New York: Cambridge University Press, 1993.

Suarez-Orozco, Marcelo M. "Everything You Ever Wanted to Know about Assimilation but Were Afraid to Ask." *Daedalus* 129 (Fall 2000): 1–30.

Suro, Roberto. *Strangers among Us: How Latino Immigration Is Transforming America*. New York: Knopf, 1998.

Swidler, Ann. "Culture in Action: Symbols and Strategies." *American Sociological Review* 51 (April 1986): 273–86.

————. *Talk of Love: How Culture Matters*. Chicago: University of Chicago Press, 2001.

Tafoya, Arthur N. *Hispanic Ministry at the Turn of the New Millennium*. Washington, D.C.: United States Conference of Catholic Bishops, 2000.

Taylor, Charles. *Sources of the Self: The Making of the Modern Identity*. Cambridge, Mass.: Harvard University Press, 1989.

Thisleton, Anthony. *New Horizons in Hermeneutics*. Grand Rapids, Mich.: Zondervan, 1992.

Tobey, Ronald, Charles Wetherall, and Jay Brigham. "Moving Out and Settling In: Residential Mobility, Home Owning, and the Public Enframing of Citizenship, 1921–1950." *American Historical Review* 95 (December 1990): 1410–29.

Tocqueville, Alexis de. *Democracy in America*. 2 vols. New York: Knopf, 1945.

Twitchell, James B. *Living It Up: Our Love Affair with Luxury*. New York: Columbia University Press, 2002.

U.S. Census Bureau. *Statistical Abstract of the United States: 2002*. Washington, D.C.: Government Printing Office, 2002.

Vatter, Harold G. *The U.S. Economy in World War II*. New York: Columbia University Press, 1985.

Veblen, Thorstein. *The Theory of the Leisure Class*. New York: Viking, 1967.

Vilbig, Peter. "Why Do They Hate America?" *New York Times*, October 15, 2001.

Warner, R. Stephen. "Approaching Religious Diversity: Barriers, Byways, and Beginnings." *Sociology of Religion* 59 (Fall 1998): 193–215.

————. "Work in Progress toward a New Paradigm for the Sociological Study of Religion in the United States." *American Journal of Sociology* 98 (1993): 1044–93.

Waters, Mary C. *Ethnic Options: Choosing Ethnic Identities in America*. Berkeley and Los Angeles: University of California Press, 1990.

Weber, Max. *Economy and Society: An Outline of Interpretive Sociology*. Edited by Guenther Roth and Claus Wittich. 2 vols. Berkeley and Los Angeles: University of California Press, 1978.

Weber, Max. *The Protestant Ethic and the Spirit of Capitalism*. Translated by Talcott Parsons. New York: Charles Scribner's Sons, 1958.

Weinstein, Dahlia Jean. "Chamber Fiesta Pays Tribute to Five Hispanic Pioneers." *Rocky Mountain News*, October 29, 2001.

Wenger, Beth. "Memory as Identity: The Invention of the Lower East Side." *American Jewish History* 85 (March 1997): 3–27.

White Jr., Ronald. *Lincoln's Greatest Speech: The Second Inaugural*. New York: Simon & Schuster, 2002.

Whitfield, Stephen J. *The Culture of the Cold War*. Baltimore: Johns Hopkins University Press, 1991.

Whitman, Walt. "Preface, 1872, to 'As a Strong Bird on Pinions Free.'" In *Prose Works*. Philadelphia: David McKay, 1892.

Whyte, William Foote. *Street Corner Society: The Social Structure of an Italian Slum*. Chicago: University of Chicago Press, 1943.

Whyte, William H., Jr. *The Organization Man*. Garden City, N.Y.: Doubleday, 1956.

Williams, Bernard. *Problems of the Self: Philosophical Papers, 1956–1972*. Cambridge: Cambridge University Press, 1973.

Williamson, David. "New Survey: Influx of Hispanics Displeases Some State Residents." *UNC News*, August 26, 1997.

Wilson, Christopher P. "The Rhetoric of Consumption: Mass-Market Magazines and the Demise of the Gentle Reader, 1880–1920." In *The Culture of Consumption: Critical Essays in American History, 1880–1980*, edited by Richard Wightman Fox and T. J. Jackson Lears, 39–64. New York: Knopf, 1983.

Wilson, Thomas C. "Cohort and Prejudice: Whites' Attitudes toward Blacks, Hispanics, Jews, and Asians." *Public Opinion Quarterly* 60 (1996): 253–74.

Wilson, William Julius. *When Work Disappears: The World of the New Urban Poor*. New York: Viking, 1997.

Wirth, Louis. "Localism, Regionalism, and Centralization." *American Sociological Review* 42 (January 1937): 493–509.

Wolfe, Alan. *The Transformation of American Religion: How We Actually Live Our Faith*. New York: Free Press, 2003.

———, ed. *School Choice: The Moral Debate*. Princeton, N.J.: Princeton University Press, 2003.

Wood, Daniel B. "Buddhist Practices Make Inroads in the U.S." *Christian Science Monitor*, November 3, 1997.

Wu, Frank. *Yellow: Race in America beyond Black and White*. New York: Basic Books, 2002.

Wuthnow, Robert. *After Heaven: Spirituality in America since the 1950s*. Berkeley and Los Angeles: University of California Press, 1998.

Wuthnow, Robert. *All in Sync: How Music and Art Are Revitalizing American Religion.* Berkeley and Los Angeles: University of California Press, 2003.

———. *God and Mammon in America.* New York: Free Press, 1994.

———. *Meaning and Moral Order: Explorations in Cultural Analysis.* Berkeley and Los Angeles: University of California Press, 1987.

———. *Poor Richard's Principle: Recovering the American Dream through the Moral Dimension of Work, Business, and Money.* Princeton, N.J.: Princeton University Press, 1996.

———. *The Restructuring of American Religion: Society and Faith since World War II.* Princeton, N.J.: Princeton University Press, 1988.

———. *Sharing the Journey: Support Groups and America's New Quest for Community.* New York: Free Press, 1994.

Wyllie, Irvin G. *The Self-Made Man in America: The Myth of Rags to Riches.* New York: Free Press, 1954.

Young, Michael P. "Confessional Protest: The Religious Birth of U.S. National Social Movements." *American Sociological Review* 67 (October 2002): 660–88.

Zurcher, Louis A. *The Mutable Self: A Self-Concept for Social Change.* Beverly Hills, Calif.: Sage, 1977.